CHRISTIANS AND SOCIALISM

ORBIS BOOKS
MARYKNOLL   NEW YORK

CHRISTIANS
and
SOCIALISM

Documentation of the
Christians For Socialism Movement
in Latin America

Translated by John Drury

Edited by John Eagleson

x

Copyright © 1975 Orbis Books, Maryknoll, New York 10545

Library of Congress Catalog Card Number: 74-78452

ISBN: Hardbound: 0-88344·059-8; Paperback: 0-88344-058-x

Manufactured in the United States of America

CONTENTS

PART IV: NATIONAL REPORTS

PART V: CONVENTION DOCUMENTS

PART VI: POST-CONVENTION DOCUMENTS

Introduction

(The following was prepared by a Chilean priest very closely connected with the Christians For Socialism movement. Because of the present situation in Chile, the writer would prefer to remain anonymous.)

In 1970 Salvador Allende became the first Marxist to be elected president through the democratic process. Ever since then Chile has been a focus of news interest; and the coup in September 1973 has kept world attention on the country. In this volume we present a collection of documents which appeared in Chile over the past few years and which reflect the thinking of a group of Latin American Christians. The group, known as Christians For Socialism, was actively engaged in the political and ideological discussions that took place during the presidency of Salvador Allende. These bare facts are enough to suggest the timeliness and relevance of this material.

Who are these Christians For Socialism? Are they really Christians, or are they Marxists? The viewpoint adopted by the Christians For Socialism led to heated debate within the Christian community, and indeed the bishops of Chile eventually forbade priests and religious to belong to the group (see Document 19 below).

The bishops recognized the ambiguity inherent in the movement. They prohibited priests and religious from participating in it, and in particular from engaging actively and openly in political activity. But they did not prohibit lay people from participating in it, nor did they condemn the movement as such. There is no doctrinal condemnation in their message. They simply point out what they consider to be errors and ambiguities, and they call upon the members to explore and reconsider their views in Christian and ecclesial terms.

For their part the members of the Christians For Socialism

group consider themselves to be Christians, and they have never contemplated removing themselves from the ecclesial community. They realize that they have entered a difficult area—political involvement with Marxists—and they feel that their vacillations and ambiguities flow from that fact. As they see it, the conflicting points of view underscored by the bishops of Chile are but part of a larger debate going on in the Church all over the world. But they have no intention of renouncing their Christian faith. Indeed some Christians, who thought they had lost their faith, have rediscovered it in this new synthesis fashioned by revolutionary Christians.

These Christians approach the gospel message in a particular way. They interpret the classic notions of salvation and redemption in terms of liberation—liberation from sin and its consequences. Their starting point is the initiative shown by God himself. As the Medellín Conference put it: "It was God himself who sent his Son in the fullness of time. He took on flesh to liberate mankind from all the shackles that weighed down on it because of sin, ignorance, hunger, poverty, and oppression. In a word he came to liberate man from the injustice and hatred that have their roots in human egotism" (Document on Justice).

Starting from this belief, Christians For Socialism see love of neighbor as effective action designed to turn Christ's liberative plan into a reality. They realize that almsgiving and other social reform efforts are not enough. It is principally through political activity, they feel, that one can effect a thoroughgoing change of existing structures. In this process they meet other people who are either in favor of liberation or opposed to it. Starting from within the Christian community, they encounter leftists, socialists, atheists, and Marxists. It is an almost inescapable dialectic in which some people are turned into enemies while others become friends.

These Christians are convinced that the existing capitalist society must be replaced with one that is socialist in inspiration. This option is not a gratuitous one. Authoritative voices in Latin America have spoken out in this vein. The bishop of Cuernavaca, Mexico, Sergio Méndez Arceo, has said: "Only socialism can give Latin America the authentic development it needs . . . . I believe that a socialist system is more in conformity with the Christian principles of brotherhood, justice, and peace . . . . I do not know what form this socialism should take, but that is the general line that Latin America should follow. In my own view, it should be a democratic form of socialism."

It was not easy for the group to take this option. Many of its members went through a profound crisis of conscience. They were torn between fidelity to traditional teaching and the need to bring about an effective transformation of society. They have had to overcome many objections and difficulties: e.g., the Church's many previous condemnations of socialism and Marxism, the totalitarian cast of various socialist countries, and the century-old opposition between Christians and Marxists.

For the moment, the military coup has silenced the members of Christians For Socialism. In this time of suffering and persecution they have had a chance to reflect and engage in self-criticism. They recognize their mistakes and regret that they were not wise enough to express themselves better.

The Christians For Socialism realize they were impatient, eagerly seeking radical solutions. They sometimes made hasty judgments, issued unfair denunciations, and fell into errors of interpretation. Their statements and declarations were published in the heat of a political and ideological debate that had gone on uninterruptedly for three years in Chile. They contained prophetic intuitions, but they also lacked doctrinal precision and were often ambiguous and incomplete.

The Christians For Socialism regret that they separated from other Christians of good will, and in particular that they were not able to dialogue with workers. They feel that they never managed to point up their continuity with the long social tradition of the Church. They did not intend to break with the past, with the hierarchical Church and other Christians. Their real intention was to move forward in line with the needs and challenges of the times.

They also realize that they were not critical enough towards developments and activities within the Popular Unity coalition. One of their aims was to act as a moral conscience within that process, to make sure that the formation of a new man and a new society remained a true goal within it. They did not do that. Or, at the very least, public opinion did not see them doing that. Their motivations and objectives were not clear to many people.

Critics of the group say that they were naive and opportunistic, that their option was a delusory one, that they were used by Allende, and that they did not manage to exert any real influence on the *modus operandi* of Allende's Popular Unity coalition.

The critics may well be right, but it is too early to make any definitive judgment. In the Church there have always been Christians who look for new pathways and who push for reforms within the Church itself. Some disappear without a trace; others have a more lasting impact.

We hope that the debate and discussion initiated by Christians For Socialism will continue and probe even more deeply. The Latin American Church has a rich social tradition, and we feel that it can be enriched by the new insights offered in these documents, which upon careful reading may be found to contain implications for Christians everywhere.

PART I

BACKGROUND DOCUMENTS

A group of Chilean priests met in April 1971 and held a workshop on the advisability of "Christian participation in the task of developing and implementing socialism in Chile." Their declaration (Document 1) had profound repercussions in various circles. It is followed here by two documents which express sympathy with the problems touched upon by the priests but reservations about their approach and their conclusions (Documents 2 and 3).

1

1

Declaration of The 80

We are a group of 80 priests who live and work with people of the working class. We came together to analyze the present situation of Chile as it begins to develop and implement socialism.

The working class is still subject to exploitation and its attendant conditions: i.e., malnutrition, lack of housing, unemployment, and limited possibilities for further education and cultural development. The cause of this situation is specific and clear. It is the capitalist system, resulting from domination by foreign imperialism and maintained by the ruling classes of this country.

This system is characterized by private ownership of the means of production and by ever growing inequality in the distribution of income. It turns the worker into a mere cog in the production system, stimulates an irrational distribution of economic resources, and causes an improper transferral of surplus goods to foreign lands. The result is stagnation, which prevents our country from escaping its situation of underdevelopment.

Such a situation cannot be tolerated any longer. It is clear to us that the working masses found great hope in the accession of the People's Government to power and in this respect they were not mistaken.

Socialism, which is characterized by social appropriation of the means of production, paves the way for a new economy which makes possible autonomous development at a more accelerated pace and which overcomes the division of society into antagonistic classes. But socialism is not just a new economy. It should also generate new values which will pave the way for a society that evinces more fellowship and brotherhood. In this society the worker will shoulder his proper role with new dignity.

We feel committed to the process that is now under way and we want to contribute to its success. The underlying reason for our commitment is our faith in Jesus Christ, which takes on depth and vitality and concrete shape in accordance with historical circumstances. To be a Christian is to be in solidarity, in fellowship, with other human beings. And at this moment in Chile fellowship means participation in the historical project that its people have set for themselves.

As Christians we do not see any incompatibility between Christianity and socialism. Quite the contrary is true. As the Cardinal of Santiago said last November: "There are more evangelical values in socialism than there are in capitalism." The fact is that socialism offers new hope that man can be more complete, and hence more evangelical: i.e., more conformed to Jesus Christ, who came to liberate us from any and every sort of bondage.

Thus it is necessary to destroy the prejudice and mistrust that exist between Christians and Marxists.

To Marxists we say that authentic religion is not the opiate of the people. It is, on the contrary, a liberating stimulus to revivify and renew the world constantly. To Christians we offer a reminder that our God committed himself personally to the history of human beings. And we say that at this present moment loving one's neighbor basically means struggling to make this world resemble as closely as possible the future world that we hope for and that we are already in the process of constructing.

We are not unaware of the difficulties and the suspicions on both sides. In large measure they have been caused by past historical circumstances that no longer prevail in Chile today. There is a long road ahead for both Christians and Marxists. But the evolution that has taken place in Christian and Marxist circles permits them to engage in a joint effort on behalf of the historical project that the country has set for itself.

This collaboration will be facilitated to the extent that two things are done: 1) to the extent that Marxism presents itself more and more as an instrument for analyzing and transforming society; 2) to the extent that we Christians proceed to purify our faith of everything that prevents us from shouldering real and effective commitment.

Hence we support the measures aimed at social appropriation of the means of production: e.g., the nationalization of mineral resources, the socialization of banks and monopoly industries, the expansion and acceleration of agrarian reform, and so forth.

We feel that much sacrifice will be entailed in the implementation of socialism, that it will involve a constructive and united effort if we are to overcome our underdevelopment and to create a new society. Obviously enough this will provoke strong resistance from those who will be deprived of their special privileges. Hence the mobilization of the people is absolutely necessary. With some concern we note that this mobilization has not been achieved as had been hoped.

We also believe that it is indispensable to lay the foundations for the creation of a new culture. This new culture must not be the mirror image of capitalist concerns and interests; it must be the real-life expression of the genuine values of our people. Only then can we see the emergence of the New Man, who will create a societal life that is truly one of fellowship and solidarity.

We note that there are large groups of workers who are in favor of the changes taking place and who are benefiting from them, but who are not actively involving themselves in the process that has already been initiated. The union of all workers, whatever their party loyalty may be, is critical at this juncture. Our country is being offered a unique opportunity to replace the existing system of dependent capitalism and to promote the cause of the laboring class throughout Latin America.

Lack of class consciousness among these workers is being encouraged and fostered by the ruling groups, primarily through the communications media and party activities. They are inculcating suspicions and fears, which ultimately lead to resistance and passivity.

We must recognize and admit that not everything being done is necessarily positive and effective. But at the same time we insist that criticism should be formulated from within the revolutionary process, not from outside it.

It is a time full of risk, but also a time full of hope. We priests, like each and every Christian, must do what we can to make our own modest contribution. That is why we have come together to reflect and to prepare ourselves in this workshop on the participation of Christians in the implementation of socialism.

Santiago de Chile
April 16, 1971

Gonzalo Arroyo
Alfonso Baeza
Martin Gárate
Esteban Gumucio
Juan Martín

Santiago Thijssen
Sergio Torres (Talca)
Ignacio Pujadas (Valparaíso)
Pierre Dubois (Coronel)

2

Letter to 80 Friends

Santiago
April 19, 1971

Dear Friends:

I have just read the declaration you published after your workshop dealing with the participation of Christians in the implementation of socialism. And I have also noted the reactions it provoked in various organs of the press.

First of all I want to repudiate the offensive caricature of your position by the daily newspaper *Tribuna*, both in its headlines and its illustration. And even though I am not a fortune teller, I can also voice my repudiation of the interpretation that is sure to show up in the weekly *PEC* [*Panorama Económico y Cultural*, an anti-Communist publication of the extreme right].

I fully agree with you that the capitalist regime is inhuman and execrable, and that a socialist regime can be more respectful of human dignity. I can even go so far as to say that a socialist regime can be more "evangelical" by virtue of its preferential concern for the "downtrodden and oppressed."

I also agree that Christians should contribute to the formation and implementation of a socialist regime in which the theoretical ideal of democracy can be effectively enjoyed by the vast majority. Today this majority is oppressed by unjust structures that make a mockery of legal liberty and equality (not to even mention fraternity).

I also agree that the collaboration of Christians and Marxists in the construction of a more just society is unobjectionable, and that it calls for the elimination of irrational prejudices and suspicions. And there are many other points where I agree with you.

But I must confess that some of the notions expressed by you have left me puzzled and disconcerted. With no other aim than to dispel misunderstandings that might confuse many Christians, and with the same pastoral and evangelical outlook that inspires your remarks, I choose to spell out the things that are of concern to me.

The first thing that perturbs me is the value that you seem to attribute to the stance you have adopted vis-à-vis the present situation of the nation. I believe that this stance is a legitimate one for a Christian (and hence for a priest). But I believe one must be very clear about the fact that it represents a political option. Any attempt to give it an added dose of theological merit is off base, it seems to me. The political option of the Christian in any set of circumstances should proceed from his faith, in the sense that he should try to make sure that his analysis of a given set of circumstances and his subsequent decision are illuminated by the absolute values which his faith receives from the gospel. But his option does not cease to be political and turn into an objectively "theological" one thereby. Such options remain subject to the inescapable risk of personal decision-making wherein the individual consciously assumes responsibility before God for his freely made decisions.

For this reason I find it difficult to subscribe to a notion such as this: "To be a Christian is to be in solidarity, in fellowship. . . . And at this moment in Chile fellowship means participation in the historical project that its people have set for themselves."

This formulation has a generalizing thrust that seems to go too far. If you had said, "The way in which we eighty people will translate this solidarity into action will be to participate in the present project," then I would have no objection. But I do not see why all Christians must adopt the same way of embodying the solidarity that is essential to the gospel. Of course it is possible that in your remark you are merely alluding to an obligation that has always been incumbent on Christians—whether in 1964, 1958, or 1938—namely, to recognize and accept legitimate authority. But since such obedience is not incompatible with a political stance of opposition (not to mention obstruction), it does not seem to me that this is what you have in mind; and it would be an obvious remark in any case.

There is another passage which embodies the same tendency to attribute objective and necessary value to the option that you yourselves have chosen. Here it is: "The union of all workers, whatever their party loyalty may be, is critical at this juncture. Our country is being offered a unique opportunity to replace the existing system of dependent capitalism . . . . " But what if the party loyalty or option of some workers consists precisely in believing that we are not confronted with "a unique opportunity to replace the existing system"? What then? You yourselves have every right to think that it is a unique opportunity. But on the basis of what principle or reason can you say that everyone else is obliged to share this conviction? To be honest and objective, I must acknowledge that here you make no attempt to ground it on any theological basis, where you yourselves or others are concerned. You simply make this statement as the fruit of a political analysis, and I am glad that you pose it thus.

The second thing that particularly perturbs me in reading the document you have published is the fact that you seem to share a class-centered outlook. To repeat it once again, I believe it is possible for a Christian to approach social reality with the instrument "for analyzing and transforming society" elaborated by Marxism: i.e., the dialectic of class struggle. But in doing this one must be aware of two things: 1) Neither its scientific validity as a sociological method nor its separability from the overall Marxist theory are universally clear and self-evident; 2) the Marxist evaluation of the proletarian class as the exclusive bearer of humanity's future does not at all dovetail with the gospel's blessing on the poor.

Any student of the gospel can readily see that the thinking of Jesus does not operate in terms of "social classes," and that his pronouncements deal with a level of human existence that is infinitely deeper, more complex and more universal than that which is defined by the antagonistic roles engendered in the economic process of production. Jesus came to save all human beings. He certainly did not picture salvation as an immanent historical process in which one social class was the protagonist. All men are saved by the grace of God that radiates from the person of Jesus—the poor in spite of their poverty and the rich in spite of their wealth. And we must not forget that the publicans, who were blessed as much by Jesus as the poor were, were rich people and even exploiters.

I do not mean to suggest that Jesus fostered exploitation. I am simply pointing out that the message of Jesus cannot be interpreted in terms of a dialectic between social classes simply because it blesses the poor (along with children, prostitutes, and publicans). Hence you will readily understand why I feel ill at ease when I see you deploring the "lack of class consciousness" in "large groups of workers." Let me make my point clear. As I see it, it is possible for a person to opt for social transformation by way of class struggle. Even though it seems to be a highly risky option, I respect you for apparently having made such an option. But let it be said clearly that this is a political option, and that it cannot be proposed as the necessary projection of the gospel in the realm of political activity.

I should also like to touch upon the uneasiness I felt over the superficial way in which you dealt with some important and complex topics. Reading your declaration one gets the impression that you slip easily from socialism to Marxist socialism, from social appropriation to state appropriation, from collaboration with Marxists in a given task to collaboration with them in the implemention of Marxist socialism. One also gets the impression that you uncritically accept certain axioms that are far from self-evident. For example, you seem to suggest that any and all suspicion of Marxism stems from "past historical circumstances that no longer prevail in Chile today." And you assert that "criticism should be formulated from within the revolutionary process, not from outside it." I must confess that I envy the frank ingenuousness that is evident in these statements.

Finally I should like to make a comment about the closing paragraph of your declaration. There you say: "It is a time full of risk, but also a time full of hope. We priests, like each and every Christian, must do what we can to make our own modest contribution." I quite agree. But in making your declaration are you simply making your modest contribution as any other Christian would? To the best of my knowledge, when eighty average lay people get together they do not usually hold a press conference and issue a statement in it. Quite clearly you have acted as priests, and you have done so to publicize an option that is legitimate in itself but that is political in nature. I do not know if this is at all consistent with the criticism levelled once upon a time at the Conservative Party and more recently at the Christian Democratic Party: namely, that they were using the weight of the label "Christian" to promote political options. Whether you intend it or not, your declarations carry the weight of the pastoral ministry with which you are invested. Hence they represent an improper foray into an area where the gospel demands that the liberty of each individual believer be respected fully. What is this curse that afflicts us curates, so that we think that Christians must always share our way of seeing things? If your document dealt with the participation of "some Christians" or "eighty priests" in the implementation of socialism, I would have nothing (or very little) to say against it. But that is not the case. Your document deals with the participation of "Christians" in the implementation of socialism. It seems to me that you have fallen into the sin of clericalism.

My friends, I have written this letter "in fear and trembling." Every day you experience at first hand the anxiety and humiliation and uncertainty and fear that afflicts the men, women, and children of this country. You, Father Esteban, have spoken to us about that fear in unforgettable terms. It seemed to me that your concrete experience might well be more valid than any of my reasons. Yet I also felt that if my reasons are worth anything at all, you will know how to make them part and parcel of your pastoral responsibility and your passionate Christian commitment.

With profound admiration and respect, I am your friend,

Beltrán Villegas, SS.CC.

3

Declaration of the Bishops of Chile

Gathered together at our annual plenary session, we the bishops of Chile have examined the present-day situation of the country. As a result of that examination, we want to issue the following statements:

1. The Church sees herself as the People of God. Her particular mission, as she sees it, is to proclaim and live out the gospel of the risen Jesus Christ in every age and place.

2. Faced with the situation that Chile is experiencing at this present moment, Christians must take as their own the overall option that was affirmed by the Latin American episcopate at Medellín. This option should be the basic criterion for their outlook and their activities. According to this option asserted at Medellín, fidelity to the gospel of Jesus Christ today requires Christians to commit themselves to thoroughgoing and urgently needed social transformations.

3. To us who live in Chile today the implementation of socialism is being proposed as a concrete way of effecting these transformations. There are sound reasons for believing that the socialism that is being proposed is predominantly Marxist in its inspiration.

4. As Vatican II reminds us, the Church, by virtue of her mission and her area of competence, is not tied to any political system. Her mission is to incarnate in every age and in every situation the good news of complete liberation for the human person and for human society. She is not competent to make pronouncements on contingent solutions of a political or

economic nature. But she does have authority to denounce anything in these solutions, which are ambivalent in themselves, that might delude or enslave man. And she is also obliged to proclaim and promote anything that would safeguard the dignity and transcendence of the human person.

5. An option for socialism of a Marxist cast poses legitimate questions. It is a system that already has concrete embodiments in history. In these concrete embodiments we find that fundamental rights of the human person have been trodden under foot just as they have been in concrete embodiments of the capitalist system. We find similar ways of proceeding that are just as condemnable. The Church, which has been sent by God to serve and liberate man, cannot remain indifferent to this fact.

6. We feel that the needs and the rights of our people call for, and should make possible, a sincere effort by all those who claim to be committed to their liberation, so that this liberation is effected in a rapid and thoroughgoing way. This poses the whole question of dialogue: its possibility, its scope, and its underlying conditions.

7. The Church is looking for dialogue and it invites others to it. Dialogue is always fruitful when the indispensable conditions for it are verified: sincerity, honesty, mutual respect. But the most pressing reason for dialogue is to be found in the expectations that the people nurture. They cannot wait hopefully forever. Nor can they be sacrificed to ideological schemes that are alien to their own original place in history.

8. To the legitimate government of Chile we reiterate the position that comes to us from Christ: i.e., respect for its authority and collaboration in its effort to serve the people. Any and every effort to fashion a more human society, to eliminate poverty by promoting the common good over private interest, demands the support of someone who is committed to man's liberation as the Christian is. The democratic tradition of this country permits us to say that this support can and should be offered through serious-minded criticism with a genuine concern for the common good.

9. The active and vigorous presence of Christians in all the organisms connected with the life of the nation, and their in-

creased effort in every sector, would seem to be urgent imperatives flowing from their real commitment to the country.

10. We greatly appreciate the repeated statements of the President of the Republic in which he has sought to respect and safeguard the rights of the religious conscience. We thank him for this cordial and considerate attitude, and we offer the same considerateness and cordiality in return.

Recently a group of priests issued a declaration, and it has been widely commented on in the communications media. With regard to their declaration we feel obliged to make the following points:

1. Like any citizen, a priest is entitled to have his own political option. But in no case should he give this option the moral backing that stems from his character as a priest. For this reason we continue to follow the tradition of the Chilean Church as exemplified by Cardinal Caro and Bishop Manuel Larraín. We have always insisted, and we will continue to insist, that our priests abstain from taking partisan political positions in public. To act otherwise would be to revert to an outdated clericalism that no one wants to see around again.

2. If the political option of the priest is presented as a logical and inescapable consequence of his Christian faith, as it was in this case, then it implicitly condemns every other option and it is an attack on the liberty of other Christians.

3. When the political option of the priest is made public, then it threatens to disrupt the unity of the Christian people with their pastors. As Vatican II points out: "In building the Christian community priests are never to put themselves at the service of any ideology or human faction. Rather as heralds of the gospel and shepherds of the Church, they must devote themselves to the spiritual growth of the Body of Christ" (*Presbyterorum ordinis*, n.6).

4. The situation that has arisen does not affect our esteem for the priests in question. Nor does it diminish our high regard for the apostolic work they, along with many others, are performing among the working class. We have touched upon this matter in

our declaration only because of the wide repercussions that their own document has had.

Finally, we reiterate and renew our hope in the liberating presence of Christ in the midst of the historical process through which we are now living. May he give us light so that we can discern and support his activity where he is struggling on behalf of the poor and the suffering. May he give us the energy of his love so that we can place it in the service of our common task: i.e., making Chile a family where every person has food, respect, and happiness.

Temuco (Chile)
April 22, 1971

PART II

DRAFT AGENDA

In the early part of December 1971, a group of priests from Argentina, Brazil, Bolivia, Colombia, Peru and Chile decided to plan for a convention the following year in Santiago, Chile. It would be a Latin American convention of those Christians who regarded socialism as a necessary precondition for the construction of a just and humane society. The idea of such a convention was promoted by the group known as The 80.

The organizers were convinced that Christians were indeed involved in the struggle of the oppressed and the laboring class in Latin America. They hoped that the proposed convention would give expression to the scope and variety and practical effectiveness of the option for revolution among some Christians on the Latin American continent. They also hoped it would provide those involved in the struggle for liberation in Latin America with an opportunity to pause for theological reflection, to exchange their personal experiences, and to offer each other mutual

17

support. The promoters felt that such a convention would not only contribute to the process under way in Latin America but also inject new vitality into the Christian faith.

The organizers appointed a committee whose first task was the elaboration of a draft agenda for the proposed convention. This agenda (Document 4) points out the aims of the convention and the methodology underlying it. It also indicates that the proposed meeting would not be officially tied to any churches or official organisms as such, but that this stance was not meant to represent a break with the official Church either.

4

Christians For Socialism:
Draft Agenda
of Proposed Convention

I. INTRODUCTION

During his recent visit to Chile, Fidel Castro met with about 120 leftist priests and religious. On numerous occasions he reiterated that Christians "are not merely tactical but also strategic allies" of Latin American revolution. Clearly these facts are signs of a new and recent time for the Church, which has frequently been marked by conservatism in sociological terms. Fidel's statement does point up a new situation on our continent. The fact is that more and more Christians are actively engaged in the struggle that the people of Latin America are waging to free themselves from capitalist imperialism. The latter has generated underdevelopment and exploitation, and this new political commitment of Christians is demanded by their faith itself.

In early December [1971] priests from Argentina, Brazil, Bolivia, Colombia, and Peru met in Santiago, Chile, with members of the Chilean Secretariat of "Christians For Socialism" in order to plan and organize the First Latin American convention of Christians For Socialism. All of them felt that at this point in history there was an imperative need to pause in their labors so that they could engage in theological reflection, exchange personal experiences, offer each other mutual support, and coordinate their commitment and activities on behalf of industrial workers, manual laborers, peasants, and students. Coordination of their commitment and activity could be a decisive factor in stimulating large sectors of Christians to involve themselves in the work of promoting the liberation of our peoples.

In view of the present political experiment in Chile, the climate of liberty existing in Santiago, and the fact that the Third Congress of UNCTAD [United Nations Conference on Trade and Development] would take place there in April, it was decided to hold the First Latin American Convention of Christians For Socialism in Santiago from 23 to 30 April, 1972. This convention would promote a twofold objective. On the one hand it would offer a chance for interior reflection and mutual support to the Christian groups involved—whether they be Catholics or Protestants, whether they be priests, ministers, religious men and women, or lay people. On the other hand it would advertise to Latin America and the whole world the fact that the gospel itself was compelling these Christians to commit themselves to the political struggle for liberation.

An organizing committee was appointed to implement these ideas. It drew up this present document and it took charge of the task of inviting all the movements, organizations, secretariats and individual Christians that identify themselves with the positions formulated here and that wish to prepare position papers or statements in line with the basic thrust of this document.

This convention will be the initiative of Christian groups that are not directly linked to institutions of the official Church or to its funding sources. Thus it will be marked by a certain austerity, which fits in well with the nature of the Christian groups participating in it. The basic idea is that each country will finance and pay for the cost of preparing for the convention within its own borders (national conventions in March, material supplies, etc.), and also for the round trip fares to the convention. The Chilean delegation pledges to provide lodging for the delegates from other countries, and to handle the material aspects of organizing the convention itself. In exceptional cases, and particularly in the case of more distant countries in Central America and the Caribbean region, the organizing committee will try to obtain funds to pay for a few plane tickets. Any suggestions in this connection will be welcomed.

We have sought public support for the convention from different notables in the Christian world who are actively involved in the liberation process as it relates to the peoples of Latin America.

Intended to be a spontaneous melding of shared hopes and desires, the convention will represent the end result of efforts and initiatives taken by various groups of committed Christians. In no way will it or should it be tied to official organisms of the Church or the government. But prominent figures in Latin America will be invited to patronize this initiative.

In this first draft agenda, which will be sent to all those invited to the convention, we spell out the objectives of the convention and we ask all those who are interested to offer their suggestions. In this way we hope to determine more accurately the goals that we all hope to attain.

II. OBJECTIVES OF THE CONVENTION

The *central* objective is:
> to exchange,
> analyze,
> and probe more deeply into the concrete experiences of Christians who are actively involved in the revolution to liberate Latin America.

This central objective of the convention is divided into two complementary objectives:
> an *external* objective
>> Through the characteristic features of the convention itself, we want to give *public* expression to the scope and variety and concrete effectiveness of the option for revolution among Christians on our continent.
>> Through this public manifestation we want to bear clear *witness* to the fact that the scope of this effort is as broad as Latin America itself.

> an *internal* objective
>> We want to make a fruitful effort at *exchanging, analyzing, and exploring* the distinctive experiences of each country. We hope thereby to be able to probe more deeply into the features they share in common.

Hence study and reflection will be involved. The common basis and point of departure for this work of analysis and exploration must be the effective real-life option of the participants in favor of liberation—an option taking concrete shape in a realistic movement towards socialism.

Thus the revolutionary process is to be the *frame of reference* in our work of study and reflection. Starting from there we shall look back at the past and forward to the future. We must take as our basic assumption the unique and comprehensive process of our people's struggle for liberation.

The revolution is one single phenomenon: it is *comprehensive and one* in character. This fact, not the parallelism of some presumed "Christian way" that is all-encompassing, is what must serve as the backdrop for examining and evaluating the value and importance of the contribution made by Christian revolutionaries.

Concrete experience has shown that it is not easy to reconcile the specific features of the external objective with those of the internal objective, the latter being regarded as the most important by all involved.

As far as the participants were concerned, the basic idea underlying the proposed convention was that it should represent Christians from every country in Latin America and from every Christian confession, provided that they evinced a real-life option in favor of the revolutionary process. These would be two essential features of the planned event. It would be Latin American and ecumenical in character.

To the convention we shall invite Christians who are committed to the revolution in the various countries of Latin America —priests, ministers, lay people. Contacts already made would indicate that such groups as the following are the kind we have in mind: Priests for the Third World, Lay People for the Third World, the Church and Change, the "Eighty," ONIS [National Office for Social Investigation], The Church in Solidarity, Golconda, the United Front, ISAL groups [Church and Society for Latin America], Christian Communities in the Broad Front, etc.

The convention is meant to take in a broad range of movements and to be representative of Latin America as a whole. We expect greater participation from nearby countries, and of course from Chile itself. We shall explore the most advisable ways to achieve the greatest possible amplitude without doing prejudice to continental representation.

The *criterion of selection* in sending out invitations will be the effective real-life option for revolution of those invited, and the ability of the potential participants to contribute to the goals of the convention.

In its draft agenda the organizing committee also presents the broad outlines of a basic document relating to the convention. They sketch some of the guidelines that might serve to shape a general framework for the discussions and suggestions of the various national conventions. They spell out the methodological lines that should be followed in our work of reflection.

Reflection should take place in three stages. These stages will enable us to break through the web of illusion that surrounds facts and ideologies and to discern the actual involvement of the Christian element in the revolutionary process. The aim is to force the participants to analyze the *reality* of the revolutionary process which Latin America is experiencing, to discover the *de facto* role that Christians are playing in it, and to distinguish that *de facto* role from the function that the "Christian element" is carrying out.

Many have viewed these sections (III and IV) as a definitive statement that expresses our thought completely and fully. But it is merely a general outline of our thinking, and it does not discuss many aspects which we considered to be beyond dispute. Thus we can understand how it might have given rise to misunderstandings and serious difficulties.

The thoughts outlined in the next two sections consist of two parts. Section III describes the three stages of reflection in a general way. Section IV offers more concrete suggestions about each of these three stages.

III. OUTLINES OF A BASIC DOCUMENT

In the preparatory meetings held so far we have gradually come to the idea that insofar as the internal objective of the convention is concerned, it will be attained through a close tie-up between three distinct stages.

First stage. We analyze the phase in which the revolutionary process is at present in each country, taking due note of the key position of some countries in the overall continental strategy of imperialism and revolution. It will be viewed primarily in terms of *the emergence of the proletariat and the mobilization of the people.* This analysis will explore in detail highly significant features: e.g., increasing acuteness of the economic crisis, political stages, typical phases of the struggle, etc. It will serve as the backdrop and framework for all subsequent reflection. Using this backdrop of the revolutionary process in action, we shall move on to analyze the role of Christians and the function of the *"Christian element"* (in its socio-cultural, ideological, and political sense) *as impediments to, or mainsprings of, the progress of the revolutionary struggle.*

The standpoint for our analysis will be determined wholly by focusing on the comprehensive nature of the process, whether we are dealing with its course within a given country or its significance on the continental level. Any and every focus of a narrower sort is thus ruled out as being too inadequate and causing too much distortion, for it tends to pass judgment on the activity of Christians without going through the necessary task of visualizing the overall process.

Right at the start we must make explicit our revolutionary option in favor of implementing socialism through the rise of the proletariat to power. Once this has been done clearly and unmistakably, then we have a set of basic criteria for judging and evaluating the role that the "Christian element" is actually playing or can play in our countries. That role may be a positive one of stimulation or a negative one of obstruction. Here is an example of what we mean. Insofar as operational politics is concerned, the very notion of "revolutionary consciousness" will include as an intrinsic component the notion of power being held by the

people—the latter being led by the proletariat—and of effectiveness as an indispensable element in the gradual attainment of
power. This entails the elimination of any and every kind of
idealism in visualizing the "Christian element," because our
focus is concentrated on the historical terrain of the actual revolutionary struggle. We are speaking of course of a directly
political focus, since it is revolutionary. On this historical plane
idealistic questions—e.g., Should the Christian take a political
stance or nor?—become totally meaningless. The option for revolution is our point of reference at all times. As an option already
made, it is also the source of our governing criteria.

Second stage. The first stage of analysis will naturally lead to a
second stage that is far more demanding in theoretical and practical terms. *We must seek out and determine, on both the theoretical and
practical level, the structural causes, the hidden whys and wherefores,
the underlying factors that account for the role which the "Christian
element" does in fact play, and can play, in the revolutionary process.*
We must make a scientific effort to take a deeper reading of
reality, to break through the surface level of appearances in both
the realm of facts and events and the realm of ideologies. To do
this we feel we cannot prescind from the posture of historical
materialism. That is, we must situate ourselves on the material
and this-worldly terrain of history and have recourse to Marxism
as an analytical tool—while remaining cognizant of the fact that
Marxism, too, is part of a historical process still going on and that
it is not a dogmatics.

Again in this second stage of analysis, the overall process of the
emergence of the struggling people must serve as the key to any
ultimate interpretation. A deeper reading of the role of the
"Christian element" is possible only insofar as it is related to this
overall process. If we are looking for keys to a deeper interpretation of the role that the "Christian element" has played in history,
we will not find them within theology—insofar as the latter is
taken as an ideological realm that can be set off in isolation. We
may indeed find related elements of much importance in theology taken as such. But it is *the structural functions that the "Christian element" actually performs in socio-economic formations* that will
best enable us to unmask the various crypto-theologies and then

move on to read the "expressed theologies." The radically historical character of our reflection on the faith means that we must
work through the medium of the "non-theological" (in the traditional sense), so that we may be able to make theology once again
a significant conduit of effectively realized love. To put it another
way: The ideological character of Christianity in its sociological
manifestations—and we mean this in the pejorative sense of the
word "ideological"—can only be unveiled through *an analysis of
the functions it performs within the framework of the modes of production and other socio-economic formations.* Only then can we begin to
understand and comprehend why and how the pristine
dynamism of Christianity in favor of liberation has been castrated
so frequently. In short, we must engage in historical analysis,
exploring the mechanisms whereby it has been apprehended and
subsumed into social systems. Only such analysis will enable us
to go beyond a mere tactical utilization of Christian elements in
the revolutionary struggle.

Third stage. In this stage we will try to get a clearer picture of the
operation of the "Christian element" in the revolutionary process. We do not want to stay solely on the tactical level, drawing
operational conclusions that are short-range in nature and directed to the immediate present. Quite the contrary is true. We
want our revolutionary praxis, viewed within the framework of
the overall revolutionary process, to be an enriching component
of revolutionary theory itself. This presupposes *a basic option on
our part:* i.e., *effective real-life participation in the revolutionary process*
on a long-term basis. To put it another way, it presupposes
strategic participation rather than mere tactical participation.
Only our real-life participation, our revolutionary praxis, will
verify the solidity and consistency of the Christian contribution to
the process of revolution. It cannot be verified by superficial and
forced presentations of the "specific contribution of Christians,"
which are wont to crop up in dialogues between Christians and
Marxists.

When we say that we do not want to stay merely on the tactical
level, we do not mean that we object to the "tactical" use of the
Christian element or to the importance that the priest has in our
societies on the cultural level. One need only have an adequate

historical outlook on the faith and its inescapable political dimension to understand the "tactical" use of the Christian element.

And yet the tactical level is often ambiguous. A tactical ally can
turn into a strategic enemy. Given the existing ties between
"sociological Christianity" and capitalism, it often happens that
groups which seem to be progressive or even leftist end up as
strategic enemies of an authentic revolutionary process in the
long run. It is along these lines, perhaps, that we must analyze
postconciliar progressivism (Medellín in particular), the positions and accommodations of certain agents of the hierarchy, and
the position of certain "leftist" Christians. Some leftist Christians, for example, generously put their talents in the service of
the revolutionary process in a way that is tactically valuable but
that nevertheless tends to peter out and even to end up as a real
check on that process.

This simple enumeration of the three stages to be followed in
planning our convention and its work of reflection has already
led us to touch upon a considerable number of substantive issues.
We hope to continue to gather suggestions so that we may eventually incorporate them into a fuller and more comprehensive
document. Indeed this may give rise to a series of auxiliary
documents as well that would prove useful in the preparation of
national conventions and our April convention in Santiago.

IV. DRAFT GUIDELINES

The brief outline in the preceding section reflects the basic
methodological line to be followed in our April convention. But of
course it is not meant to fix in advance all the details of its
program and its organization. And that is all the more true for the
national conventions that are to take place in March. Taking due
account of the points outlined in the preceding section, we would
suggest the following draft guidelines for various national groups
in the preparation of their national conventions in March. It is not
our intention at all to make these guidelines mandatory. We
simply want to give a concrete illustration of the practical possibilities of the focus we have chosen.

First stage. The first step is to situate the experience of a given nation within an overall framework: i.e., the historical process of Latin America. Within the Latin American process, the emphasis will be on *the emergence of the proletariat and the growing mobilization of the people*. By way of example here, we shall merely touch upon some elements of this *overall framework*.

At the present time Latin America finds itself engaged in a revolutionary struggle replete with the hallmarks of a long and difficult journey. Political events bear witness to reformist and populist efforts that failed (e.g., the "revolution in liberty" attempted by the Christian Democrats in Chile from 1964-1970), as well as to repression and subversion (e.g., in Brazil, Uruguay, Argentina). The roots of this struggle are to be found in the *mode of production* that typifies most of Latin America, a mode of production based on *dependent capitalism*. Within Latin America it is centered in certain centers of industrial growth which have been spawned by foreign capitalism and which vary in strength depending on the availability of natural resources and the dynamism of the overall economy (compare Uruguay and Brazil, Costa Rica and Venezuela).

This mode of production based on dependent capitalism leads to economic crises, causes vast sectors of the public to lead an alienated and marginal life, and leads to political and social disintegration in our nations. This disintegration is more or less acute and obvious, depending on the nation involved. Meanwhile international capitalism, led by the United States, continues to progress at an accelerated pace—in technological and economic terms at least.

Within this overall framework of underdevelopment, only touched upon superficially here, we find that attitudes and perspectives of liberation are alive today. These perspectives were opened up a decade ago by the Cuban revolution, and they are now beginning to take concrete shape in some countries. Even in countries dominated by rightist political regimes we find a growing national consciousness; it is a reaction to the economic domination of the United States and to its unsound foreign policy. Progressivist governments have arisen through military coups (e.g., the government in Peru and that of Torres in Bolivia). In Chile a Marxist president has come to power through the democratic elective process. He is backed by the laboring class and he plans to implement a program that will overcome the system of dependent capitalism and legally inaugurate a socialist regime.

But the struggle for liberation has its failures too. Dictatorial and repressive regimes continue to flourish in some countries. Others seem to be moving backwards after taking some forward steps (e.g., in Bolivia). This gives rise to a heroic and sorrowful revolutionary struggle, reduced to the level of guerilla subversion in some countries. This revolutionary struggle intensifies revolutionary awareness and keeps repressive governments on tenterhooks (e.g., in Uruguay); but it does not manage to bring power to the people over the short run. Yet Latin America is "on the move" politically, and a new anti-capitalist and anti-imperialist consciousness is on the rise.

Within this overall framework, again sketched only briefly above, the churches are also subjected to profound changes. In some countries, for example, the Catholic Church is freeing herself from the traditional image. This traditional image pictured her as a clerical and monolithic entity, deeply bound up with the capitalist system and, at the very least, favoring the *status quo*, with an apologetic and triumphalist outlook in theology and a bent for sectarian conquest in temporal matters. As significant segments of the Church became involved with the laborer and the peasant, they evinced a growing awareness of the people's oppressive poverty and its structural cause: i.e., the system of dependent capitalism, which perpetuates economic and social evils.

This is not the place to analyze, even briefly and sketchily, why this process of change in the Church and of a growing commitment to the revolution in certain church segments is not solely generated *internally* by its own process of updating and *aggiornamento* (Vatican II, and Medellín which has given rise to a new theology of liberation) and why it is rather *conditioned by the economic and political happenings* mentioned briefly above. The convulsive dynamism of social deterioration gives rise to a series of internal crises within the Church. It divides Christians with opposing political stances; at the same time it creates a climate for rapprochement between Catholic and Protestant Christians who previously had little to do with each other. The class struggle seems to mark a new dividing line between Christians; at the same time it seems to be erasing or at least weakening other dividing lines that once separated Catholics from Protestants and Christians from Marxists.

This overall framework of structural analysis must be grounded on, and thoroughly verified by the reality of each country. Within this basic overall framework, however, it might be well to pose such questions as the following:

1. At what stage of the economic, social, and political process is your country?
2. Starting with Medellín, in what *significant happenings* on the national or global level have the Christians of your country participated?
3. Which of these happenings have served as a check or restraint on the process of revolutionary social change?
4. Which of these happenings have served as stimuli to this same process?
5. Which significant events seem to help to accelerate the revolutionary process in the short run, only to retard it later on? For example, have the movements of Christian origin or inspiration moved towards greater revolutionary commitment?
6. Which happenings that seem to be "reactionary" strengthen and consolidate a more long-range process?

Second stage. In the first stage you analyzed certain significant happenings on the level of descriptive history. Now these same happenings should be analyzed in terms of theoretical principles that will help you to determine their structural causes on the practical level. Some useful questions at this stage might be the following:

1. What "theological" positions are the inspiration for the significant happenings under discussion?
2. Is there a real correspondence between formal declarations and practical positions regarding these happenings (especially with regard to the revolutionary process now in gestation)?
3. What ideological elements do you find when you examine the content of sermons and the ministry of the sacraments?
4. What relationship do you detect between the factors analyzed above and the socio-economic setup of the country? To what extent does the preaching of the Christian message fill the role of camouflaging or concealing the real social situation?

5. To what extent are seemingly doctrinal elements put to ideological use in the significant happenings analyzed above? Consider
   such concepts as "Christian charity," "social peace," "Christian liberty," "natural law," and the "interior life."

Third stage. The main goal of this stage is to move on from the
analysis undertaken in the two previous stages to detect and
analyze a Christian contribution that can enrich the revolutionary
process. This is the objective of the convention itself. This does
not mean to imply that we are to overlook or disregard the tactical
outlook that Christians should adopt in a given country or in
Latin America as a whole.

PART III

MOVEMENT-HIERARCHY DOSSIER

The Declaration of The 80 and their subsequent activities provoked a variety of reactions in Chile. Among these reactions the basic stance of the Chilean hierarchy merits attention—particularly with regard to the proposed convention of Christians For Socialism. The interchange of communiqués between the bishops and the coordinating committee of Christians For Socialism served to clarify the views of both. Despite clear differences of opinion on certain issues and tactics, an attitude of respectful accommodation seemed to prevail.

On January 12, 1972, a memorandum was circulated to the bishops of Chile by the Permanent Committee of the Chilean Episcopate. It provided background information on The 80, reiterated the basic stance of the Chilean hierarchy towards political activity by priests, and stressed the fact that the proposed convention had no official approbation from the hierarchy (Document 5). The rest of the documents in this section represent an interchange of views between the members of the Secretariat of Christians For Socialism and the Archbishop of Santiago, Cardinal Raúl Silva Henríquez. On February 10 Father Gonzalo Arroyo invited the Cardinal to be a patron of the upcoming convention (Document 6). In a letter dated March 3, Cardinal Silva declined the invitation and expressed serious reservations about the doctrinal thrust of the Draft Agenda (Document 7). On March 20, the Secretariat responded to Cardinal Silva, criticizing his personal remarks to Father Gonzalo Arroyo and answering his objections point by point (Document 8). Cardinal Silva replied to their letter on April 13, indicating that he was pleased with the substance of their letter but also defending himself against what he regarded as unfair accusations against himself (Document 9). On April 28, an interview took place between Father Giulio Girardi of the Secretariat and Cardinal Silva. It was felt that this interview helped to clear up several points, and that a published summary of the Cardinal's views would counterbalance false interpretations that had appeared in the press. Father Girardi drew up a summary of the Cardinal's views, as expressed during their interview, which was then checked by the Cardinal himself before publication (Document 10).

5

Confidential Episcopal Memo on Upcoming Convention

Santiago
January 12, 1972

My Fellow Bishops:

By authority of the Permanent Committee of the Chilean Episcopate I am sending you some background information regarding the upcoming convention of priests from various Latin American countries. The convention is to take place in Santiago, Chile, in April. It has been convened by a group of Chilean priests known as "The 80" or "The Priest Secretariat of Christians For Socialism."

1. *Origin of the group known as "The 80."* In April 1971 a group of between sixty and seventy priests met in Santiago. They belonged to the archdiocese of Santiago and other dioceses in the country. They examined the socio-political situation of Chile and decided to commit themselves to the construction and implementation of socialism, opting *politically* for the *Popular Unity* regime. At that time they published a document in which they explained their point of view. That document has had profound repercussions on the national and international level.

The Chilean episcopate was meeting at the same time, holding a plenary session in Temuco. Faced with the convention of the priests known as "The 80," it formulated its position on their stance in these terms [see above Document 3]:

a. *Like any citizen, a priest is entitled to have his own political option.* But in no case should he give this option the moral backing that

35

stems from his character as a priest. For this reason we continue to follow the tradition of the Chilean church as exemplified by Cardinal Caro and Bishop Manuel Larraín. We have always insisted, and we will continue to insist, that our priests abstain from taking *partisan political positions* in public. To act otherwise would be to revert to an outdated clericalism that no one wants to see around again.

b. If the political option of the priest is presented as a *logical and inescapable consequence* of his Christian faith, as it was in this case, then it implicitly condemns every other option and *it is an attack on the liberty* of other Christians.

c. When the political option of the priest is made public, then it threatens to disrupt the unity of the Christian people with their pastors. As Vatican II points out: "In building the Christian community, priests are never to put themselves at the service of any ideology or human faction. Rather, as heralds of the gospel and shepherds of the Church, they must devote themselves to the spiritual growth of the Body of Christ" (*Presbyterorum ordinis*, n.6).

d. The situation that has arisen does not affect our esteem for the priests in question. Nor does it diminish our high regard for the apostolic work they, along with many others, are performing among the working class. We have touched upon this matter in our declaration only because of the wide repercussions that their own document has had.

2. *Activities of The 80.* Afterwards The 80 organized themselves to form a priest secretariat entitled "Christians For Socialism." It is an active group which makes decisions, issues public statements, drafts documents, and organizes meetings. It is trying to establish ties with similar groups in other countries, and *its political collaboration with the Popular Unity government in Chile becomes more and more marked. It even goes so far as to make concrete pronouncements about political elections.*

3. *Relations with the hierarchy.* Practically all of the priests in this group maintain their relationships with their bishops. The latter have not sought to break off ties with the former, even when their attention has been called to the fact that the activities of the priests run counter to norms that have been laid down by the Chilean episcopate.

To be specific, *the group known as The 80, as such, does not have the approbation of the Chilean episcopate* because *we feel* it is not the function of the priest to evince *a political commitment that confuses and divides the faithful.* This is a *pastoral judgment* made by the episcopate. After studying the concrete situation in Chile, we have reiterated this judgment several times in recent years: in September 1970, in April 1971, and in our presentation to the synod of bishops.

4. *Another group of priests.* In July 1971 another group of priests was formed, known as "The 200." They met to engage in reflection, prior to the next synod of bishops. This meeting was organized by priests of "The 80" group. The outcome of their reflection contained valuable elements which the Chilean episcopate accepted. The document drawn up by The 200, bearing witness to the thinking of a group of priests, was added as an appendix to the documentation that the Chilean episcopate presented at the synod of bishops.

The group known as The 200 wants to distinguish itself from the group known as The 80, because its objective is not directly political. It seeks rather to exert internal pressure within the Church in order to achieve certain reforms. Lately, however, it seems that this group is re-examining its own aims and goals.

5. *Convention of Latin American priests.* The group known as The 80, or as the Priest Secretariat of Christians For Socialism, is organizing a Latin American Convention in conjunction with similar groups of priests. The convention will take place in Santiago, Chile, from April 23 to April 30 of this year, at the same time that the third congress of UNCTAD is being held in Santiago. The announcement of this proposed convention, dated December 16, 1971, was sent to the Cardinal Archbishop of Santiago by Father Gonzalo Arroyo, S.J., the Secretary General of the group known as The 80. The convention is solely the initiative of this group, which has provided only limited information about the convention itself.

Receipt of this announcement does not mean that the Cardinal or the Chilean hierarchy approve this convention. Such approval has not been sought. And how can approval be given to a convention whose program, objectives, and participants are unknown? We do not want our silence to be interpreted as approval of this convention. Nor do we want our *silence* to be used to obtain the presence or participation of *representatives* from other episcopates at this convention. That is the reason behind this present communiqué. However, *we would very much like to know the opinion* of our fellow bishops in our conference concerning: 1) the organization of these groups of priests; 2) their ties with the local hierarchy; 3) the upcoming convention in April.

Finally, we want to express our firm hope that we will have a dialogue with these priests at an opportune time . . . .

Carlos Oviedo Cavada
Auxiliary Bishop of Concepción
Secretary General of the
Episcopal Conference of Chile

6

Letter of Invitation
to the Archbishop of Santiago

Executive Secretariat
Christians For Socialism
P.O. Box 117
Santiago 14
February 10, 1972

Cardinal Raúl Silva Henríquez
Archbishop of Santiago

Dear Cardinal:

As we indicated in our announcement letter dated December 17, 1971, the First Latin American Convention of Christians For Socialism will take place in this city from April 23 to April 30 of this year. Invited to it are various Christian movements, secretariats, and organisms of a progressivist nature as well as individuals who are in agreement with the basic formulations concerning the convention that appear in the attached document.

We have the honor of inviting you to be a member of our committee of patrons for this convention. We want it to represent a broad sector of Catholics and Protestants who are trying to follow Christ's summons "to proclaim release for prisoners and recovery of sight for the blind; to let the broken victims go free" (Lk 4:18). At present Latin America is engaged in a revolutionary struggle to liberate itself from its economic dependence on capitalist imperialism and from the underdevelopment generated by that imperialism. We believe that the contribution of Christians to this struggle can be a decisive one.

At the convention we hope to analyze the political experiences of the different individuals and groups which are seeking the liberation of the peoples of America; to evaluate the role that Christians have played in this process so far and that they should play in the future; to engage in theological reflection on this role; and to consider ways of coordinating our efforts and our support so that our action might be more effective.

This convention is not tied up with any official organism of government or the Church. It is an initiative sponsored by persons associated with the ONIS movement in Peru, the Third World movement in Argentina, and the continental ISAL movement. They, along with the Secretariat of the Christians For Socialism movement in Chile, have felt that such a convention is necessary, useful, and even desperately needed.

To carry out this convention, we are at present relying solely on the funds provided by the individual national groups. They are to finance their own round-trip journey. In turn the Chilean delegation has offered to find lodging for foreign delegates and to finance the cost of their stay here. The modesty of our resources will impose a certain degree of austerity on the convention. But we feel sure that this fact will highlight more clearly the demands of the gospel in our turbulent Latin America, where in many instances new hopes of liberation are being spawned among industrial workers, manual laborers, peasants, and students.

The response to this invitation has been favorable so far. Apart from the groups mentioned above, various theologians of note have promised to attend; and we also hope to have some bishops in attendance, lending their weight to the proceedings. We hope that you too will honor us with your presence and active participation at the upcoming convention in Santiago.

Gonzalo Arroyo
for the Organizing Committee

7

Initial Response of Cardinal Silva
to Gonzalo Arroyo

Santiago
March 3, 1972

Rev. Gonzalo Arroyo

Dear Father:

This is in reply to your invitation on behalf of the Organizing Committee that I become a patron of the convention you plan to hold from April 23 to April 30 of this year under the designation "Christians For Socialism."

I have carefully studied the Draft Agenda of the proposed convention which you sent me and which I already had in my possession. From my study of this document I am convinced that you are going to hold a political meeting and that your aim is to commit the Church and Christians to the struggle on behalf of Marxism and the Marxist revolution in Latin America. As you see it, Marxism is the one and only way to liberate man.

As you can readily appreciate, my dear friend, it does not seem at all proper to me to patronize a convention of priests who have taken a stance which in my opinion is not the stance of the Church, and who make affirmations and engage in actions that are at variance with explicit declarations issued by the national episcopate.

I believe that you, motivated by the lofty desire to liberate our people from oppressive structures, are embarking on a road which is not the best one in my judgment. As I see it, this pathway is in fact causing you to renounce your Christianity and it will not lead to the liberation for which you hope.

I appreciate your generosity. I fully share your manifest yearning for the liberation of our people. But I do not at all share your idea that one must choose Marxism as the one and only solution for the problems of our America. While there is no doubt that there can be many points of contact with Marxists in working for the liberation of our peoples, I think it is absolutely necessary that Christians do not renounce their Christianity. Instead they must contribute the spiritual values of Christianity to this struggle for liberation, so that the eventual outcome will in fact be the one they hoped for.

In order to make my observations concrete and specific, I will present six points that touch upon your Draft Agenda and that offer support for my position on this matter. I want you to know the thinking of a pastor of souls who does not want to deviate one bit from his principles and who is sure that only Jesus Christ makes us free.

1. You propose anonymous Christianity without the Church.

The aims of the proposed convention are framed in the context of anonymous groups of "committed Christians": "Intended to be a spontaneous melding of shared hopes and desires, the convention will represent the end result of efforts and initiatives taken by various groups of committed Christians. In no way will it or should it be tied to official organisms of the Church or the government."

There is no reference at all to the gospel and, in particular, to the Church. But there is no Christianity without the Church and a hierarchical priesthood. The danger lies in setting up an opposition between Christianity and Institution. The new visage of the Church since Vatican II is unity and plurality. In this hazardous time it is more important than ever that the Christian community be a "sacrament of unity" and that the hierarchy be a service to that unity.

Within this pluralism the pope and the bishops maintain the role of safeguarding and serving as a "sacrament" of the universal communion. Their role guarantees the unity and liberty of every Christian.

As the bishops of Chile have pointed out in their episcopal conference, those whose role makes them official representatives of the Church must serve the simultaneous effort of all Christians to live the gospel from within any and every legitimate political stance. For this reason these official representatives cannot publicly "take sides with one specific group or party." At the same time, however, Christians do not act as "anonymous Christians" within the different groups and parties; they act as "seeds of resurrection" in order to "flesh out the fundamental option of the gospel." And they do this in unity and continuity with the Church and her hierarchy, without which there is no true and faithful proclamation of Jesus Christ.

2. You propose a narrow formula of revolution as the only way.

In the eyes of those who drew up your Draft Agenda, the only formula for liberation is "revolution." And this revolution is "one single phenomenon . . . *comprehensive and one* in character." It has to do with the rise of the proletariat to power as they struggle to liberate themselves from socio-economic exploitation and every other form of bondage.

This outlook is well on the way towards becoming Marxist. It evinces a class-based attitude and it evaluates human liberation in terms that are too strictly economics-oriented.

In equating a commitment to "the process of socialization" with a specific program of "socialism," and in equating service to the cause of liberating the "poor" and the "masses" with a class struggle of the "proletariat" you oversimplify the problem and the reality. It is a superficial outlook that does not mesh well with a Christian and priestly outlook.

You state that you must "have recourse to Marxism as an analytical tool" and to its dialectic of class struggle. This leads me to two conclusions that have already been stressed by the bishops of Chile [see Document 2]: "1) neither its scientific validity as a sociological method nor its separability from the overall Marxist theory are universally clear and self-evident; 2) the Marxist evaluation of the proletarian class as the exclusive bearer of humanity's future does not at all dovetail with the gospel's blessing on the poor."

And Pope Paul VI tells us: "One can indeed look at Marxist doctrine, as it is implemented in real-life action, and make distinctions between these various facets and between the various questions it raises for Christian deliberation and action. But it would be foolish and dangerous on that account to forget that they are closely linked to each other; to embrace certain elements of Marxist investigation without taking due account of their relation with its doctrine; and to become involved in the class struggle and the Marxist interpretation of it without paying attention to the kind of violent and totalitarian society to which this activity gradually leads" (Apostolic Letter *Octogesima adveniens*, May 14, 1971, n.34).

3. You reduce Christianity to the revolutionary class struggle and to the historical situation.

You talk about analyzing "the role of Christians and the function of the 'Christian element' . . . as impediments to, or mainsprings of, the progress of the revolutionary struggle." This leads you to "the elimination of any and every kind of idealism in visualizing the 'Christian element.' " Your focus is concentrated "on the historical terrain of the actual revolutionary struggle." Your point of reference at all times and the source of your governing criteria is "the option for revolution."

The Church, as the community of believers, has made a fundamental option that is the *raison d'être* of her whole existence and mission. She has opted definitively and ineradicably for the risen Christ, as a bride for her bridegroom.

In Jesus Christ she has opted for everything that is human and for the gospel as her supreme criterion in the tasks connected with liberation. All human beings without exception enter into this option. If she shows any favoritism or preference at all, it is for those most in need of liberation and for the criterion of love as the supreme inspiration of all methodology in praxis.

Of its very nature, this humanist commitment of the Church is far deeper and more complete than that presented by Marxism. Indeed the latter is excluding and unilateral. Its schemas seem to be Manichean in inspiration because they divide human beings into good and bad, oppressed and oppressors, solely on the basis of economic factors and social differences.

The Church's commitment to liberation starts from a more radical exigency and it strives for a more integral liberation insofar as it tries to clearly reveal, at every level of its activity, him who alone is capable of giving salvation to the world: Jesus Christ.

4. You reduce theology to ideology in a superficial way.

Theology is not simply material for philosophical analysis. It expresses the faith of the Church. It asserts the paradoxical proposition that Jesus is the Christ. And it also examines the presuppositions and further implications of this assertion.

Theological existence gives expression to the existence of those who are possessed by the Spirit in the bosom of the Church and who have received the Word of knowledge and widsom.

Marxists certainly do teach Christians to stop being mere word-mongers, to leaven and set in motion those sources of energy that can be most effective in bringing about changes: e.g., young people and the common people as a whole. It is in these milieus in particular that political activity and any commitment to it must rest on the basis described by Pope Paul VI: "Political activity . . . should be grounded on a formulated picture of society that is consistent in itself with regard to the means it will use and the plans from which it will operate. These plans should proceed from a full-fledged awareness of man's vocation and of the different forms it assumes in society" (*Octogesima adveniens*, Apostolic Letter, 14 May 1971, n.25).

To reduce everything that is not socio-economic transformation to ideology is to greatly oversimplify the problem. Faith is not ideology. It is a reality superior to any and all ideologies, capable of criticizing them and perceiving both the positive and negative elements in them. It helps ideology to truly serve man.

5. You reduce Christianity to a single dimension: socio-economic transformation.

It is indeed true that if Christianity estranges man from society and its struggles, then it is not authentic. Faith always leads to social and political involvement.

But the essential commitment of Christianity is evangelization. And that means proclaiming Christ and suffusing all temporal values and commitments with the spirit of the gospel. The two aspects are inseparable. Any and every unilateral interpretation leads to dualism and is therefore alienating. Exclusive focus on the first aspect turns Christianity into an intellectual pronouncement. Vatican II expressly stated that the divorce between faith and historical commitment was one of the major errors of our age. Total emphasis on the second aspect, on temporal values, can cause man to forget the spirit of the gospel that should animate them.

We must stay cognizant of the fact that our proclamation of Christ should entail historical commitment, and that our commitment in history should be vivified by the spirit of the gospel. Thus if people dedicate themselves to party politics, they are not Christians insofar as they engage in politics; they are Christians insofar as they engage in politics in the spirit of the gospel.

6. In general, you reduce Christianity to something that is purely sociological and that has no element of mystery in it.

The preponderant sociological thrust of your document is prejudicial to the deeper reality of the mystery. In the view it expresses we do not find any place for those values that are peculiar and essential to Christianity: incarnation, redemption, the sense of sin, prayer, contemplation, the presence of the Spirit. At the same time historical horizontalism, with all its ambiguity, predominates.

Thus your document represents an individualistic interpretation of the Church, the mystery of faith, and Christianity. It evinces no deeper biblical interpretation of God's pedagogy in history.

As you can see, my dear friend, many serious doctrinal differences separate us. I believe that you are turning Christianity into a ridiculous caricature by reducing it to a socio-economic and political system. It thereby loses its lofty religious values. I cannot subscribe to that nor can I patronize a convention of priests who, for all their good will, seek to do just that. Please excuse me, my dear friend, for not being able to accept your invitation. I would ask you to erase my name once and for all from the list of possible patrons for this convention.

Before I close, I would like to say a personal word to you, dear Father. You are a member of the Society of Jesus, an Institute commissioned to defend the Catholic Church, which was founded by Jesus Christ, and to spread its beneficent influence throughout the world. After pondering the points of this letter and your own efforts to promote this Convention of Christians For Socialism, I must confess that I am a bit scandalized. In all frankness I must say that your activity seems to be destructive of the Church. That you hold these ideas is not so disturbing, because we all can make mistakes. But an Institute such as yours has many members who have had a solid formation and who are deeply versed in Christian thought. And it seems to me that they should not allow a public action of such undeniable impact on the Catholic Church before examining it carefully and getting approval of the event and the doctrines underlying it. If your Institute is not capable of guiding the activity of its members in favor of the Church, I think it has betrayed the deepest reasons underlying its own origin.

Pardon me, dear friend, for this frankness. You know my character and the way I work. No motive of pettiness is behind these reflections of mine.

Your servant in Christ,
Raúl Cardinal Silva H.
Archbishop of Santiago

8

Response of the Coordinating Committee to Cardinal Silva

Santiago
March 20, 1972

Cardinal Raúl Silva Henríquez

Dear Don Raúl:

We have read your letter of March 3 to Gonzalo Arroyo, turning down the invitation to take part in the First Latin American Convention of Christians For Socialism. Since Gonzalo Arroyo was not acting in his capacity as an individual but rather as a member of a team and as the duly chosen Secretary General of our organization, we wish first of all to indicate that we all are in solidarity with him.

Secondly, speaking respectfully but quite frankly, we must say that we are in total disagreement with the personal reference you make at the end of your letter. Just as you say you are scandalized by Gonzalo's attitude, so we are scandalized by the attitude of a pastor who would pass such severe judgment on a priest when the latter, motivated by good intentions and following the appeals of the Church itself is engaged in the struggle to bring the poor and the oppressed to their liberation in Jesus Christ. We are even more scandalized by the way you do this—making a personal reference in a letter that you circulated to the other bishops in our episcopal conference and that has come to the attention of other priests and lay people. Of course Gonzalo can make a mistake—as you can, as we can. But we have every evidence of his good will and his love for the authentic Church of Christ. Hence we simply cannot accept the statement that his activity is destructive, and we also find it unacceptable that this statement should be made in a letter that was circulated within the Church. This approach, it seems to us, is totally out of line with the trust and openness that should exist between a pastor and his priests. Hence we think that you should think the matter over and offer an explanation to Gonzalo, for the statement in your letter may not have been a fortunate expression of your own thinking; and it openly contradicts what you said to him in a private conversation a few days before.

Moving on to the heart of the matter, we want you to know that we have given much thought to your letter. We have also consulted with various members of the Secretariat of Christians For Socialism whose philosophical and theological background could help us best to elucidate doctrinal questions.

When we re-read your letter, we saw even more clearly something that we had noticed before: namely, that our Draft Agenda omits important features of Christian thinking about liberation, and that these points are precisely the ones you bring up in your six observations. *But we do not deny what we have omitted.* On the contrary, we take these things for granted. It did not occur to us to explicitate those things because they are part and parcel of our life and activity as priests. So we spoke about the things which were *new* to us and which therefore required greater elaboration: namely, *the sociological and political aspect of the Christian faith.*

As a result our document is to some extent a one-sided one, and it could upset readers who were unfamiliar with the presuppositions we take for granted. But our document makes no claims to completeness. Its basic scope is clearly outlined in a preliminary note concerning that document: "The sole aim of this document is to provide a cursory sketch of some *basic guidelines* that might serve as a basic framework for the suggestions and discussions that will crop up at the various national meetings. It is in no way meant to be a strict delimitation of the agenda for the Convention. If the preparatory phase does in fact confirm that

these guidelines are central points of interest for everyone involved, then they will be spelled out further in some sort of Basic
Document that might serve as an auxiliary draft during the preparatory phase."

It should be evident from this statement that the Draft Agenda
is hardly a complete and finished embodiment of our thinking.
We are in complete agreement with the following statement you
make in your letter: "While there is no doubt that there can be
many points of contact with Marxists in working for the liberation
of our people, I think it is absolutely necessary that Christians do
not renounce their Christianity. Instead they must contribute the
spiritual values of Christianity to this struggle for liberation, so
that the eventual outcome will in fact be the one they hoped for."

At the same time, however, there are things in your letter that
are far from clear. We believe that everyone would benefit from
further elucidation of them. And we also feel that important
sections of our Draft Agenda have not been comprehended in
their authentic sense.

1. "You propose anonymous Christianity without the Church."

In your letter the term "anonymous Christianity," which does
not appear in the document you criticize, appears to be quite
unclear. In any case its meaning in your letter seems to have little
to do with its meaning in contemporary theological discussions
(see the works of Karl Rahner).

If in fact there is no (explicit) reference to the gospel in our Draft
Agenda, the reason is that in it we are not claiming to speak
"theologically" about the entire *content* of the "Christian element" as such. We are simply trying to delineate the objectives
and mechanics of a convention centered around the cultural and
political function that the "Christian element" could or does in
fact play in the present-day operation of Latin American society.
It is a methodological necessity that these objectives and
mechanics be posed in a sociological and political framework. We
fully agree with you when you say: "There is no Christianity
without the Church and a hierarchical priesthood. The danger

lies in setting up an opposition between Christianity and Institution." But we do not see why or how the stated non-association of the planned convention with any official organisms of the Church or the hierarchy can be interpreted as a rejection, on the part of the convention organizers, of any and all reference to the institutional Church and to the hierarchical priesthood insofar as their understanding of Christianity is concerned. Your letter would seem to suggest that it is licit for Christians—priests and lay people—to meet and talk about the implications of their faith only when they are officially called together by the hierarchy. What is more, we have in fact approached you, the Permanent Committee of the Episcopate, and other Latin American bishops. We have asked all of you the same thing: to be present at the convention in whatever way you deem suitable. This concrete position could hardly be compatible with rejection of the institutional factor in the Church. There is a wide distance between holding a convention not convoked by the hierarchy and actually rejecting the hierarchy.

There is another reason for this type of meeting not being the result of official initiative. The reason is the hierarchy's function of unity which you yourself mention. It is indisputable that the episcopate and the priesthood are a "sacrament of unity." But this fact does not reveal to us the concrete form in which this service to unity should be exercised. There are epochs of social consensus and epochs of social dissent. In the former it is easy for the hierarchy to echo the existing consensus, to formulate it and express its deeper underlying import. In the latter the primary task is to help to create a unity that does not exist or that is seriously impaired. Everything becomes more difficult for the priest in such instances. In carrying out his task of leading people to unity, he must often tread unexplored pathways, seek new and unforeseen solutions, and run the risk of making mistakes. But doesn't the good shepherd do the same thing in searching for the lost sheep? The task of bishops is even more difficult. In such epochs it is to be expected that free discussion among Christians will be allowed greater room, even when it comes to the concrete forms of expressing their faith.

2. *"You propose a narrow formula of revolution as the only way."*

That in Latin America we cannot have liberation without revolution and the implementation of socialism, that "revolution"
and "socialism" cannot be just theoretical options but rather
must entail (critical-minded) commitment to a concrete process
that is in fact at work—these are convictions that have already
been arrived at by a significant sector of Latin American Christianity; and many bishops are included in this group.

When we say that "the revolution is one single
phenomenon . . . comprehensive and one in character," we are
trying to say that it is necessary for all who truly desire revolution
to join forces and unite. And we are thereby rejecting any attempt
to stress some fudamentally different option: e.g., a Christian
revolution that would stand as an alternative or an option opposed to a Marxist revolution. The Latin American experience
has taught us that the external forces opposed to our liberation
are very powerful, so powerful that liberation is feasible only if
we achieve a broad-based union among those sectors—both
Christian and Marxist—which truly desire revolution.

Insofar as the scientific analysis proposed by Marxism is concerned, we fully agree that it is partial and incomplete. That is
true of any form of scientific analysis. If someone is looking for an
all-embracing statement about man, then he or she must turn to
philosophy, theology, art, or religious experience—as the case
may be. Despite the fact that any scientific method is partial and
incomplete, there is a permanent temptation to turn it into a
philosophy and ultimately into a religion. Paul VI shrewdly
noted this fact in section 38 of *Octogesima adveniens*. But there he
notes this fact as a general tendency. He does not say it is a
peculiarity of Marxism; he says it is a feature of the sciences in
general, and at present of the "human sciences" in particular.

We also agree that its scientific validity as a sociological
methodology is not "universally clear and self-evident." But in a
recent document the bishops of Chile do point out the positive
contributions made by this methodology. These contributions
are enough to satisfy us. In the present circumstances of Latin
America we believe that this methodology, more than any other,

clearly spotlights the all-embracing and interrelated character of the different phenomena blocking our liberation. We believe that there is indeed a real temptation to view Marxism as a cure-all. Hence we expressly add a proviso when we talk about using it as an analytic method: " . . . remaining cognizant of the fact that Marxism too is part of an historical process still going on and that it is not a dogmatics."

Our Draft Agenda does not in any way affirm that the Marxist valuation of the proletariat coincides with the gospel's blessing on the poor. There is no doubt that such an indentification, aside from being a gross anachronism, would empty the gospel of its religious marrow on the one hand and, on the other hand, over-look the originality of the Marxist analysis in the socio-economic realm. Yet today it seems difficult for anyone to flatly deny any dovetailing between the Marxist evaluation and the gospel's blessing on the poor. For recent exegesis has brought out the social and economic dimensions surrounding the religious valua-tion of poverty and oppression in the Jewish, biblical tradition; and we must interpret the gospel within this context.

The novel aspect of Paul VI's treatment of Marxism is his shift of emphasis from doctrine to concrete options. This shift was anticipated by John XXIII: "It is perfectly legitimate to make a clear distinction between a false philosophy of the nature, origin, and purpose of men and the world, and economic, social, cul-tural, and political undertakings—even when such undertakings draw their origin and inspiration from that philosophy. True, the philosophic formula does not change once it has been set down in precise terms, but the undertakings clearly cannot avoid being influenced to a certain extent by the changing conditions in which they have to operate" (*Pacem in terris,* n.159). Right from the start of *Octogesima adveniens,* Paul VI focuses on the variety of options available: "In the face of such widely varying situations, it is certainly difficult for us to enunciate one way of thinking which will provide a suitable solution for all parts of the world . . . . Christian communities should determine the courses of action and the tasks which should be undertaken to effect the social, political and economic changes that appear necessary and that often will brook no delay"(n.4). Referring directly to socialism later on, he says: "Keen and discerning judgment is called for . . . . Socialism finds expression in different ways: as a generous desire and quest for a more just society, as an historical movement with a political organization aim, as a body of doctrine that professes to give an integral and independent consideration of man. Distinctions must be made between these forms of expression, so that selectivity may be exercised in concrete circumstances . . . . This discernment will enable Christians to appreciate to what extent they may involve themselves in these plans" (n.31).

What is the reason for this "keen and discerning judgment"? It is that the passage of one hundred years means something. The Marxists we meet today in the flesh have been affected by the continuing history of the world and of their own nations. It would be naive—and also anti-Marxist—to think that they have not learned anything from history. There is no reason to think that they accept unreservedly everything that Marx wrote a century ago. There are things in Marx's view that relate to his situation as a man of the nineteenth century and that are anachronistic today. On the other hand we should not think that the passage of history has transformed it so much that there is no trace of the classic formulation Marx set forth. And so *Octogesima adveniens* urges caution: "One can indeed look at Marxist doctrine, as it is implemented in real-life action, and make distinctions between these various facets and between the various questions it raises for Christian deliberation and action. But it would be foolish and dangerous on that account to forget that they are closely linked to each other; to embrace certain elements of Marxist investigation without taking due account of their relation with its doctrine; and to become involved in the class struggle and the Marxist interpretation of it without paying attention to the kind of violent and totalitarian society to which this activity gradually leads" (n.34).

In short, one cannot simply take over this doctrine; one must create it anew. In the course of history Christians have taken over the most varied kinds of thought, some of them being greatly at variance with the Christian faith: e.g., gnosticism, pantheistic neoplatonism, Averroist aristotelianism, materialistic darwinism, atheistic psychoanalysis. But it has not been a purely mechanical operation in which some things have been adopted and others rejected. Instead it has been a work of re-creation. Christians have not simply taken over some item and incorporated it into the "Christian synthesis." They have re-thought the "Christian synthesis" in the light of the new elements taken in. Paul VI summons us to do this, warning us against a mechanical and unimaginative assimilation of Marxism. That is the underlying intention of his remark.

In the ideological and political context of Latin America, the same warning should be given to those who adopt an anti-Marxist position. To what extent may such a position indicate that Christianity has been contaminated by bourgeois ideology and by concrete complicity with an established form of violence?

3. "You reduce Christianity to the revolutionary class struggle and to the historical situation."

When we talk about the role of Christians and the function of the "Christian element" in the revolutionary struggle, we are speaking in sociological and political terms about the real-life Church as it exists in concrete individuals, groups, and institutions in our historical context. When you say in your letter that the Church has opted in Jesus Christ for all that is human and for the gospel as the supreme criterion of liberation, you are speaking in theological terms; and the further implications of these terms require much greater clarification. The two languages are not necessarily opposed to each other. But as they are framed in your letter, there is a danger that they will never get together at all.

In our document, by contrast, the terms spring from a desire to mediate between the two. We ask about the real-life existence and impact of the "Christian element" in the praxis of history; and this praxis must entail concrete options with their inevitable risks. We do feel that we need to elaborate a new theological language which allows for an encounter between the language of sociology and the traditional language of theology.

We agree with you when you say in your letter that the Christian vision of liberation is more profound and complete than the

Marxist vision. But it should be noted that Marxist thinkers themselves have noticed the incomplete character of their social
analysis. Today they are making an effort to spell out their thinking about the individual (e.g., Adam Schaff, Herbert Marcuse,
etc.). But the Christian does go even deeper, planting and posing
liberation in terms of man's relationship with God. On this level
human beings do not simply liberate themselves; they integrate
their efforts into the liberation achieved by Christ. But while
Christianity does have a more clearcut vision of the overall perspectives of liberation, it also has much to learn from Marxism,
psychoanalysis, and other disciplines about the concrete
mechanisms through which liberation works itself out at different levels.

4. "You reduce theology to ideology."

We feel that you level this charge against our document in a
gratuitous way, using the same line of argument cited earlier: i.e.,
if something is not affirmed explicitly, you assume that it is being
denied. It is true that theology is centered around the risen Christ
and wells up from the activity of his Spirit, as does the faith which
is its source and which it claims to serve. But it is no less true that
it is conditioned by socio-cultural factors and that it inevitably has
socio-political implications. If it did not have such implications,
rulers would not have evinced such a preoccupation with theology throughout the history of the Church. (Constantine played
such a preponderant role at the Council of Ephesus, not because
he was a devoted student of theology, but because the questions
debated there about Christ and the Virgin had implications directly relating to the political unity of his empire.)

But the fact that theology has *conditions* surrounding it does not
mean that one can conclude that it *can be reduced* to those conditions. The free act has many conditions surrounding it—social
conditionings, psychological conditionings, physiological conditionings, and so forth. But it is not reducible to these conditions.
In the present case we propose to make a critical study of the
conditionings and implications imbedded in the present-day

situation of Latin America. But this does not mean that we deny or reject the other aspect: the essential truth of theology. In your letter you state that Christ inspires temporal tasks and that he is the liberator of history; you do not say anything about his divinity. Yet it is clear that you do not deny or reject his divinity.

In our document we expressly allude to the ideological factor. At one point we say: "If we are looking for keys to a deeper interpretation of the role that the 'Christian element' has played in history, we will not find them within theology—insofar as the latter is taken as an ideological realm that can be set off in isolation." But shortly after that statement we add: "The radically historical character of our reflection on the faith means that we must work through the medium of the 'non-theological' (in the traditional sense), so that we may be able to make theology once again a significant conduit of effectively realized love." To put this less abstrusely: Instead of fashioning a theology that is isolated from its conditioning factors and naively unaware of them, we want to fashion a theology that incorporates these factors. Further on we talk about exploring the possibility of "ideological elements" in the content of sermons and the ministry of the sacraments. Clearly this suggestion does not reduce sermons and the sacraments to nothing more than ideology. And the same obviously holds true when we talk about apparently doctrinal elements being "put to ideological use." What we are seeking to do is to detect the possible abuse of such concepts as Christian charity, social peace, Christian liberty, natural law, interior life, and so forth. For that matter you yourself are concerned about making a distinction between authentic doctrine and apparent doctrine. In a recent interview program you discussed how people abuse such a traditional and worthwhile notion as the "interior life."

It is an obvious historical fact that theologies or theological elements have often been used ideologically to justify the existing socio-economic system during the two-thousand-year history of the Church. That this has been true, and continues to be true, in the concrete history of Latin America is no less a fact. It is verified by the real-life experience of critical-minded Christians of all sorts in Latin America, and this experience has been attested to by many documents—including some documents issued by the hierarchy in recent years.

5. "You reduce Christianity to a single dimension: socio-economic transformation."

Here again we are confronted with two types of language that do not get together but that are not opposed either. You talk about "the essential commitment of Christianity," and you say that "faith always leads to social and political involvement." These statements in turn are grounded on the major premise that "if Christianity estranges man from society and its struggles, then it is not authentic."

The projected Convention takes this major premise for granted and begins directly with the minor premise. It wants to find out in what way and to what extent Christians of Latin America are alienated from society and its struggles by their beliefs and real-life practices, and also alienate others. It wants to find this out precisely to combat the divorce between faith and real-life commitment in history that was criticized so severely by Vatican II. And it wants to do this precisely because its organizers are convinced that authentic Christian faith has a great deal to contribute to the liberation process now under way on our continent.

6. "You reduce Christianity to something that is purely sociological and that has no element of mystery in it."

This objection, which sums up the others, does not seem justified to us. In proposing a socio-cultural analysis of Christianity as it exists *in the concrete* in Latin America, we are not at all claiming to offer a comprehensive view of what Christianity is in itself. We are not proposing to examine all the elements that are essential for a full and complete understanding and practice of it. (See our observations above.)

We repeat: The fact that something is not affirmed does not mean that it is denied. But we do agree that our Draft Agenda could have contained a few more explicit references to the overall dimensions of Christianity even though it did not propose to treat them directly.

You reproach us for an individualistic "interpretation" on the one hand, and for reducing Christianity to its social and political dimensions on the other hand. We do not see how you can reconcile these two criticisms.

We choose to take seriously the socio-cultural and political dimension of Christianity in present-day Latin America. In so doing we believe that this tack not only includes a biblical examination of God's pedagogy in history but also is demanded by it.

One passage in your letter has left us perplexed. You say this about our document: "In the view it expresses we do not find any place for those values that are peculiar and essential to Christianity: incarnation, redemption, the sense of sin, prayer, contemplation, the presence of the Spirit. At the same time historical horizontalism, with all its ambiguity, predominates."

Most of us members of the Secretariat of Christians For Socialism are priests. Some of us are parish priests directly under you. Every Sunday we celebrate the Eucharist in the midst of a Christian community, and we proclaim the word of God to it. It would indeed be a serious situation in the Church if in all that there was no trace of the incarnation, the redemption, and the other realities you mention. That you would think of us in that light is what disconcerts us most. We realize that your reading of a full and complete document arouses your suspicions, that you feel there are things which should be spelled out more clearly, and that you are showing us what we should spell out more fully. But we simply cannot understand how you can suppose that the essential core of Christianity does not form a part of our lives.

We feel that you can well presume we have much more than an immense "good will." You are aware of the extremely austere kind of life that is led by not a few priests who make up this Secretariat. How could one live such a life if he did not lead it out of love for Jesus Christ, out of a desire to shoulder his cross and thus participate in his redemptive work? If we were engaged in a political effort at consciousness-raising, we could live just as well in the best section of town. On this point we simply do not understand you, and we feel that there is need for more contact and conversation between you and us. That is what all of us desire most.

After this lengthy commentary on the six points you felt obliged to make about our document, we feel that there is no validity in this statement of yours: "From my study of this document I am convinced that you are going to hold a political meeting and that your aim is to commit the Church and Christians to the struggle on behalf of Marxism and the Marxist revolution in Latin America." This conclusion is based on a distorted reading and a mistaken interpretation of our Draft Agenda, and hence it grieves us. Most of your statements and objections are based on the argument from omission.

However, we want to say the following. If by "political" you are referring to the handling of the public affairs, to the struggle for power and the exercise of such power, or to opting for a specific party, then the convention will not be "political" because it does not have any of those objectives.

Now if a group of Christians get together to reflect on the unjust situation in Latin America, on the liberation of the oppressed, on the behavior of Christians in the struggle for liberation and the involvement of faith in this process, then their act of getting together will inevitably have political repercussions (as did the Medellín Conference).

We are not interested in forming factions designed to lead the masses of the people to take over the power now held by a few. That undoubtedly is "political." But now the word has a meaning that is quite different from the restricted sense it is usually given.

In short, we would agree that our meeting is political if by that term you are referring to the great transformation of this continent into a society of human beings who are truly equal in the rights they have. We would not agree that it is political if by that you are referring to the petty game of party politics whereby each group seeks to grab power and dominate others.

Our convention does not seek to propagate a specific ideology or to fight for Marxist parties. What interests us is the liberation of the people. It is one thing to believe that Jesus Christ is the only one in whom we find man's total liberation. It is something else again—something not opposed to the first belief—to concern oneself with the human instruments of a socio-economic liberation that is not alien or inimical to Christ's liberation.

Here we have tried to answer your comments and objections at length, after giving them deep study and thought. We can only regret that you will not be present in any way at our Convention. On many occasions your public stances have inspired us to commit ourselves more generously to work on behalf of our fellow men, the oppressed in particular, and on behalf of our society. This time around we will not reckon with your support. But we do hope that this dialogue—harsh as it may seem—will help to ensure that on other occasions we will be able to be together in the difficult task which the Church has entrusted to us among the laboring class, the peasants, and others struggling for their liberation.

Sincerely yours,
Coordinating Committee
Secretariat of
Christians For Socialism

Gonzalo Arroyo
Alfonso Baeza
Juan Casañas
Martín Gárate
Esteban Gumucio
José Gutiérrez
Diego Irarrázaval

Juan Martín
Antonio Mondalaers
Mariano Puga
Guillermo Redington
Pablo Richard
Sergio Torres
Santiago Thijssen

9

Response of Cardinal Silva to Coordinating Committee

Santiago
April 13, 1972

Gonzalo Arroyo and
Members of the Coordinating Committee of the
Secretariat of Christians For Socialism

My Dear Friends:

On returning from my trip to Rome, I found your letter of March 20 in which you respond to my previous letter to Gonzalo Arroyo. Despite the polemical passages it contains, and despite the harsh and in my opinion unjust judgments it expresses, I accept the substance of it which strikes me as being quite positive.

You acknowledge that your document "omits important features of Christian thinking"; that it is "hardly a complete and finished embodiment" of your thinking. You agree that your Draft Agenda "could have contained a few more explicit references to the overall dimensions of Christianity." You admit that in practice the revolution is not one single thing, that what you are proposing is "a broad-based union among those sectors . . . which truly desire revolution." The kind of politics you are interested in is not the "handling of public affairs" or "opting for a specific party"; it is politics in the manner of the episcopal conference at Medellín. You state that your convention "does not seek to propagate a specific ideology or to fight for Marxist parties."

These and other similar remarks have clarified your thinking a great deal. It is too bad, in my opinion, that those who formulated your response to me had not drawn up the Draft Agenda in the first place. It might have spared us this exchange of letters.

Before I conclude, I want to explore three statements you make in order to obviate serious misunderstandings. Firstly, you criticize me severely for stating that the political activity of some of you is destructive of the Church. On this point the doctrine of the church magisterium is clearly and authoritatively expressed by Pius XII: "When men in politics—including members of the Church—seek to turn the Bride of Christ into their ally or *to use her as a tool of their national or international political combines, they thereby do damage to the very essence of the Church and to her very life.*" Even in the loftier type of politics to which you refer in your letter, the Church cannot end up judging "on the basis of exclusively political criteria."

Secondly, it seems unjust and out of line with a true Christian outlook for you to misrepresent the facts, to accuse me of not wanting the liberation of the peoples of Latin America, and to say that your work on behalf of this objective is the thing I am objecting to in some of you. My public statements, my pastoral commitments, and my entire life clearly express what I think and feel. They indicate how unjust and unmerited is this accusation.

Thirdly, you claim that I make personal charges against some of you who are my parish priests and who lead lives entailing great sacrifice. Read my letter carefully and you will see that no such charge can be gotten out of it. In my response I analyzed a doctrine, and there is no doubt that personal positions can differ greatly from the doctrine.

Finally, there is nothing strange in the fact that I should bring these letters to the attention of the episcopate. We bishops, too, work in a team. That is all I have to say. I believe in the good faith of many of you. I pray God that the fears which I basically feel about the outcome of your convention will not prove correct; that your convention will represent a real forward step in the liberation activity of Christians in Latin America.

Raúl Cardinal Silva Henríquez
Archbishop of Santiago

10

Authorized Summary of Cardinal Silva's Views

1. The Cardinal does not feel called upon to direct politics nor to recommend a specific economic or socio-political system. He simply expresses the judgment merited by the various systems that are being offered to the peoples of Latin America today. In line with what the bishops of Latin America stated at Medellín and what the bishops of Chile have stated repeatedly, he feels that liberal capitalism, based on the unrestricted quest for profit, is an outdated system responsible for very many of the ills that afflict our countries. He thinks that what Latin America probably desires is some type of pluralistic and democratic socialism; and that if the people opt for this type of organization and government, the Church will have no difficulty in accepting it and collaborating loyally with it.

2. In analyzing the social process under way, the Christian, like any objective human being, discovers the fact of class struggle. In describing and interpreting this fact, however, he must avoid sectarianism and any species of dualism that would divide human beings into good and evil and that would equate a judgment on classes with a judgment on individual persons.

In recognizing the fact of class struggle, the Christian cannot accept it as a permanent state of affairs. Rather, he must work to supersede it. This means being dedicated—with the weapons proper to the gospel—to the creation and strengthening of structures which effectively assure the equality of rights and opportunities.

3. Christianity can never be reduced to an ideology. But one must recognize and admit that in history Christians have been

influenced by the structures and ideologies of the society in which they live—in particular by the structures and ideologies of a capitalist variety. It is an urgent necessity for Christians to liberate themselves from these influences, which condition their way of evaluating and judging many problems and attitudes, and to opt for new pathways in the light of the gospel.

4. The quest of Christians for new ways of pondering and living their faith should take into account all the valuable contributions of human thought and science. As far as Marxism is concerned, they can utilize some of its features in the analysis of society. But they should maintain a critical attitude towards it, thus relativizing its tendency to absolutize economic factors and rectifying the materialist ideology that serves as its basis.

5. To foster these investigations, it is both legitimate and desirable for priests and lay people to sponsor initiatives on their own authority, to organize meetings that will pose the new problems and explore new pathways. The hierarchy respects this liberty. In turn it asks that its own liberty be respected as well, when it abstains from taking part in ways that might be interpreted as approbation.

These kinds of meetings provide the hierarchy with valuable material for study and reflection. But the hierarchy must remain sufficiently free to be able to step in and possibly offer correctives.

6. Insofar as the upcoming convention of Christians For Socialism is concerned, the hierarchy wanted to stress in a letter that the convention was undertaken on private initiative and that it did not have any special approbation. It also expressed its concerns about the doctrinal orientations of the upcoming convention, which appeared to be ambiguous. The letter of the hierarchy does not in any way represent a change in its position. It looks with sympathy and expectation on the attempts to fashion more just and liberating structures in our country.

More recently the organizers of the upcoming convention have provided further clarifications and explanations. The present attitude of the hierarchy is not one of disapproval but of expectation. It hopes that the proceedings of the convention will prove that its earlier fears were without foundation.

There is no doubt that Christians ought to involve themselves in the liberation of human beings, combatting any and every oppressive structure no matter what label it may wear. Insofar as the concrete forms of this involvement are concerned, it is only natural that there should be diverse options and that these options should be embraced with liberty, sincerity, and mutual respect.

Santiago
April 28, 1972

PART IV

NATIONAL REPORTS

The Draft Agenda for the proposed Latin American Convention of Christians For Socialism suggested that preliminary conventions be held on the national level, and that the delegates draw up a report on the role of Christianity in the life of their own nation. These reports were presented during two days of the international convention (April 23–24, 1972). A sampling of these reports is provided in this section.

The report of the Chilean delegation is particularly interesting for several reasons. It seems to be the most full-fledged attempt to follow the guidelines of the Draft Agenda, and it was drawn up by a committee from the Secretariat of Christians For Socialism. Thus it is a concrete illustration of what the convention organizers had in mind. The Chilean delegation held a preliminary national convention in Padre Hurtado on March 24–25, 1972. The conclusions of that convention were amplified by outside informational material to provide the basis for the final Chilean report.

11

Chile

Following the pattern suggested in the guidelines of the Draft Agenda, the report of the Chilean delegation will be given in three sections that correspond to the three stages of analysis mentioned in that document. In Part One we shall attempt to describe the present phase through which the Chilean social process is passing, indicating some significant happenings in which Christians contributed to the furthering of the people's revolutionary undertaking. In Part Two we shall try to determine more precisely the function of the "Christian element" within the Chilean social setup—the dominant characteristic of that setup being a dependent form of capitalism that has spawned underdevelopment. In Part Three we shall sketch some theological conclusions and lines of action that issue from the experience of leftist Christians in Chile.

We should point out that we were not able to make the complete and finished analysis that we had wanted to make, and we apologize to our fellow delegates from other countries for this fact. Deeply involved in the tasks attending the liberation of the people of Latin America, as we ourselves are, you will certainly appreciate the fact that in pre-revolutionary epochs intellectual effort suffers when people are confronted with the urgent need for commitment.

PART ONE

1. Introduction

Any analysis of the significant happenings in which Christians have served as protagonists in the social arena should be made within the present-day process going on in Chile. That process is aimed at making a start on the road towards socialism. In some respects Chile offers an example of particular interest in the whole area of analyzing the political activity of Christians. This is true for two reasons.

Firstly, the "Chilean road" to socialism is a program advanced by the Popular Unity coalition of Marxist parties and some Social Democrats, and it was initiated in 1970 with Salvador Allende's accession to the presidency of the nation. But this took place after the failure of another experiment that was begun in 1964: i.e., the so-called "revolution in liberty" advocated by the ruling Christian Democrats. It is clear that the 1964 experiment was directly inspired by Christian social thinking and strongly influenced by the social doctrine of the Church; hence Christians played a major role in advocating it. But there are Christians involved in the present political program of the Popular Unity coalition. And even though they do not predominate, they are actively participating with Marxists in government activities and political action among the masses. So we have two successive models of Christian involvement in Chilean society, and this gives us an opportunity to get a clearer grasp of the specific nature of the Christian contribution to the process of liberation.

Secondly, the so-called "Chilean way" of revolution starts from the presupposition that the journey towards socialism can be made through the legal process. "It presupposes that we can establish the institutional foundations for a new form of social order in a context of pluralism and liberty. The task is extraordinarily complex because there are no precedents to serve as our inspiration."[1] In other words, the idea is to respect the rules of a bourgeois democracy and, with the power won in the election, and with the power of a mobilized people, to use at least part of the existing legal structure to transform our bourgeois democracy into a people's democracy.

It is not our purpose here to analyze the viability of this particular model for effecting a transition to socialism. It is enough to establish the fact that the Chilean program for revolution seems to be less opposed to the traditional doctrine advocated by the hierarchical Church up to now—that doctrine being clearly opposed to the use of violence. It is opposed to violence despite the fact that in 1968 it took a look at the situation in Latin America and forthrightly acknowledged the existence of "institutionalized violence" in the existing system, where the popular majorities are under the dominion of privileged classes,[2] and where there is a close tie-up with the "international imperialism of money" denounced earlier by Paul VI.[3] For this reason, however, the participation of Christians in the struggle to implement socialism —even socialism that is Marxist in inspiration—is explicitly recognized as something legitimate by the bishops of Chile despite the reservations they feel about the Marxist model.[4] Thus the *de facto* presence of Christians in the political process of Chile is quite significant already and it is potentially even more significant. This is in marked contrast to the other experiments at socialist revolution in past history.

2. The "Chilean Road" to Socialism as a Program

Any judgment about the present-day process in Chile should be made in terms of the program of the Popular Unity coalition, and particularly in terms of its central objective: initiating the transition to socialism.[5] This central objective is based on a scientific certainty that is confirmed by concrete experience: i.e., that Chile's underdevelopment is the inevitable consequence of its entanglement in the worldwide capitalist system and that, in economic terms, the development of the dependent nations requires a breakaway from this system and the construction of a socialist society.[6]

The program of the Popular Unity coalition is not a socialist one. A correct analysis of the interrelationship of political forces in 1970 led to the conclusion that such a program could not be advocated successfully. But contrary to the opinion of the extreme left, dubious about the possibilities of triumph, control of the government was won by a coalition of proletarian parties and representatives of the lower middle class. Reactionary attempts were made to prevent Allende from assuming the presidency, these attempts culminating in the assassination of General Schneider. But the attempts were quashed by the massive support of the people and by the errors of the right wing itself. In the program of the winning coalition it was considered important to unite the largest number of forces in order to attack the chief enemies that were putting obstacles in the way of national development and the people's liberation. These enemies are the foreign companies that have been controlling certain basic resources—copper and iron in particular—the huge national and foreign monopolies, and the plantation owners who have been exploiting the peasantry for centuries.

So the program of the Popular Unity coalition sought to clear the road for later attempts to build a socialist society. At the same time it promised a series of measures that would benefit the popular majorities and win further support for the government: e.g., income redistribution, access to new levels of basic consumption, increased educational opportunities, housing programs, and so forth. To effect these goals the Popular Unity coalition considered making alliances with small and medium-size business people in urban and rural areas, whose interests cannot be equated with those of the foreign conglomerates, the national bourgeoisie, or the large plantation owners. In the view of the Popular Unity coalition, consolidating the power of organized labor and increasing support for its program through alliances with the lower and middle bourgeoisie is the only way to overcome the principal enemies and to initiate the first phase of the journey towards socialism. That first phase would include the socialization of a segment of industrial economy, the nationalization of banks and distributors, and agricultural reform.[7]

3. The General Economic, Social, and Political Situation

After a year and a half of rule by the Popular Unity coalition, opposition criticism centered around two principal points: economic problems and the alleged threat to constitutionally guaranteed liberty. Criticism based on economic realities stressed inflation, increased money in circulation, diminishing reserves, lack of supplies, and so forth. The fact is that this criticism ignores three blunt facts: a 1971 increase in the gross national product by 8% and of industrial production by 12%; a decline in inflation and unemployment; and larger earnings for broad sectors of the population. Apart from this fact, however, the criticisms would be valid from our point of view only if these economic problems put obstacles in the way of the transition to socialism advocated by the Popular Unity coalition.

Hence we cannot analyze the economic situation without considering its tie-ups with the political situation. After a year and a half of rule by the Popular Unity coalition, it is evident that important gains have been made. Progress has been made in its central objective to fashion a socialized sector of the economy. Copper and iron have been nationalized. Banks have been socialized—along with the monopolies in the cement, steel, and textile industries. Agrarian reform has moved ahead, and is now at the point of eliminating the large landed estates. Income has been redistributed and the economy has been reactivated after the situation of economic depression that existed when Frei turned over the government to Allende. Nevertheless the phase of easy economic expansion is almost over, especially insofar as it is based on idle industrial capacity and the utilization of fiscal policies. Accelerated economic transformation necessarily produces imbalances in the area of production (copper, nationalized industries) between supply and demand. Supply is increasing, but not sufficiently in some sectors. This causes a lack of supplies at the higher levels of consumption. This situation also puts pressure on the balance of payments with foreign countries since we must have recourse to imports, particularly agricultural and cattle products, in order to satisfy the increased demand for food supplies.

There is no doubt that the economic situation is a ticklish one, and that the short-range outlook for 1972 and 1973 is less clear than the intermediate-range outlook for the years ahead when the nationalization policies will achieve their goals. The lack of flexibility in the government apparatus for implementing the new economic policy (CORFO, CODELCO, etc.), the need for new investments to maintain production, the foreign debt and its maturing payments, and other such factors are the challenges facing us at this stage. The opposition has quickly utilized them to convey the impression that we are on the edge of starvation on a grand scale and total economic chaos. In addition, since last

December the opposition has begun to coordinate its resistance. Monopoly enterprises and the communications media have joined together, and parliamentary battles have helped to cause economic deterioration. The reverses suffered by the ruling coalition in the complementary elections of last summer give a clear indication of the advances made by the forces of reaction. So it would be wise for us to describe the political situation in which we now find ourselves.

It is quite likely that the foreign delegates to this convention felt a bit confused and disconcerted when they arrived here a few days ago. Despite their wise reservations about the news they receive from the capitalist news media, they may well have been influenced unconsciously by the image of our country that these media project. Our country is depicted as one under the thumb of a Marxist dictatorship, on the verge of suppressing freedom of expression, and sinking into total economic chaos with the threat of mass starvation on the horizon. To their surprise the delegates find that our so-called Marxist government takes pride in respecting our Constitution and laws; that there is total freedom of the press and the airwaves for the opposition, which uses these media every day to attack and even insult the government and leftist groups; that this same opposition is able to organize public rallies; that the cost of living is relatively low; and that the bulk of the population has an adequate level of supplies despite shortages of some specific items.

Perhaps the most surprising thing is that Chile, characterized as a socialist country by the media, does not appear to be very different from other underdeveloped capitalist nations on this continent. Like them it has minority segments that have entered the era of consumption which typifies the developed countries; and it also has three segments of the population, living in marginal neighborhoods and rural areas, who live on a subsistent and impoverished level because of unemployment, illiteracy, exploitation, and social discrimination.

At the same time, however, foreign delegates assembled here will undoubtedly see something in the whole Chilean process that distinguishes it from other countries. They will see a test-tube model of a society agitated by an intense ideological struggle which mirrors the political struggle and the reality of the class struggle. And the model may well be clearer and on a larger scale here than in other countries. You need only listen to the radio. A large number of stations are clearly lined up with the government or in opposition to it. In both cases political propaganda fills the air as if we were on the eve of an election. There is talk about the problems of nationalization, the participation of workers in the social area of the economy, the lack of supplies, agrarian reform, marches against the government, or marches in favor of the government by parties allied with the Popular Unity coalition or by the Workers' Central. This impression is undoubtedly confirmed when one makes contact with middle-class families in the fashionable section of Santiago, where one may find a paroxysm of verbal aggressiveness and emotional excess.

There have been two opposition marches since the disconcerting election defeat in 1970. They represent one phase in the open offensive of the reactionary forces in Chile against the initiatives of the government—in particular, against its program of establishing a socialized area made up of nationalized industries. The "march of the saucepans" started out apparently as a protest of housewives against the lack of supplies. In early December it gave way to disorders and seditious uprisings instigated by fascist groups. The success of this march was utilized to make a constitutional attack on the Interior Minister in parliament, and he was subsequently deposed. The march for "democracy and liberty" on April 11 cannot be interpreted solely as the mobilization of the bourgeoisie in defense of its economic interests, which were threatened by the government's program of socializing monopolies, banks, and natural resources. In these marches there is also a new factor, an emotional discharge that is the real mobilizing factor. What we have is a psychological purification of the bitterness felt by a minority segment of the population, which sees itself losing its privileges, its bourgeois way of life, and its capitalist style. This feeling is undoubtedly shared by other segments of the lower middle class and even by some laborers, who are egged on by the communications media which are broadly utilized by the economic right-wing and the opposition parties.

The power of the dominant ideology is such that these sectors are being mobilized to defend "democracy," "liberty," "order," and "supplies." These are ideological slogans which shrewdly conceal the real interest involved—those of the privileged minority—which are certainly opposed to those of the popular sectors that are being mobilized by the right.

So far the religious factor has not intruded into this ideological struggle—at least not in the open and decisive way it did in the fall of Goulart in Brazil, and even in the fall of Juan José Torres in Bolivia. The stance of the hierarchy and the existence of significant leftist sectors in the churches has prevented any intense utilization of religion as a counter-revolutionary force—at least on a massive scale. But a certain strain of anti-communism lies buried deep within Christians, and ultimately it is grounded on religion. Anti-communist propaganda, the "fright campaign" preceding elections in particular, relies for its effectiveness on this latent anti-communism that is especially strong in women.

The political warfare of the opposition is centered in parliament, which it controls. The most powerful party in electoral terms is the Christian Democratic party, whose presidential platform called for "communitarian socialism." But lately, on such decisive issues as the attack on the Interior Minister and parliamentary elections, it has sided with the right. The leftist sectors, followers of Tomic, have been displaced, especially since the breakaway of the Christian Left group from that party. This occurred with particular reference to the Hamilton-Fuentealba proposal for constitutional reform, which involved a tacit alliance between the Christian Democrats and the right (P. Nacional, Democracia Radical) that is opposed to the government. This proposal establishes the area which is to be socialized and that which is to be mixed, and it determines the enterprises that will make up each area. In practice this opposition reform measure, already approved by the full congress, paralyzes the whole process of nationalizing monopolies. If it were promulgated, the state would be required to restore most of the requisitioned firms to their former owners, firms which now make up the socialized area of the economy and represent the seeds of the future socialist society. As of this moment the question is not settled. The President vetoed the measure and sent it back to parliament. The veto will probably be rejected by a majority, but parliament will be unable to attain the necessary two-thirds majority.

Now there is a juridical battle over the interpretation of the constitution. What is required to overturn a presidential veto? A simple majority or a two-thirds vote? This juridical battle has great political importance. Congress seems inclined to reject the interpretation of the executive branch, that is, to deny that the Constitutional Tribunal has competence to settle the issue, and to call for a plebiscite on the matter. The executive branch, supported by leftist groups, is inclined to promulgate the reform on the basis of its own criterion, in the event that the Constitutional Tribunal is in fact declared incompetent. This could lead to a constitutional charge against the President, designed to deprive him of his office. Even though the opposition does not have sufficient strength in parliament to carry this through, it would represent an important step forward for the reactionary forces. The struggle clearly tends to divide Chilean society into two antagonistic blocs.

From this analysis it is evident that the process going on in Chile has not reached the point of no return. It is reversible. The breakaway from capitalism in the transition to socialism depends on workers taking over power not only in the executive branch but also in congress and the judiciary.

4. Self-criticism by the Left

So far we have pointed out some of the achievements of the Popular Unity coalition in trying to carry out its central objective of moving ahead on the road to socialism. We have highlighted its struggle to establish a socialized area in the economy despite the efforts of the bourgeoisie to prevent this. The confrontation is played out in parliament, in the communications media, in debates, in schools, on street corners, and even in the home. There is no doubt that the roots of this conflict lie bedded in the economy. There we find a conflict between the interests of capitalist monopolies—linked up with international capitalism, as the secret papers of ITT clearly show—and the interests of wage-earners in urban and rural areas. Behind the opposition parties are the capitalists and their foreign allies (Confederación del Comercio y la Producción, Sociedad de Fomento Fabril, etc.). They have won over other sectors of the lower and intermediate middle class, of the city and the countryside, by fronts that seem to be trade-unionist in character (e.g., FRENAP) and by the failure of the Popular Unity coalition to truly cement its policy of alliances with these sectors.

In order to analyze possible ways out of the political confrontation between the Popular Unity government and the opposition, we must take due account of certain concrete conditions surrounding the whole process. In particular, one must consider the ticklish economic situation in the short run. This is especially true if there is a boycott by the threatened Chilean bourgeoisie and North American interests, and this leads to an intensification of the so-called battle over production. And it is even more true if the government has to resort to certain measures of a populist cast, not only to solve real problems besetting the poor segments of the population, but also to maintain and bolster its base of popular support.

Secondly, there is the necessity of operating within the Constitution and legal structures because that is what the "Chilean way" to socialism demands, and because that is what is demanded by the existence of professional armed forces whose doctrine is to maintain political neutrality while the government in power conforms to the constitution.

Thirdly, we must not underestimate the cultural reality of the Chilean people, their marked attachment to juridical forms, their electoral political tradition—all this inculcated by a long-standing practice of Western bourgeois democracy. The cultural horizon of the Chilean person is probably quite closed to the idea of seeking political solutions by violence; and there is little socialist consciousness in many segments of the proletariat and the peasantry. The former have been led astray by a tradition of labor unionism that is economics-oriented to a large extent, and the latter are attached to the ownership of land. The subculture of the laborer and the peasant reflects values that are part and parcel of the dominant bourgeois ideology.

The present political confrontation between the government

and the opposition will be resolved in favor of the former only to the extent that organized laborer and the people are mobilized politically to defend what they have won and to move on towards the full takeover of power so that the transition to socialism becomes irreversible.

Inadequate participation by workers and the masses is one of the criticisms that the Popular Unity government voices about itself. At the El Arrayán meeting it declared: "Our response to the foreseeable restrictions should not be to stop but to move on further and more rapidly to carry out our program completely."[8] And this entails "carrying the process to a deeper level by truly incorporating the working class into it in a massive way at every level of decision-making."

In the enterprises that are part of the socialized and mixed sector of the economy, the participation of the workers has been initiated. They have now been included in the management boards. However, there is a tendency to restrict them to matters of secondary importance and concern. And one can also notice a tendency towards sectarianism working not only against those who do not belong to Popular Unity but also against some members of the left itself.

In enterprises in the private sector of the economy, critical study of the workers by production watchdog committees has not been articulated adequately. The trade-union structure itself must be extended into small and medium-size businesses to form branches, so that mobilization can be accomplished through class directives issued by the Workers' Central. In the farm sector, the formation of peasant councils proceeds fitfully; and the participation of peasants in the planning of agrarian reform is still meagre.

Other forms of participation would integrate vast segments of the population into local health committees, neighborhood councils, centers for mothers, price and supply boards, and voluntary services. They would help to mobilize the people around the program aimed at introducing socialism. The government services dealing with health, education, and housing also require reforms in their structure and modes of functioning so that many concrete tasks are entrusted to the people. This will allow room for their "participation," which in turn will gradually change the nature and character of the government.

As the Popular Unity coalition puts it, socialism must be constructed from the grass-roots level up.[9]

These are some of the self-criticisms voiced by the Popular Unity coalition. And there are other criticisms voiced by leftist segments that are not a part of the Popular Unity—MIR [Movement of the Revolutionary Left] in particular.

The central political problem faced by the country right now is the mobilization of the popular sectors in order to change the power setup that has ruled our system and still does. There is general agreement on this point. The present political dispute centers around power, the power that a privileged group possesses in Chilean society and that it sees threatened by the actions of the Popular Unity government. This unstable, conflict-ridden situation calls for some kind of solution, and the mobilization of the masses is that solution.

How to go about it is a question that we have not yet been able to define clearly. The parties in the Popular Unity front are aware of their achievements, which are noteworthy to some extent. But in implementing their program they have also come to see that the process lacks homogeneous direction. MIR and other groups have criticized the ambiguity of certain leftist policies and the signs of vacillation as consequences of a lack of unified direction. This type of criticism also showed up at our national convention in preparation for this convention.

People have also noted certain failures to appreciate where the process is at this moment; this deficiency stems from a failure to appreciate the present situation in Chile correctly. As some see it, the conquest of the executive branch of government by Popular Unity signified its takeover of social and political power as well; hence the task to work on now is the construction of socialism. This outlook would direct all efforts into activities that are under government control: e.g., centralized planning, government involvement on all fronts, and so forth. The end result of this approach would be to more or less separate the government from the activities of the masses. It would lead to bureaucracy and to the imposition of policies with no direct link to the aspirations of the people at large. Those who operate along these lines forget that the whole question of power is in dispute in our country.

They act as if they actually held it. The continuing appearance of obstacles indicates that the power of the Popular Unity government is relative; that the use of bourgeois legal structures as the instrument for transforming these very structures has its limits; and that such transformation will only be verified in the activity of the mobilized masses, not in the use of a legal structure that runs counter to this transformation. An example of how this whole process might go astray is the battle over productivity when it is completely dissociated from real power. Such a battle would tend to reduce the combativeness of the masses.

Another tendency, which crops up fairly frequently in radicalized segments of the left, sins in the opposite direction. It underestimates the role being played by the government now in power, and hence it poses the whole problem of power in an abstract, a-historical form. People sometimes forget that it is through the existence of the Popular Unity government that we confront the concrete possibility of moving along the road towards socialism. They stress the mobilization of the masses on all fronts, paying no regard to certain lines of strategy that have been worked out or to the complexity of the concrete process now under way in Chile. This concrete process makes the whole question of power complex in two ways. On the one hand the existence of the ruling government—as distinct from the State —is a necessary precondition for moving towards socialism in the present situation of Chile. On the other hand the activity of the masses and their struggle for power is the precondition for accomplishing this goal and reaching the point where the process becomes irreversible. Those who stress the mobilization of the masses but overlook the task of working out the government's role and activity do focus on an important and central point, but they lack concrete political vision. It is that kind of vision that will enable us to move towards the construction of a more just and rational society and to escape underdevelopment. An example of deviation in this direction would be the indiscriminate occupation of rural lands, factories, and so forth. Such actions break with the whole legal structure, and they cost the government politically. They also take no account of the program which makes specific the overall strategy leading towards socialism.

With its interests affected, the bourgeoisie defends itself; and that is only logical. In a recent declaration, our bishops have stated that any effort at bringing about change must confront the opposition posed by the privileged minority that will lose its present status.[10] The members of this group will defend themselves, and they have been doing precisely that. Now even though these defensive actions may intensify the mobilization of the masses and increase their combativeness at a given moment, if these reactions are not framed within a program, they can prove to be politically counter-productive insofar as the overall process is concerned.

The people need socialism in order to be able to liberate themselves from the exploitation attendant upon capitalism. There is no room for naiveté or abstract idealism here. We must recognize and correct errors, of course, but we cannot pretend that we will gain political power and construct socialism with a flourish of the pen or on the strength of good will and enthusiasm. The mobilization of the masses is a task that calls for patience and delicate handling; in effecting it we must use all the instruments and tools that science and scholarly discipline offer us. We cannot fashion a majority favoring such changes by using moral imperatives, mass propaganda, and grandstand plays. The impact and effectiveness of such methods is temporary and dubious. The people must advance step by step, maintaining ties with their political vanguard and using a clearly worked out strategy for taking over power and establishing a people's state that will permit them to fashion and implement socialism.

Imbedded in this overall task is the task of fashioning an authentic socialist awareness in the masses. This awareness will serve as the foundation for the New Man and the new society we seek to form. The potential impact of Christians in this area is of special importance, as we shall see in Part Two.

PART TWO

The Christian Element in the Present Historical Process

In Chile today, Christianity seems to be neutral or reactionary to some people, subversive to others, and renovative to most. In our history we find that Christianity has followed a political trajectory. On the one hand it has ended up in reformism and the mass man created by that approach. On the other hand it has moved towards faint sparks of revolutionary Christianity. If we sketch a typology of Christians in terms of the whole process of change, the Church, and faith, their respective class positions show up clearly.

If we want to comprehend social Christianity on the one hand and revolutionary Christianity on the other, we do well to analyze their respective logics as well. The differences between these two structured ways of thinking show up clearly when we compare how each relates theory to praxis, when we note that one has an empirical line of thought whereas the other has a dialectical line of thought, and when we see that one has an abstract sense of history while the other has a concrete sense of history.

1. The Evolution of Chilean Society and its Christianity

It is apparent that the capitalist structure of the country and its dependent underdevelopment have evolved over the course of time. It is also apparent that the class struggle has become more acute, and that the people have solidified and organized into parties and labor unions with their own strategies. The socio-political statements and expressions of Christians have been situated within the system of domination over and over again, to the point where they have come to be the principal pseudo-revolutionary alternative standing in opposition to the socialist forces.

A. Christian Conservatism

In the violent centuries of colonial rule, a "Christian society" was established. Religion gave it cultural legitimacy. The economic and social organization, along with the whole colonial institutional setup, took on a sacred character.

The process of winning independence from Spain and the ideology of liberalism put Christianity on the defensive. The agrarian and commercial oligarchy imposed a new form of violence on the country: i.e., the democratic system as a subsidiary of the nascent international capitalism. The Christian forces re-grouped into a confessional party (the Conservative Party) and into institutions of an educational, cultural, and charitable nature, complying with the interests of the dominant class.

In the political arena, the practice of Christianity came to be the work of developing the established order and bolstering the legitimacy of democratic liberty. So today we find a traditional sector of the dominant class, which proclaims itself Christian for the most part, religiously defending traditions and private property, and resorting to reactionary violence. Even though Opus Dei and a small segment of the hierarchy supports this sector, Christian social forces have stripped the banner of Christianity away from it. But popular religiosity, as the internalization of national tradition on the mass level, lends strong support to this conservatism.

The oligarchic segment feels that the Church has betrayed it, that her posture of renewal tolerates "Communist" segments within her borders. Its members criticize the hierarchy—in particular, those priests who do not stay within the spiritual realm and who attack the culture and class interests of this group. These people picture Christianity as the institution of truth and the sacred, and faith as relationship to God and acceptance of his doctrine. They picture God as the guaranty of order and morality, the order and morality of their own class. They have used religion to launch an intense anti-Marxist campaign. This successful campaign has induced large segments of the people at large to regard revolutionary activities as demoniacal.

Much more significant is the preservation and maintenance of traditional Christianity in the religious consciousness of people at large. The saints and God have the power to solve the concrete problems associated with their oppressed situation. The Protestant churches which have burgeoned among the middle and marginal classes represent a socio-cultural refuge, and they foster abstention from politics.[11] In these and other ways the forces of popular religiosity, both Catholic and Protestant, exert a negative influence on the poor, preventing them from liberating themselves from structural oppression.

B. Christian Reformism

Since the beginning of this century progressive advances have been made in labor-union movements and in working-class parties. The middle classes and the army responded with a succession of populist projects (A. Alessandri, Frente Popular, Ibáñez). A process of industrialization was initiated which consolidated Chile's underdevelopment and its dependence on North American and European capitalism. In practice the Christian sector once again took its place within the reformist current of the intermediate classes, which were being used as tools by the dominant class.

The painful situation of the exploited marginal masses, growing numerically all the time, and Christian social awareness prompted discussions of the "social question" in small circles of Christians. Groups and institutes of Christian inspiration cropped up under the impetus given by some priests (F.Vives, A.Hurtado, Bishop Manuel Larraín), young professional people, and workers. Christian labor unions and cooperatives appeared. The Falange and the Christian Social Party came into being. Later came the IER (Institute of Rural Education) to promote education and unionism among the peasantry, and DESAL to promote developmentalist studies and activities.

Agrarian reform was initiated on church lands before it was initiated by the government. For the most part, Christian churches were financially and ideologically dependent on the developed countries. Catholic Action was organized within the Catholic Church. It formed many militant Christians who took a prominent part in reformist political activity. This combination of attitudes and activities projected the image of a Church that was progressive through and through. In reality, however, only an elite corps was involved. This group engaged in initiatives for change; but they were incomplete and deceptive in nature, operating within a pervasive structure of exploitation and dependence.

The doctrinal backdrop for all these initiatives was Christian social doctrine.[12] Its principles, deeply infected with bourgeois ideology, provided moralistic criticism of certain social injustices. But it did not pose the structural problem of capitalism, and it was decidedly anti-socialist and anti-Marxist. Hence it defended the capitalist mode of production and it condemned the revolutionary efforts of the oppressed.

Christian reformism culminated in the so-called "revolution in liberty" sponsored by the Christian Democrats. It arose as a separate approach, opposed to Marxist and popular forces and allied with the conservative forces. Most of the Catholic hierarchy and Christians in general committed their loyalty to this program of the Christian Democrats. This party appealed to principles of Christian inspiration in order to propose a new system: communitarianism. It led to concrete reforms in agriculture, education, housing, and economic planning. But it did not lead to any real structural change in the economy or in society. It merely bolstered neocapitalism and its ideology of liberty and democracy that are the weapons of the ruling class. It developed a policy of integrating the marginal urban laborers and rural peasants into the structure that was oppressing them. It made significant inroads among the people through organizations operating as part of the system and through mass diffusion of its reformist ideology. In this way it reconciled the popular sectors with the bourgeoisie and divided the laboring class.

This new Christian political program is therefore incapable of resolving the contradictions of a neocapitalist society, with its exploitation of the nation's majority and its growing chasm of underdevelopment. Although the Christian Democrats lost the presidency in the last election, they have bolstered their strength through the support of the right and of "independent" elements. They now represent the opposition, despite the fact that certain progressive and popular segments remain in their party which could unite with the left.

The broad segments of social-minded Christians maintain and strengthen their sectarian institutions or those that are Christian in inspiration. Whatever the intent may be of parishes, Protestant sects, and the cultural and educational centers of Christian affiliation, in practice they fashion an ideological policy which reinforces the reformism of the ruling class. The vigor of the Christian

Democratic faction and the sacral character of bourgeois values makes it unnecessary for the churches to engage in direct political action. That is why these segments advocate a church that does not get involved in politics and condemn leftists priests and ministers as "politicians." They envision and seek to fashion a communitarian church, emphasizing interpersonal relations, reform of church structures, and adhesion to Jesus Christ as the savior. [13]

As these sectors see it, there are values relating to man and society that derive from the faith. In fact these values represent a new version of the bourgeois ideology. Their Christian humanism inspires them to develop an awareness and a line of action that will lead to the transformation of the existing society. The chief images of God center around love for all and personal commitment. This bypasses the whole reality of conflict and implies that the efforts of the ruling class are aimed at unity and peace. Proponents of this position declare that they are both anti-capitalist and anti-Marxist. They propose a democratic and pluralistic approach which comes down to being an alliance of classes around the bourgeoisie and a sacralization of reality. The majority of Christians, both Catholic and Protestant, adopt this posture in practice—including the hierarchy and the laity. Given this fact, there is little reason to hope that Christianity on the mass level will be a revolutionary factor.

2. Christians in the Socialist Revolution

Towards the end of the last decade, various groups of leftist Christians began to organize and speak out in various social sectors and in various parts of the country. Starting from an evangelical and political commitment to the cause of the working class, Christian social awareness has become radicalized, and it has taken on the task of analyzing the whole matter of class struggle.

Even though these groupings are recent in origin, there have been revolutionary Christians around for some time. The most notable one is Clotario Blest, the first President of the CUT (Central Unica de Trabajadores—Workers' Central), who has fought for the revolutionary unity of the people for over fifty years. There have been other isolated cases in labor unions, leftist parties, and other militant fronts. But they have not managed to really break up the predominant structure—a conservative or reformist Christianity allied with capitalism.

With the growth of the Christian Democratic party, the student and worker factions of Catholic Action entered a period of crisis. A large segment of its militants moved into partisan political activity. By the end of the last decade, however, some segments of this movement were radicalized and came out in favor of socialism. On August 11, 1969, lay people from the rebel wing of the Christian Democratic party and the "Camilo Torres" movement joined with some priests of Catholic Action to "take over" the Santiago Cathedral. Their cry was "for a Church on the side of the people and their struggle." The Young People's Church arose in Santiago, and the People's Church arose in Valparaíso; both attacked capitalism and denounced the structure of power and wealth dominating the Church. This gave public evidence of the real division existing between Christians. Now many Christians—students, workers, professional people, young people—are abandoning Christian reformism as isolated individuals or as organized groups.

In the 1960s, various priests entered the production lines of large industries and smaller workshops. It was in this context that the whole issue of revolutionary commitment to the working class arose for them. Some priests and nuns have gone to live with villagers and peasants, sharing their living conditions and sometimes involving themselves directly in their political struggle. Some Protestant ministers, too, together with their communities are expanding their religious awareness and moving towards social commitment. In all these instances, concrete experience of structural injustice has generated new evangelical commitment to the poor. Political action with and for the working class has gradually become an imperative of charity itself.

This shift of Christians towards the revolutionary effort of the people has taken concrete shape in the formation of new leftist parties. MAPU [United Popular Action Movement] arose in 1969, drawing off a sizeable group of peasants, students, workers, and professionals from the Christian Democrats. It describes itself as a proletarian party espousing a Marxist interpretation of reality. It was part of the Popular Unity coalition which captured the presidency in 1970. In 1971 another group withdrew from the Christian Democrats, rejecting the latter's alliance with the right. It comes to the Chilean left as a Christian segment contributing socio-cultural elements of Christian inspiration to the revolutionary process. These two parties attack the religious and Christian character of capitalism in decisive fashion. They also destroy the false idea that one must choose between Marxism and Christianity, stressing the contradiction existing between exploiters and exploited.

This Christian participation in the effort to construct socialism makes it more difficult for the owner class to continue using Christianity for its own interests. It also counteracts the notion that Christian reformism is the only platform of action for Christians. But it should also be pointed out that in recent years some Christians, following the heroic example of Camilo Torres, have joined MIR; and that others at the grass-rooots level are militant members of Marxist parties, the Communist Party, and even more in the Socialist Party.

In April 1971, there was a meeting of about 80 priests who live and work with the people in Santiago or in the provinces [see Document 1]. Their public declaration was an important step forward in the ideological struggle. They attacked private property and the capitalist system, declaring their personal commitment to the working class. Their faith in Jesus Christ, their solidarity with the exploited, and their scientific analysis led them to call for socialism. The group known as "The 80" has continued to grow, forming additional groups in various sections of the country. They have formed a "Secretariat of Christians For Socialism" which issues documents, provides for the interchange of personal experiences, and coordinates groups at the grass-roots level. Its contacts with groups in three countries led to the idea of holding a Latin American Convention of Christians For Socialism.

In March 1972, the Secretariat organized a national convention here in which some 200 people participated: workers, students, professionals, priests, ministers, nuns, and lay people. They made a critical analysis of the process going on in Chile, with particular reference to the mobilization of the people and the ideological struggle. Various political positions were voiced, but the participants agreed on the need to solidify the present process so that it would be irreversible, and on the necessity of increasing Christian participation in the revolution.

Christians participating in the move towards socialism are moving beyond Christian social ideology. In varying degrees they share the struggle and theory of the working class.[14] In general, their concrete Christian experience is turning into revolutionary practice with a utopian outlook. Hence they generally evince criticism within the process itself. Even though they are a minority of Christians in numerical terms, they are having a profound impact on the national consciousness and they are destroying myths. The forces of the left, the government, and the communications media are putting a large spotlight on leftist Christian sectors. Their declarations and actions are erasing the indentification between reformism and Christianity and thus helping to destroy the religious legitimation of capitalism to which most people in the country are accustomed.

Leftist Christians want the most weighty portion of the churches to take the part of the oppressed, and they want to see the disappearance of those institutions of Christian inspiration which the ruling class has created. They see that many reforms (pastoral, catechetical, administrative, etc.) and the political thrust of grass-roots communities often bolster the established system. They are subject to pressure and to subtle but effective persecution by their hierarchical officials and their communities. Leftist Christian leaders are kept out of official and semi-official organizations of their churches. (Some, for example, were positively excluded from the Medellín Conference. Obstacles are placed in the way of leftist educators and pastors. Institutions such as Adveniat, Misereor, and the Latin American Division of NCWC (United States)[15] deny economic aid to initiatives undertaken by leftist Christians; and the middle classes do not back them up in seeking such aid. They are not invited to participate in the redaction of official documents of the Church.)

When Christians at the grass-roots level see that the organisms of the Church do not pay heed to their positions, many of them lose interest in official Christianity. They want to have serious, critical dialogue with their hierarchies. The latter, despite some gestures of good will, tend to show great distrust towards them. So these Christians see themselves left on the sideline by official Christianity on the one hand; on the other hand they are gradually discovering evangelical Christianity and the combative face of Jesus Christ. The pastor, be he Catholic or Protestant, is valued in terms of his understanding of the gospel to the poor and of his involvement in the struggle for a new society. Recognizing their socio-cultural impact, leftist priests and ministers are committing themselves to serve the concrete process of liberation that is going on in Chile.

In coming to make a distinction between faith and ideologized religion, leftist Christians go through a "crisis of faith." For many of them, political involvement with the working class constitutes the concrete expression of faith in Jesus Christ. Their evangelical hope is a critical impulse in the process of constructing socialism. Since there is only one history, the revolutionary process is the privileged place in which to exercise Christian love. So these Christians situate Chrsitian action in the struggle of the oppressed class; and their horizon is the "new heaven and earth" which is the joint work of God and the revolutionaries.

3. Social Christianity and Revolutionary Christianity

In considering how these two types of thinking operate, we can make three observations that will serve to introduce the matter.

A. Social Christianity has a clear physiognomy which has taken shape and been refined over the course of some forty years. It finds expression in documents ranging from the collective pastoral of 1932 (*La verdadera y única solución de la cuestión social*), to the working draft of 1971 (*Evangelio, política y socialismos*). Important landmarks along the way are the documents issued in 1962 (*El deber social y político en la hora presente*) and in 1968 (*Chile, voluntad de ser*).

The physiognomy of revolutionary Christianity is less clearcut, since it does not have a history. There are some public statements, such as the Declaration of The 80 (1971). But since this line of thought is still in the early stages of burgeoning personal experience, it finds expression mainly in the private forum (e.g., personal remarks or rough outlines designed to be used in group discussions). When the statements are public, they are the responsibility of the author or the small group of signatories.

In the documents of the hierarchy there is frequent reference to the great social encyclicals of Leo XIII, Pius XI, Pius XII, John XXIII, and Paul VI. In fact, the hierarchy sees its own documents as the *application* of these encyclicals to Chile. *Rerum novarum, Quadragesimo anno,* and *Populorum progressio* are the end product of a lengthy process of elaboration. Hence they represent a finished line of thought. By contrast, revolutionary Christianity really does not have sources which it can site. It is a line of thought in search of itself. An important consequence flows from this fact. One cannot apply the same criteria of interpretation to the two sets of affirmations, just as one would err in applying the same line of interpretation to the language of a conciliar constitution and to the long process of oral and written preparation that preceded it.

B. If we move from the texts themselves to the authors of them, we will have another useful clue in trying to interpret them and to understand the different attitudes of Catholics towards the revolutionary process in Latin America. The men who have composed the papal encyclicals and those who have composed the pastoral letters of the Chilean bishops often had a twofold formation: in social sciences of a non-Marxist type, and in scholastic philosophy and theology. In the last twenty years Catholic theological faculties have incorporated the whole problem-complex of phenomenology and existentialism into their own reflection. The assimilation of Hegel and Freud has occurred in more limited circles. Discussion of the questions raised by Marx, Nietzsche, the philosophy of language, and structuralism is a more recent innovation. Needless to say, most bishops are far away from that world; it is difficult for them to appreciate what all that could represent for a better understanding of Christian faith and practice. That is why many connotations in Paul VI's Apostolic Letter *(Octogesima adveniens)* to Cardinal Roy went unnoticed here in Chile. One need only compare this papal document, which was worked on by men whose philosophical and social training is quite up-to-date, with the working draft of the Chilean bishops entitled *Evangelio, política y socialismos.*

The formation of revolutionary Christians takes another route. For the majority of them, direct contact with peasant or working-class leaders plays a decisive role. They often share the people's way of life, living in their neighborhoods or joining them at their job sites. Most of them have only just begun to learn how to use the Marxist set of instruments for making a concrete analysis of a revolutionary process. Theory and theoretician are a late arrival on the scene of revolutionary Christianity. As is true in all areas of life, one must undergo a certain amount of practical experience before one begins to theorize about it. The formation of these theories shares something in common with that of the theories of social Christianity: i.e., a philosophical and theological base. But there is one difference: The Christian theoreticians of revolution have generally had some deep, impressive contact with some great modern author. This fact is fraught with more consequences than one might glimpse at first glance. To begin with, this difference in formation creates serious difficulties for dialogue within the Church. People use the same words, but they speak out of different logics. Often one party does not grasp or even glimpse the logic that the other is using.

C. Under Pius XI and Pius XII, the social doctrine of the Church was a clearcut matter. Starting with John XXIII, Christian thought began to look for a new way to relate to what was going on in human society. To a man like Oswald von Nell-Breuning, who played a key role in earlier papal pontificates, *Populorum progressio* represents the first hint of "decadence" in the social doctrine of the Church.

More recent documents of the papacy and the Chilean hierarchy are more groping in nature. Even their authors do not have a clear idea of the kind of thinking that is at work in them. It is indicative that Paul VI did not choose to commemorate the eightieth anniversary of *Rerum novarum* with an encyclical, as Pius XI had done on the fortieth anniversary. He was content to issue an Apostolic Letter *(Octogesima adveniens)*, which lists the various problems, offer some signposts on the road towards a solution, and makes some suggestions as to how they might be tackled.

The bishops of Chile chose the format of a "working draft" to discuss the gospel and socialism. This form of presentation is significant:

> The general lines of this document were established at the plenary session, and they accord with the thinking of the Chilean episcopate. But the final composition of the text was entrusted to the pastoral commission, so that the commission could present it as a "working draft": i.e., a doctrinal orientation designed to enlighten and stimulate the reflection and the personal commitment of Christian groups. We hope that people will *work* with it in church circles—groups, organizations, communities, etc. In this sense it is an *internal* church document and it is directed especially to priests, religious, and those lay people who have directive roles in pastoral action. We urge them to study it personally and in groups, and to convey its contents—insofar as that may be necessary—to all those over whom they have charge (pp.5–6).

The document has been published in the newspapers, and politicans have made much use of it. But this does not alter the fact that it was conceived by its authors as an "internal" church document. It is less clear as to what "working draft" means. The bishops ask people to "work with it." But how? By assimilating its contents and conveying those contents to others, and no more? Or by discussing and debating it as well? Whatever the subjective intention of the bishops—or of some of them—might have been, the written document is objectively ambiguous. It does not solve the question.

The fact is, however, that these documents are often read by people who were formed in the style of thinking that characterized the social doctrine of the traditional Church. Even when an attempt is made to say something new or distinctive in them, the reader tends to interpret the statement within the framework of the reformist line of thought. That is why we want to try to describe what is clear: i.e., the Social Christian way of thinking and the Marxist way of thinking.

The latter has influenced revolutionary Christians in different ways. But human beings are made of flesh and blood, and they are not as neat and clearcut as abstract schemas. They come fresh from the tenets of social Christianity or they are, in varying degrees, on their way towards adopting Marxism. In some cases the assimilation of Marxism is a mechanical thing, in others it turns out to be creative. In no case is the end product chemically pure.

Having made these preliminary observations, let us move on in the next section to give a brief description of the two styles of thinking. Here we are not referring directly to the content of these two thought styles. We are interested in the general way that the mind operates in dealing with these contents. Our analysis will focus on three major points: the relationship between theory and praxis, empirical thinking and dialectical thinking, and the concrete sense of history.

4. Relationship between Theory and Praxis

In the two modes of thinking we find that two different kinds of logic are operative.

A. The logic of social Christianity is not peculiar to it alone. It has been at the foundation of occidental thinking since the time of the ancient Greeks. In this logic, theory is fashioned *prior* to the concrete praxis of history. Henri Lorin, the President of the French *Semaines Sociales*, expresses this mode of thought clearly when he described the guiding ideas of social-minded Catholics in the following terms. He said that these ideas have not been worked out under the pressure of contemporary situations and circumstances. They are not the work of a day in response to the desires of a day. They flow directly from the dogmas of creation, original sin, and redemption—revealed dogmas of which the Church is the trustee.[16]

Christian social thinking is not totally *a priori*. It *follows logically* from philosophical reflection on man's essence in general. It is also subsequent to the interpretation of divine revelation provided by the Church's magisterium. But it is *prior* to any concrete consideration of history. In large measure, Christian social ethics is based on the model of what Saint Thomas calls "practical reason." Time and again his *Summa Theologica* explains how this practical reason operates. Starting from self-evident first principles, it moves *deductively* to proximate conclusions and then to remote conclusions. History does not enter in the picture at all.

B. A different logic was established with the advent of Hegel, and of Marx in particular. It starts from the basic fact that the human relationship is essentially one of conflict. The first act is not reflection on the essence of man and its first principles. It is the recognition that man finds himself in the midst of a conflict, without even having looked for it. Daily life confronts man with problems that he has not chosen, and he is forced to solve them in an order which he often cannot choose either. Man's conscious response to this conflict is what is called "praxis." But praxis is not something arbitrary and whimsical. It presupposes reflection, and this reflection is called theory.

Let us see how the two different logics confront the matter of cooperation between Christians and Marxists. In an earlier day, the encyclical *Divini redemptoris* rejected the possibility outright: "Since communism is intrinsically evil, those who wish to save western civilization from ruin cannot be allowed to collaborate with it in any area at all"(n.60). The working draft of the Chilean bishops is more subtle. It does not reject collaboration with Marxists outright, but it hems in such collaboration with repeated warnings. As one author points out:

> With the hope of a new road before us, we find that in section III alone of this document (*Los cristianos y el socialismo*) such words as "danger," "risk," and words with similar connotations ("seduction," "preoccupation," "uneasiness," "caution," "fear") are used twenty-six times. This creates a certain atmosphere which is clearly opposed to any kind of initiative or enthusiasm. Even more serious is the lack of such references to capitalism, perhaps because that was taken for granted. In any case these words are applied twenty-four times to socialism, once to capitalism and socialism, and only once to capitalism alone. Terms denoting dehumanization are used fifteen times: e.g., "dehumanization," "inhuman," "antihuman," "destructive of man," "mutilating," "crushing," "cruel." Twelve times they refer to socialism, and twice to both. [17]

The context surrounding the publication of *Divini redemptoris* was the policy of the hand outstretched in friendship. In 1936 the communists said: "Let us join forces in the face of the fascist threat looming over Europe." The Pope's answer was: "No,

because communism is intrinsically evil." *Before* any consideration was given to the historical situation and its concrete dangers,
the response had already been formulated: "We cannot ally ourselves with you for reasons of principle."

The situation is not so simple in the document of the Chilean
episcopate (*Evangelio, política y socialismos*). Right off it admits that
Christians can collaborate with Marxism. But then it sets down
conditions: "To do this one must have a good idea of the *objective*
risks that collaboration with Marxism may entail both for the
Christians involved with it and for the country as a whole. If
someone feels that he cannot overcome these risks, then in conscience he cannot collaborate with Marxism. People can collaborate on the other hand, if they feel they can resist these dangers to
themselves and diminish their effect on the country as a whole
precisely through this sort of collaboration which they feel is
suffused with the spirit of the gospel" (n.32).

The novel feature here, in contrast to *Divini redemptoris,* is that
the conditions for some sort of possible collaboration enter into
consideration. *Divini redemptoris* said that such collaboration was
not possible; the document of the Chilean episcopate says it is
possible under certain conditions. But what does this new feature
really amount to? Don't the majority of Christians come under
the heading of those who feel they "cannot overcome these risks"
and hence in conscience "cannot collaborate with Marxism"?
Once the condition is met, such collaboration is all right. For most
Christians, then, the answer continues to be that such collaboration is not possible.

Let us try to go more deeply into the why and wherefore of this
negative response insofar as the majority of Christians are concerned. The bishops of Chile make this remark in their document:
"The dehumanizing effects of capitalism are something that we
have experienced over a long period of time; we know where they
lie. What is more, the popes and we ourselves have denounced
them many different times in the past. And Paul VI denounced
them once again in his Apostolic Letter, *Octogesima adveniens.* On
the other hand, many Christians do not know precisely which
aspects of Marxism call for special caution in the light of a Christian vision of man and humanism"(n.31). But what exactly is the

situation of a considerable majority of Christians, specifically those who are closer to their bishops and priests? For many years they have heard much talk about the atheism, materialism, and practical "economicism" of the Marxist approach. They have heard talk about its attacks on the dignity of the human person, about the evils of a Marxist dictatorship, and about the persecutions suffered by Catholics under its rule. While there may be "many Christians" who do not know precisely what the questionable aspects of Marxism are, this group still constitutes a minority. Most Christians can pinpoint the dangers of Marxism very well.

But while the majority of Christians can pinpoint the dangers of Marxism, it cannot be said that they can accurately visualize the "dehumanizing effects of capitalism." And this is true in spite of the fact that the popes and bishops may have denounced them on repeated occasions. The fact is that our bishops underestimate the lack of perception evinced by the majority of Christians when it comes to the existing dangers of capitalism, and overestimate the lack of perception evinced by a minority of Christians when it comes to the dangers of Marxism. How are we to explain this difference in valuation? The reason, in our opinion, is that the *a priori* scheme of thinking is still operative in a subtle way. In other words, theory is formulated prior to concrete historical praxis. The emphasis of our bishops is not influenced by the present status of capitalism or Marxism in Chile; it is dictated by a theoretical judgment on the errors of Marxism.

The logic of revolutionary Christianity operates differently when it reflects on such matters. In many cases man does not invent his problems, he runs into them. Every solution entails risks, and man does not pick his risks. To a large extent the risks and dangers are imposed on him whether he chooses them or not. If we are confronted with a fire, there is not a great deal of room for deliberation. The task confronting us is to put it out. Nor do we have much choice in picking our risks. We can get drenched or we can get burned to a crisp. The revolutionary Christian looks at the objective situation in Latin America and sees it as a conflagration. He cannot afford the luxury of choosing his allies. He must take those that life offers; there are no others.

In the ranks of revolutionary Christians there certainly are some people who are politically naive; but there are others who are quite clear-eyed. Their clear-eyed awareness of the risks does not prevent them from shouldering them.

The Christian knows that there is a root core of atheism and materialism in Marxism. He knows that this leads to repercussions that are visible to us: e.g., a society of men without God in Russia. He also knows it leads to unseen repercussions that are far more difficult to analyze. At the same time, however, he knows that history is not reduced to the application of theories which were elaborated in an *a priori* way. Such theories do influence history, but they are strongly influenced by history in turn. The future is not something spelled out in advance from the very start. If one were to maintain that the future was already determined, he would hardly be voicing a Christian outlook. He would be rejecting out of hand the creative role of the Holy Spirit in history. The revolutionary Christian knows that the future will take the form given to it by those who actively shape it. He wishes to be involved in the construction process, and from within that framework he is willing to accept the risks entailed and to make every effort to transform them into a new form of the Spirit's presence.

5. Empirical Thinking and Dialectical Thinking

Our analysis here must be made on two levels: in terms of the socio-economic process and in terms of social consciousness.

A. Social Christianity proposes correctives for the abuses of the capitalist system, and it also proposes that we go beyond the capitalist system as such. These proposals were presented in a more systematic way in the documents issued by Pius XI and Pius XII, and in a more empirical way in the documents that have appeared more recently.

Under Pius XI and Pius XII, the Church proclaimed that it was necessary to correct the abuses of capitalism in such areas as property ownership, wages, the right of workers to defend themselves, government intervention, and so forth. The suggestion that we get beyond capitalism took the following line: The capitalist system, whose essence is the wage contract, is just in itself in spite of its recurrent abuses; but it is not the best system. It should be replaced by a different system whose cornerstone would be the contract of association. When an attempt was made to talk more concretely about this proposal, suggestions were made to reform business and professional life. The business enterprise should gradually and progressively become that of its workers. Society should be structured, not as classes that stand over against one another, but as professions which bring men together in unity. [18]

The denunciation of capitalism and the urgent need for reform are more strongly stressed by Paul VI: "We must make haste. Too many people are suffering. While some make progress, others stand still or move backwards; and the gap between them is widening" (Populorum progressio, n.29). He goes on to reject revolutionary uprisings "except where there is manifest, long-standing tyranny which would do great damage to fundamental personal rights and dangerous harm to the common good of the country" (n.31). And then he says: "We want to be clearly understood on this point. The present state of affairs must be confronted boldly, and its concomitant injustices must be challenged and overcome. Continuing development calls for bold innovations that will work profound changes. The critical state of affairs must be corrected for the better without delay" (n.32).

But what reforms are we talking about? The Medellín Conference spelled out the situation that we must now work our way out of. It referred to such factors as the following: various forms of marginal living and alienation; excessive inequality between different social classes; the continuing and increasing frustration of people's expectations; the unjust exercise of repressive power by certain ruling segments; tensions resulting from the dependence of our countries on some center of economic power; the growing imbalance and perversion of international trade; the flight of economic and human resources; the evasion of taxes by various foreign companies; the flight of dividends and profits from our countries; steadily rising indebtedness; international monopolies and the international imperialism of money; political imperialism of whatever ideological stamp, and so forth. [19]

That is the situation from which we must escape. But what road are we to take? The system of liberal capitalism and the Marxist system would seem to squelch any possibility of transforming our economic structures. Both systems attack the dignity of the human person. The former presupposes the primacy of capital, its power, and its discriminatory utilization for the sake of profit. The latter maintains a humanism on the ideological level; but it is more concerned with collective man and, in practice, this concern is translated into a totalitarian concentration of power in the hands of the State. We are obliged to denounce the fact that Latin America sees itself hemmed in between these two positions, and that she remains dependent on one or the other power center into which her economy is channeled.

And we make an urgent appeal to business leaders, to their organizations, and to the political authorities. We ask that they radically modify their values, attitudes, and standards with regard to the organization, functioning, and purpose of business enterprises. Support should be given to all those businessmen who, as individuals or as members of an organization, make an effort to orientate business enterprises along the lines suggested by the social directives of the Church's magisterium. It is a matter of fundamental importance if socio-economic change in Latin America is to move towards an economy that is truly humane.

Neither the increased investment of capital, nor the utilization of the most advanced production techniques, nor economic planning will truly be in the service of man until the workers are allowed to involve themselves in the running of a business enterprise. Leaving room for "the necessary unity of operations," we must make room for "the active participation of everyone . . . in appropriately determined ways" (Gaudium et spes, n.68). And the same holds true on the macro-economic level in trade between nations (see Populorum progressio, n.59–60).

Moving on to an analysis of the whole matter of social consciousness, we see that the logic of social Christianity operates within certain categories: justice and peace (see Populorum progressio, n.5); a humanism of development that is simultaneously individual and communitarian (ibid., n.14–18); universal charity (ibid., n.66–74); universal solidarity (ibid., n.80; see also

Gaudium et spes, n.23–32). In this brand of logic, social consciousness is in conformity with these virtues and in opposition to other
attitudes such as egotism, injustice, and violence. Social consciousness here is synonymous with ethical conscience; it is the
moral conscience operating in one of its dimensions, that concerned with social life.

Social Christianity does perceive the phenomena, but it does
not adequately perceive the connections between them. Hegel
was the first to highlight a set of connections that have proved to
be of great importance to thought and action in our age. He saw
that phenomena do not exist in isolation, that they form an
interconnected whole in which contradiction plays a major role.
He also saw that there are surface-level phenomena, and deep-
level phenomena, that the real causes of what is going on at the
surface level are far removed from there, existing on a distinct
level that we may not even be aware of. Hegel also saw that
philosophical and theological thinking is profoundly conditioned
by what takes place in the socio-economic structure. Finally, he
saw that it makes no sense to pose the question of ethics independently of the overall movement of reality, that it is impossible
to give commandments that deal with the surface level and expect them to replace injustice with justice, that one must get
down to the hidden roots. To this type of relationship Hegel gave
the name "dialectics." The opposite of grasping things dialecti-
cally is grasping them empirically, that is, as they are given to us
in concrete experience.

Hegel is only the founder of the dialectical method. After him it
was developed in different directions. Freud developed it in the
area of the unconscious. Marx, Lenin, and Mao developed it in
the area of analyzing economics, society, and politics. Today
some people are trying to integrate both types of analysis. Others
are taking another look at the whole matter from the viewpoint of
philosophy and theology. One may disagree with the concrete
analyses made by these authors. One may even disagree with
their most basic presuppositions. But it is becoming more and
more clear that they have made a significant contribution to the
analysis of human reality. Their contribution may be open to

refinement, reworking, and even radical change. But it cannot simply be shunted aside.

We have described social Christianity as an empirical line of thought, and thus set it up in contrast to the dialectical cast of revolutionary Christianity. Our reasons for doing this will become clear as we spell out the features of revolutionary Christianity, which arose as an attempt to overcome the inadequacies of social Christianity.

B. Marx was the first to see capitalism as an interlocking whole. In this whole, there was constant dialectical interaction between the parts: production, social classes, government, law, ideology, and conscience. We cannot contemplate one of these items without keeping all the others in mind as well. Nor can we contemplate them in some intellectual ivory tower, some island of neutrality, where we would be able to see what is going on "objectively."

In the decade of the sixties, Christians began to realize that social Christianity ended up being the exact opposite of what it sought to be, precisely because it had ignored this approach. Social Christianity sought to liberate man from the evils of capitalism. In practice, however, capitalism was stronger; it ended up using social Christianity for its own ends and taking complete control over the latter. So Christians began to look to Marxism—the naive approaching it naively, the clear-eyed approaching it with clear eyes.

The capitalist system has demonstrated a surprising vitality and capacity for adaption in the face of the novel twists and turns of history. By contrast the reform-minded social Christian, failing to recognize the logic involved, has been nearly always a Johnny-come-lately. In 1931 Pius XI felt proud because significant advances in social justice vis-à-vis the European worker had taken place—thanks in part to *Rerum novarum*. What had really happened was that capitalism had changed the chief object of its exploitation, shifting from the European sphere to the realm of its colonies elsewhere. Around 1970 the term "imperialism" begins to show up in papal and episcopal documents. But the fact is that Lenin had analyzed the phenomenon of imperialism fifty years earlier. Now the Church is getting around to denounce the imperialism of money and the injustice practiced by the affluent nations; but the fact is that the key focus of exploitation has shifted once again to technological know-how, the capacity to handle it, and the multinational conglomerates. The latter are often more powerful than nations themselves. Now that this fact is beginning to dawn on people, the key focus of exploitation is again shifting—towards ideology, and the educational and communications media that transmit it.

The movement of history is carrying the struggle for liberation into the realm of conscious awareness—an area where the Christian really does have more to contribute. But this presupposes that he has a correct idea of what social awareness is. It is not primarily the ethical conscience that social Christianity made of it. If that is anything at all, it is a false conscience. In order to be able to do a good job of exploitation, capitalism must misrepresent the real situation to both the exploiter and the exploited. The Christian exploiter hears many sermons and exhortations from his bishops, and we can presume he also has humane feelings. If he felt that he were exploiting people, he would experience a conflict in conscience at the very least. But if he does not suspect that he is doing such a thing, then he can listen to countless appeals for generosity and love without ever being upset by them. The neat thing about ideology is that it presents *de facto* exploitation as something that is respectable and "in conformity with the natural order of things." *Mutatis mutandis,* it plays an analogous role vis-à-vis the exploited.

Here revolutionary Christians have a privileged area of work for themselves. They must unmask the various ways in which the Christian way of life has been ideologized, examining such realities as faith, hope, charity, the sacraments, and Christian institutions. This work would presuppose two things at the outset: 1) Faith, the sacraments, and Christian institutions cannot be reduced to ideology; 2) each one of these realities, however, is subject to the threat of ideologization to some extent. To explain this point more clearly, we shall use an example that is highly significant both for the revolution and for concrete Christian experience: i.e., the class struggle.

The documents issued during the pontificates of Leo XIII, Pius XI, and Pius XII explicitly mention the struggle between the classes and reject it. In these documents it is always associated with the notion of hatred: "The Communists maintain that the conflict which is moving the world towards its final synthesis can be accelerated by man. So they try to exacerbate the differences existing between the different social classes and to make the class struggle, with all its hatred and destructiveness, look like a crusade on behalf of man's progress" (*Divini redemptoris*, n.9). Pius XII reiterates the same thought and stresses the need for collaborating with other social classes.[20] The term "class struggle" or "class warfare" disappears from the encyclicals of John XXIII and Paul VI. It reappears in Paul VI's recent Apostolic Letter, but this time the notion of "hatred" is not associated with it: "One can indeed look at Marxist doctrine, as it is implemented in real-life action, and make distinctions between these various facets and between the various questions it raises for Christian deliberation and action. But it would be foolish and dangerous on that account to forget that they are closely linked to each other; to embrace certain elements of Marxist investigation without taking due account of their relation with its doctrine; and to become involved in the class struggle and the Marxist interpretation of it without paying attention to the kind of violent and totalitarian society to which this activity gradually leads" (*Octogesima adveniens*, n.34).

This is the teaching of the popes. Now let us see how this teaching has been reflected in Chile. In 1932 the bishops of Chile issued a pastoral letter dealing with the one and only authentic solution to the social question (*La verdadera y única solución de la cuestión social*). In it no explicit mention is made of communism and socialism, even though these doctrines had been condemned in *Rerum novarum* and *Quadragesimo anno*. Clearly enough, these two doctrines were not temptations for Christians, who were solidly enmeshed in Manchesterian liberalism; so the pastoral letter directed its criticism at the latter doctrine. But it is worth noting what advice and admonitions are given to workers in this letter. Workers are obliged "to abstain from the use of force in defending their own rights; never to mount seditious insurrec-

tions; to avoid joining forces with wicked men who offer gran-
diose promises and unconscionable hopes that only lead to useless regret and the ruin of one's personal fortunes." Interspersing
passages from *Rerum novarum* in their text, the Chilean bishops
go on to say:

> Exercising this natural right of association, workers have formed
> countless associations. There has never been so many as there are
> now. But do these associations seek the real welfare of society and
> their members as their goal? Are they animated by a spirit of justice
> and peace? This is not the place to consider whence many of these
> associations spring, what they seek, and what road they are tak-
> ing. At bottom, however, it seems very likely that they are ordinar-
> ily directed by hidden chieftains who organize them in a way that
> hardly dovetails with the name of Christian or with the well-being
> of the State. Gaining a monopoly over every industry,they force
> those who do not wish to join them to pay for this resistance with
> wretchedness and poverty. They are organizations of resistance
> and force, and violence holds sway in them. Their heads are
> dictators, and the membership groans under dictatorial rule. The
> members cannot withdraw because they would be subject to per-
> secution, so they are forced to follow pathways for which their
> conscience reproaches them. Christian workers are faced with one
> of two alternatives: to give their name to associations which will
> jeopardize their religion, or to join together and form their own
> associations so that they can free themselves from that unjust and
> intolerable oppression. Only a person who is willing to endanger
> man's highest welfare would hesitate to choose the latter alterna-
> tive as the only viable choice. Good Catholics have come to realize
> this. With zeal and enthusiasm they have begun to organize
> working-class societies that are animated by the Christian spirit,
> free of despotism and demagoguery, and highly beneficial in every
> way to the members and to civil society. Hopefully bishops will
> offer them support and protection. Under their authority and
> auspices, many individual priests in religious orders and in the
> secular clergy are trying to administer to the spiritual needs of the
> members in these associations. And some wealthy Catholics, at-
> tempting to join the workers as comrades, are spending them-
> selves and a great deal of money to establish and propagate these
> associations in many different areas. With the help of these as-
> sociations and their own labor, the workers will be able to obtain
> some comforts in the present and the hope of a decent rest in the
> future.

Thirty years later we find little change in the substance of our
bishops' thinking. Class struggle is directly linked with hatred,

envy, and destructiveness. One document (*El deber social y político en la hora presente*, n.20) reproduces the passage in section 9 of *Divini redemptoris* that we cited earlier. That encyclical still remains in force in Chile even though it had been written twenty-five years earlier. The document of the Chilean bishops was published on September 18, 1962, and it was to exert a real influence on the election campaign that ended in victory for Frei. After that, the term "class struggle" disappears from the episcopal vocabulary although they continue to speak out against hatred and violence.[21] But the association had already been made, and several generations of Christians have grown up under its influence. The term "class struggle" crops up once again in a section of a more recent episcopal document (*Evangelio, política y socialismos*, n.53) where direct reference is made to Paul VI's Apostolic Letter (*Octogesima adveniens*, n. 34). This time there is no mention of "hate." The term "class struggle" is introduced as a key element in the overall logic of Marxist thought.

Two things show up quite clearly from the detailed citations we have just indicated. Firstly, no indigenous ideas have been introduced into Chilean reflection on the class struggle. The documents of the Chilean bishops merely reproduce or restate pertinent sections of papal documents. Secondly, insofar as they emphasize the matter of hatred, the papal documents bypass the essential point. The class struggle does engender hatreds, but that is not the root of the matter. Take war, for example, which also engenders hatred. War is not waged to give people an opportunity to vent their aggressiveness; it is waged to win power. The class struggle is a particular form of war. As such, it is a political concept, not a psychological one.

If a person slanders other people in a certain group, he may set the members against each other. In so doing, he "sows hatred"; and that may well be the aim he has in mind. Our situation here is different. Hatreds develop, not because someone is "sowing" them but because the objective situation of inequality brings them out when people take conscious notice of it, when it ceases to be hidden in unconscious obscurity. Moreover, hatred and envy are generally considered to be traits of those who do not possess something: the have-nots. Up to now the usual thing was for the have-nots to feel hatred when they opened their eyes. But there is a moment in a revolutionary process when the subjective feeling of hatred shifts to the other side. The "haves" begin to nurture hatred when they feel that their interests are being threatened. At the same time the "have-nots" begin to nuture feelings of hope, although we must readily admit that the long history of resentment cannot be wiped out with a stroke of the pen.

The ideologizing of charity and the sacraments finds its clearest expression in the Eucharist. It operates in three ways: 1) by equating class struggle with hatred and disunion completely, it tends to turn Christians away from that struggle; 2) by hiding the nature of the struggle for justice under a methodology of its own, it confuses the Christian and makes it hard for him to pinpoint the real enemies of justice; 3) by fostering and promoting a specifically Christian way of struggling for justice, it undermines the unity of the working class that is so necessary for a successful outcome in the struggle.

The work of "de-ideologizing" should operate on all three fronts. It is true that the innate preference of the Christian is for peace and unity. But this preference cannot be the outcome of naive desires. The preference of a sick person is obviously for health. But if this preference is to be achieved in reality, the sick person must start with a lucid awareness of his condition as a sick person. Naturally the Christian wants to see unity among all. But if this unity is to be made possible at all, he cannot start off by taking it for an already accomplished fact. The unity which he longs for is not a unity that already exists; it is a unity that must be constructed. The preference of the Christian is for peace, but the battle often does not conform to his preference. The dosage of violence is determined by those who resist being deprived of their privileges. Marxist strategy plans have been pointing this out for a long time. And this view has been amply confirmed by the events that have taken place in Chile since September 4, 1970.

Insofar as the struggle is concerned, Christianity must take up the problem of the justice of the objectives and the justice of the means—not of some abstract justice but of a concrete justice subject to the dialectical movement of history. A remark of Lenin is pertinent in this connection:

(Marxism) recognizes the most varied forms of struggle. It does not "invent" them. It simply generalizes, organizes, and injects conscious awareness into the forms of revolutionary class struggle that arise spontaneously in the course of the whole movement. Marxism rejects unconditionally anything in the nature of abstract formulas or doctrinaire recipes. It demands that one pay most attention to the struggle of the masses *in operation* . . . . That is why Marxism does not reject any form of struggle outright. It does not restrict itself completely to the forms of struggle that are present or possible in a given moment. It recognizes the *inevitable* need for new forms of struggle which may be unknown to people acting at a certain period of time but which may appear when a given social setup changes. In this sense we might say that Marxism *learns* from the concrete practice of the masses. Nothing could be further from its mind than the notion that it is to *teach* the masses certain forms of struggle that have been worked up and criticized by ivory-tower systematizers . . . . If one proposed to give a simple "yes" or "no" to a specific means of struggle without giving detailed consideration to the concrete situation of the movement in question at a given stage, that would be equivalent to withdrawing from the terrain of Marxism altogether.

We would make two observations on this passage. First of all, Christianity will not accept any and every form of struggle. For example, it will not accept calumny. Secondly, Marxism will not reject *a priori* the collaboration of someone who imposes certain limitations on himself in the struggle. The entry of significant groups of Christians into the revolutionary struggle can contribute qualitatively important transformations to that struggle. Everything will depend on how numerous and how creative these groups are.

In the Middle Ages, for example, the Church found herself in the midst of a barbarous society where the age-old custom was for men to do battle with each other and wage war. The Church did not limit herself to lyrical proclamations about her preference for peace. Taking human beings as she found them, she tried to create a style of warfare which somehow reflected the spirit of the gospel. One writer of that period put it this way: "The Christian is the man who passes through the field of battle with a flower in his hand." That is what the revolutionary Christian tries to avoid. He has not sought out the battlefield; he has been propelled into it by life. Flowers are not completely out of place, but one must know enough to wait for the right moment to use them and fight in the meantime.

Finally, the Christian must fight for the unity of the working class. Such unity is the key to victory. It is within this area that he can display his preference for unity in the most creative way, by trying to overcome myopic factionalism. The unity of the working class is, in large measure, a task related to the ideological struggle. The temptation of consumerism is one of the great factors causing division among the workers. It drives them into competition with one another, inducing them to seek benefits for themselves or their particular group. Thus there are tasks that are very proper to the Christian. But they presuppose that he will situate himself inside the revolutionary process rather than outside it.

6. Concrete Sense of History

A profound sense of history is what marked off the Jewish community, and later the Christian community, from the other peoples of antiquity. The members of these two communities knew that life is a journey towards liberation—a liberation still in the future or a liberation that had been achieved in substance but still had to be implemented. But while the Christian has always had a pretty clear idea of the grand coordinates of historical time, the same has not been true of particular coordinates in the concrete trajectory of history. The fact is that the science of history is a recent invention. Hegel, Marx, and Heidegger—among others—have opened the road in different directions.

A. The absence of a concrete sense of history in social Christianity is the logical result of the factors discussed earlier: i.e., theory is established prior to any consideration of historical praxis, and the praxis of social Christianity is empirical rather than dialectical. Its theory operates in the realm of necessity, but it is an a-historical necessity. It is the necessity of the essence of man as known by metaphysical reflection or by the revealed word. Its praxis, on the other hand, is the realm of pure contingency. There is no intervening factor to provide order or to establish something akin to a logic of history. Social Christianity offers principles and commandments in social ethics, but it does not say how we are to move towards the fulfillment of these tenets. The latter matter is left to the technicians and "experts." As a result, when social Christianity ends up in charge of the government, it is devoured by the logic of the capitalist regime even when it claims it is moving beyond that logic.

This has not happened on the level of the individual. Quite early there arose a spirituality alongside dogma and moral principles. Spirituality is the science of the concrete path that man takes in his quest for union with God. The mystics and the great spiritual writers have described this itinerary and the dangers along the way. It developed a practical theory about temptation, decision-making (the "discernment of spirits"), the ways to confront difficulties, and so forth. In short, from very early times the Church has had a sense of the concrete history of the individual. What has been lacking in social Christianity is a sense of concrete social history.

B. Once again this is what revolutionary Christians have looked for in Marxism: a strategy and a set of tactics. As is true in the case of the class struggle, it is not a matter of taking them over mechanically but of shouldering them in a way that recreates them anew

A short time ago, the ITT papers were published. It was a revelation for many Christians. It was not that for people trained in the Marxist method of analyzing history. Those familiar with Lenin's analysis of imperialism would have expected some such attempt as the one planned for September–October 1970. And on the basis of this expectation they could point their investigation in the right direction. That is precisely what the Popular Unity front did on that occasion. The bishops would not have hesitated to condemn any such rash attempt to plunge the country into civil war; but they could not do that because they lacked an anticipatory framework that would have allowed them to gather the information needed in order to act.

In the exact sciences one can predict with a high degree of accuracy. Today, in fact, we can land artifacts on the moon with almost pinpoint accuracy. Obviously the accuracy of the Marxist science of history is much less. It operates in the realm of liberty, where the margin of the unpredictable is far larger. But it operates in the realm of a structured liberty, where the margin of the foreseeable and the predictable goes far beyond the mere conjecture of someone with a good historical eye.

PART THREE

Guidelines for Action

The process going on in Chile spotlights certain priorities for Christians who are working on behalf of socialism. While the ruling class is bolstering its alliances with "independent" groups, attracting popular segments, and thus developing into a growing opposition, the revolutionary forces are moving ahead slowly and with great difficulty. The people are divided. Only a small segment of the people is at work in an organized, revolutionary way—though this segment is aware and active in an effective way. So we face the major task of mobilizing the people and unifying their combative strength in order to consolidate the process of moving towards socialism.

This political effort cannot be separated from the cultural urgency of the ideological struggle. The outlook and behavior of the bourgeoisie has seeped into the masses, making it difficult for the working class to take cognizance of their situation. Bourgeois culture has religious features in it, and it is bolstered by the ideology of social Christianity. The ideological battle is proving to be of prime importance right now, and it involves the religious ideology of the majority of Chileans.

In this transition to socialism in Chile, the vocation of the people to fashion a new society shows up in striking terms. Leftist Christians recognize the historic summons that God is now issuing to the people of Chile: to free themselves from the chains of neocapitalism and fashion a new society. In the present revolutionary struggle they see a journey towards the kingdom of God, because in this conflict-filled history God is accompanying the poor towards their liberation as he has always done. Responding to God's summons to liberation, which is now awakening in the hearts of the people, leftist Christians are committing themselves more and more to the struggle of the working class.

1. The Quality of Christian Commitment

Christian love for one's neighbor is concrete and universal in one's commitment to the working class and its historical project. For it is from the people themselves, organized as the working class and guided by the rationale of revolution through their leaders, that the strategy for constructing socialism has arisen. Solidarity with the working class—industrial workers, peasants, manual laborers—becomes truly effective and revolutionary charity because the socialism which they have generated will help to liberate all the people. Thus Christian commitment is to the cause of the workers, and it is there that the Christian will share in Christ's liberative work that gives shape and structure to history.

The workers have their own class-oriented organizations, parties, and movements. Leftist Christians involve themselves in these battle fronts; they do not form parallel organisms of their own. Real, authentic commitment to the workers implies that one will adopt the discipline and strategy of their organized forces. Fighting alongside their worth by the caliber and effectiveness of their activity, they are scattered among their comrades. But whatever their position in the Chilean left may be, Christians see the cause of unity as an imperative for them. Unless the whole left is united, the people will be defeated.

The working class possesses a sense of brotherhood that cannot be found elsewhere, and this sense is growing all the time. Though it does indeed suffer from tragic divisions and sectarian splits, in its long and heroic journey through history it is fashioning a unity that points the way towards brotherhood in the future. This fraternal order impels it to destroy the established disorder of neocapitalist society. In this struggle for fraternal equality and within the context of the class struggle, leftist Christians take their place in the midst of the oppressed class. On the one hand they strip the rich man of his instruments of exploitation so that he might cease to be rich and become a brother of the poor man. On the other hand they stand united with all the oppressed of Chile, so that the latter might be able to break their chains and fashion real equality.

Grounded in the revolutionary action of the working class, in which the New Man is being formed, leftist Christians celebrate the Eucharist. Christ, the New Man, was sent to liberate the oppressed (Lk 4:18–16). Sharing the body and blood of the Lord, revolutionary Christians join the poor as their brothers and shoulder their struggle and their goal.

2. Mobilization of the People

Around those Christians who are participating actively in the revolutionary process we find a mass of people who look on as spectators or who actively oppose the process. Numerous segments of the populace have been won over by the forces of the right; they have surrendered to reformist practices or to conformism. Other segments are on the defensive; they do not participate because they reject the traditional political game and its abuses.

Faced with this situation, revolutionary Christians take on the task of incorporating elements from these sectors into the revolutionary process. They feel that the conditions of structural exploitation to which the people have been subjected will be overcome if the people take cognizance of them and act in a revolutionary way. The vast majority of the people possess a religious conscience that has been ideologized. Frequently they have been dispirited by groups that claim to be "Christian." Leftist Christians set themselves the task of helping these people to move away from their passivity and misapprehension and motivating them to undertake liberative action.

Since the neocapitalist system and the ruling class have left the country immersed in all sorts of problems and contradictions, the process of moving towards socialism must overcome huge obstacles. Moreover, the working class itself is divided; it has not achieved sufficient revolutionary unity to insure victory. Hence it will take much sacrifice on the part of the people to break away from their bourgeois aspirations and their individualism, and to overthrow the forces that are oppressing them. Motivated by faith and by political realism, revolutionary Christians do not indulge in promises of immediate wellbeing. Instead they proclaim the need for sacrifice and for disinterested effort on behalf of the welfare of the working class as a whole.

Christians involved in the transition to socialism know that it is a long-term struggle, and that certain conditions are imposed on them and others in the short run. In an immediate sense the working class is overcoming the injustices of capitalist society and enjoying the minimum standards of a human way of life. But in order to achieve complete power, it will be necessary to face up to the difficult and demanding tasks of revolutionary change. There is a persistent dynamism at work in the people, a dynamism imposed on them by capitalist society. It tempts them to turn back to the security of dependence. Taking due account of all that, leftist Christians accompany the mass of the people and offer them encouragement both in their immediate advances and in the strategy for total liberation.

Hope sets a decisive imprint on the activity of revolutionary Christians. The exodus from a situation of oppression to a socialist society calls for a political praxis that is simultaneously realistic and "utopian." They realize that if the people are not mobilized, there will be no revolution. But they also realize that if the goal of total liberation is not part and parcel of this mobilization, then the people will remain caught in the grip of reformism. Thus Christian hope becomes the driving force behind the activity of leftist Christians. Their activity is directed along the lines of permanent revolution, so that there will be no turning back on the road to socialism and to a society that is truly egalitarian and fraternal.

The real objective of the mobilized people is a new heaven and a new earth. To achieve this end, the God of the Exodus voices a persistent and perduring plea to leave injustice behind and to keep moving forward towards a new society—a society that is the joint work of the God of Jesus Christ and of the revolutionaries. In the Chilean process of moving towards socialism, dehumanizing structures and relationships are being generated still. A continuing battle against these things is being waged by those Christians who are involved in the struggle of the working class.

3. Development of a New Consciousness

With its tools and media for cultural and educational domination, the neocapitalist system imposes an ideology that creates alienation in the people. Following the guidelines of this system, the mass of people develop a subculture that is dependent and reformist. Revolutionary consciousness develops only if the people act in some organized fashion, both in rural and urban areas. It is when the workers mobilize as a class that they develop their class consciousness and their plan of socialism. Class consciousness must be bolstered if we are to ensure the success of the process now going on in Chile. A primary task of leftist Christians is to collaborate in the effort to acquire this new consciousness through revolutionary activity, to develop it in themselves, in their comrades in the struggle, and in the masses of the people. Consciousness-raising does not lie solely in the verbal or ideological area, therefore; it also lies in the area of political and cultural praxis. So it is very important for us to expand and solidify the socialized area of the economy, agrarian reform, and popular participation in leftist activities and organizations.

The bourgeois ideology utilizes the Christian faith, converting it into a religion that legitimizes domination and offers pseudo-Christian values. A sacred character has been given to democracy and liberty, and "charity" has been turned into something that is incompatible with revolution. The rights of the human person now function as rights of the ruling class; and in this version they are defended as essential elements of Christianity. In such forms as these, the ideology of social Christianity is diffused far and wide.

In recent decades an anti-communism has taken root which has a religious cast at bottom. It diverts people's attention away from the fundamental problem of exploitation and underdevelopment and towards the whole problem-complex of Marxism; it also stresses a false brand of nationalism. Reacting to these facts and many others, revolutionary Christians attribute primary importance to the ideological battle. They do so because they have a deep appreciation for the gospel and for the faith they have received. They refuse to allow the destruction of Jesus Christ, his Church, and his sacraments; to permit them to be turned into defenders of neocapitalism and the interests of a minority. They participate in the work of a de-ideologizing also because the religious character of the existing cultural domination must be challenged so that the people can liberate their own awareness and conscience. Through the witness of their evangelical and revolutionary involvement, Christians can facilitate the participation of the Christian masses in the process of constructing a new society. This is particularly true for ministers, pastors, religious men and women, priests and bishops. To the extent that they help to render the gospel present in the process, they help to further the participation of other Christians.

As we indicated above, a considerable number of Christians have participated in the socialist program of the working class since the end of the 1960s. Even though they represent a minority in the various churches, and even though the "Christian element" continues to be reformist for the most part, these Christians have had a profound impact on the national consciousness. Being a revolutionary is no longer incompatible with being a Christian; nor is the union of the two something that occurs only in isolated cases. Some revolutionary Christians, sensing the necessity of mutual support and challenge, have come together for reflection, discussion, and liturgical worship. But these activities must be intensified as quickly as possible, and more and more Christians must participate in them.

In their interchange and correlation of personal experiences, in their communal celebrations of thanksgiving, and in their common quest for the paschal demands of Jesus Christ, these Christians have sensed the growth of an astonishing hopefulness and brotherhood. They have no desire to set up a political movement of their own. They work and struggle within the ranks of manual laborers, salaried workers, professionals, peasants, and students. Nor do they have any desire to form a front in opposition to their communities or their hierarchies. Thanks to the discernment of spirits in the Church, the search is a common task which calls for positive and perduring dialogue with the hierarchy. The cause of liberation seeks the destruction of capitalism and the construction of socialism as a fundamental step towards the arrival of God's kingdom. Because of their solidarity with the struggle of the oppressed, and on the basis of a scientific analysis of the process, they work on behalf of socialism. Because of their faith and hope in the God of Jesus Christ, they live and act in a revolutionary way.

Leftist Christians are motivated by their love for Jesus Christ and his Church and driven by their unconditional solidarity with the oppressed. So they invite all the Christians of Chile to participate actively and constructively in the historical program of the working class. If Christians collaborate concretely and effectively in the transition form neocapitalism to socialism, they will be giving a faithful response to Christ's summons to fashion a brotherly, egalitarian society.

Because we cannot "serve God and Money" (Lk 16:13). Because "whoever cares for his own safety is lost; but if a man will let himself be lost for my sake, that man is safe" (Lk 9:24). Because "when Christians dare to give full-fledged revolutionary witness, then the Latin American revolution will be invincible" (Che Guevara).

NOTES

1. Salvador Allende Gossens, First Address before Congress in full session, May 21, 1971.

2. Medellín Conference, Document on Peace, n.16, October 1968.

3. Paul VI, Encyclical *Populorum progressio*, n.26.

4. Bishops of Chile, working draft entitled *Evangelio, política y socialismos*, Santiago, 1971, n.48.

5. Presidential campaign of Salvador Allende, *Programa Básico de la Unidad Popular*, the first forty measures.

6. See *Chile Hoy*, Ed. Universitaria, Santiago, 1971; in particular, "Estructura económica: algunas características fundamentales," by Sergio Aranda and Alberto Martínez.

7. See an analysis of this problem-complex in *Problemas y perspectivas del socialismo en Chile* (*Cuadernos de la Realidad Nacional*, Number 10, December 1971) and *Materiales para el estudio del área de propiedad social* (*Cuadernos de la Realidad Nacional*, Number 11). See also Gonzalo Arroyo's report on the CEREN-CESO Symposium, *Transición al socialismo y la experiencia chilena*.

8. "Nuevas tareas para el Gobierno Popular y el Pueblo de Chile" (Acuerdos de "El Arrayán"), Santiago, February 9, 1972.

9. "To study and resolve everything with the masses: that will be our fundamental line of action, and it will be deepened and generalized more and more. It is not just general revolutionary impulses that are to emanate from the people at the grass-roots level. From there should also come specific decisions, whose execution should be performed and checked by the masses more and more directly" (Acuerdos de "El Arrayán").

10. The bishops of Chile, Punta de Tralca, April 11, 1972.

11. Lalive D'Epinay, *El refugio de las masas*, Ed. del Pacífico, Santiago, 1968.

12. Gonzalo Arroyo, "La Iglesia en la década del 70," in *América 70* (edited by Carlos Nandón). Edición Nueva Universidad, CU of Chile, 1970.

13. Pablo Fontaine, "Situación actual de la Iglesia Chilena, " *Mensaje*, August 1971, 201:367–71.

14. José Pablo Richard, "Renacimiento socialista y verificación histórica del cristianismo," *CEREN*, CU of Chile, April 12, 1972, pp. 144–53.

15. Translator's note: The National Catholic Welfare Conference is now known as the United States Catholic Conference (USCC).

16. Cited by Jean Villain in *La enseñanza social de la Iglesia*, Madrid, Aguilar, 1957, p. 21.

17. Juan Luis Segundo, *La Iglesia chilena ante el socialismo*.

18. See Jean Villain, *La enseñanza social de la Iglesia*.

19. "Iglesia y liberación humana," in *Los documentos de Medellín*, Editorial Nova Terra, Barcelona, 1969, pp. 68–73.

20. Pius XII, Address to Catholic Associations of Italian Workers, June 29, 1948, n.21–23.

21. See *Chile, voluntad de ser*, n.36; and the more recent episcopal Declaration of April 11, 1972, n.3,4,5,8.

12

Peru

In general, Peruvian society has all the characteristics of an underdeveloped society. It is dependent in the international sphere, and its socio-economic structure is marked by domination. We do not think it is necessary to describe these facts in detail because that is the basic situation of almost all the countries in Latin America.

Right now Peru is governed by a military junta. The armed forces took over political power in a coup on October 3, 1968, deposing President Belaúnde. To explain the circumstances surrounding this coup, we must refer briefly to the government of Belaúnde.

In 1963 Fernando Belaúnde was elected President of the republic with the backing of a front composed of segments from the middle and lower bourgeoisie. He was also supported by some leftist sectors and had substantial popular support. His program was a "reformist" one. His rivals were the APRA (American People's Revolutionary Alliance, ordinarily a leftist party but at that time allied with the dominant sectors in the country), and a former dictator who was supported by segments of the old oligarchy in the nation.

The election of Belaúnde was viewed very sympathetically by significant segments of the armed forces. He initiated his regime with an energetic effort at reform, but this effort was hampered by his lack of control in parliament, where the opposition right was in the majority. Faced with this situation, President Belaúnde gradually moved towards an "understanding" with the opposition right, and his government eventually ended up as a totally reactionary one.

During the reign of Belaúnde a process of political radicalization took place in the country. Among the causes for this were the rekindling of hopeful expectations among the people, which were caused by the promises of Belaúnde himself, but were later frustrated. There was also the outcrop of armed leftist uprisings. While these uprisings were rapidly put down by the armed forces, they made clear to significant segments of the population—including the armed forces—the necessity for structural changes.

That brings us to 1968, when the country suffered an acute economic crisis that was accompanied by political scandal. Government figures were found to be involved in a huge smuggling operation. Certain concessions that had been taken over improperly were handed over completely to the International Petroleum Company, the local subsidiary of Standard Oil. This solution was shared both by the executive branch and by the opposition in parliament.

These circumstances led to a full-blown political crisis. The reformist political parties had failed, and there were no partisan alternatives. Popular organizations began to form, but the left did not represent a viable alternative in the short run or the intermediate run.

Faced with this situation, the armed forces took over political power in the country. They exercised this power in an institutional way and informed the country that they were taking over executive and legislative power in order to move the process of change forward.

At first it was clear that the military government was not operating on any clear-cut ideological basis. It indicated that it would effect necessary structural reforms while maintaining an independent international policy, and it also affirmed the necessity of restoring order and social peace.

Right away it annulled the transfer of petroleum deposits that had been made by Belaúnde. This action represented a strong stand against imperialist interests and confirmed its nationalist approach. Subsequently the military government set forth a series of political and economic laws and measures that bore a markedly reformist tinge. We shall only mention them here without going into any detailed analysis:

In the area of international politics, it extended its

diplomatic and commercial relationships with almost all the socialist countries, and it broadened its ties with the countries of the Third World.

It supported the principle of ideological pluralism within continental organizations.

It formulated a policy whereby underdeveloped nations would defend their natural resources (especially with regard to territorial waters).

It gave ample support to a policy of independence for the nations of the Third World.

It reserved to the government of Peru the commercialization of its fishing grounds, and the commercialization and refinement of its mining production.

It reserved to the government all basic industry, and it progressively nationalized foreign investments, setting limits on their participation.

It reinforced the role of government banking, established control over some private banks, and set forth measures to restrict and control the use and exchange of foreign currency.

It passed an agrarian reform law which did away with the large landed estates and sought to turn the land over to those who work it. It favored cooperative forms of production on expropriated lands.

It passed an education reform law, which sought to democratize the system and to train people for their work.

It passed a law establishing a labor community in the areas of fishing, industry, and mining. This institution brought together all the workers in an industry or enterprise so that they would share in its ownership, management, and profits. A set percentage of these profits would be set aside for the acquisition of stock in the company, up to 50% of the shares. Thus the workers would gradually be incorporated into the process of controlling and managing an enterprise and its capital.

That is a brief list of some of the most significant measures passed by the Peruvian military government. As far as their implementation is concerned, the pace varied from one case to another. There is no reason to discuss this point in detail here. In general, we can say that the decision-making process embodied in the promulgation of laws proceeds more briskly than the implementation of these same laws. This is particularly true when the laws in question entail substantial modifications of the socio-economic structure.

Another important factor must be taken into account in any analysis of the Peruvian process. The fact is that the measures and actions do not move in a single, straight-line direction. Contradictory measures appear simultaneously or follow one another. The implementation of the agrarian reform law is a case in point. The law was promulgated on July 24, 1969. Between that date and November 1970, there were more than eighteen labor-union conflicts. Labor leaders were jailed, some of them were exiled from the country; later they were released from jail, and the exiles were permitted to return.

From all this it is clear that the Peruvian process has its own unique character that makes any definitive evaluation difficult. This fact shows up with particular clarity when one tries to make political evaluations on the basis of the tools provided by the social sciences, for these sciences tend to stop a reality in a "still shot" so that they can formulate some judgment about it. But it is clear from the facts of life that the political dynamism of the regime does not allow any static evaluation of it. Take the laws establishing the labor community, for example. When they were promulgated, it was thought that the business model proposed for the Peruvian situation was that of conciliation between capital and labor. In his annual message of July 1971, however, President Velasco pointed out that the labor-community setup was not the model envisioned by the government in general. It was simply a model for existing enterprises. The government was trying to design a model based on social ownership for the new enterprises that would be created in line with the requirements of national development.

Insofar as this societal model is concerned, it is important to underline the evolving nature of its definition. At the start the government stated that it was not pursuing a course of liberal capitalism or a communist regime. The former had demonstrated its failure by subjecting the vast majority of the nation's people to subhuman living conditions within a formal democracy; and the latter had led, historically, to centralized regimes fraught with bureaucracy. Now the government has come around to quite a different formulation. It claims it is seeking the construction of a social democracy with full participation, one inspired by the best elements in the humanist, libertarian, and socialist tradition and by the most advanced elements in Christianity.

Despite what it says, however, it is clear that in reality the power of governing is now exercised by the armed forces, acting as an institution. The military puts its representatives in various organisms of the government. They exercise the executive and legislative functions, and final decisions are made by the armed forces who govern in the people's name.

In recent months we have seen the creation of a governmental entity whose aim is to support popular mobilization. With this aim in mind, it is supposed to help to create the organization of the people along territorial and functional lines, in both the social and economic areas. Because of its recent creation, its results cannot be evaluated as yet.

Another noteworthy point is the length of time envisioned for the continuation of the military junta in power. Its most representative spokesmen have indicated that the term is still indefinite; and also that they will not step down from power until they have advanced the process of change so far that their handover of power to others will not mean a return to former conditions.

At present, political organizations take one of three positions vis-à-vis the military junta. We will present them briefly here, even at the risk of oversimplifying:

—Open and total opposition. This opposition is divided between two extremes. The economic and political right opposes the government because it sees its interests threatened. At the other extreme, some Marxist groups start from the position that the government is reformist and oppose it completely; these Marxist groups are of little weight numerically.

—Full support. This position is particularly evident among the middle range of the bourgeoisie. These people feel that it is important to consolidate the gains already made and not to go any further.

—Support intermingled with criticism. Important segments of the population support the process because they maintain that the military government has initiated a process of change in the country. But they also feel that it can evolve towards greater radicalization and seek to move it in that direction. They seek to do this by exerting influence on the various levels of governmental decision-making and also—even more basically—by creating channels of popular pressure. This position is maintained by militants formerly in the reformist political parties, Marxists, labor leaders, technicians, intellectuals, a few organizations of the Marxist left such as the Communist Party, and one of the factions that follows a Maoist line.

The Situation of the Church

1. The life of the Peruvian Church in recent years has been conditioned internally by a wide-scale process of fermenting ideas and group formation. Groups of lay Catholics and priests within the various apostolic movements have gradually been radicalizing their options. Externally the Peruvian Church has been conditioned by two factors: the impact of the Medellín Conference and of the Peruvian political process. The ecclesial reform envisioned at Medellín in connection with the oppressive situation of the Latin American people was initiated in Peru itself within the new social and political context created by the ruling military junta. This latter context, appearing concomitantly with the thrust towards internal Church reform, has profoundly influenced church life; to a large extent it explains the peculiar nature of the way church life has evolved.

2. It is clear that, in the beginning, ecclesial renewal moved in the direction of intra-ecclesial reformism pure and simple, and that it still continues in that direction to a large extent. It operates with the naive assumption that it can continue to be a-political. This brand of ecclesial reformism looks with sympathy on a political policy of developmentalism and modernization that

does not call into question the system created to benefit only a few.

3. At the same time, however, new vigor has been injected into already existing groups of Christians—both priests and lay people—who see a political dimension in the presence of the Church and the proclamation of the gospel. The priests' movement ONIS and the Movement for a Church in Solidarity are the most important groups of this sort. Their influence is growing. Conscious of the class struggle that is going on in Peruvian society, they feel that their option for the oppressed classes and for the construction of socialism is something demanded by their faith. By 1968 the ineffectiveness of reformist parties along the lines of Acción Popular ("People's Action") and the Christian Democrats was evident. Since then, there has been a growing tendency to make openings to leftist groups and to get involved personally with them.

4. The hierarchy has shown a certain amount of openness to some of this uneasiness and restlessness. The whole issue of the people's liberation has been given consideration in such documents as that of the 1969 episcopal conference and that presented to the 1971 Synod (*Justicia en el mundo*). These documents are among the elements that have helped to criticize ideologies, to point out lines of commitment and involvement, and to facilitate the adoption of more radical stances by many Christian groups. The adoption of these more radical stances has stirred up unwonted hostility in rightist Catholic sectors, and it will help to polarize opinions and options within the Church. It will make clear the fact that the class struggle cuts through the ecclesial community itself.

5. The groups mentioned in section 3 above keenly feel the serious flaws in our pastoral effort. Up to now this pastoral effort has been directed mainly towards the ruling class and the middle-class sectors. It has alienated the common people as a whole or left them on the sidelines. This is proved by the disproportionate number of militant Christians coming from the middle classes and the scant number of such Christians coming from the ranks of laborers and peasants. If we are to have a more authentic Church, it is urgent that we engage in evangelizing activity among the common people and their classes.

13

Puerto Rico

Political Colonialism

To understand Puerto Rico correctly, we must place it within the context of its history, a history of almost five centuries of colonialism. In this age of de-colonization, Puerto Rico still remains an example of a dependent political colony. Under the deceptive smoke screen of the title "Commonwealth," it is the Congress of the United States that wields power over Puerto Rico. This power found expression in 1917 when American citizenship was imposed on Puerto Ricans. Later on it found expression in the "blood tribute" of compulsory military service, whereby Puerto Ricans were obliged to serve as mercenaries in the wars of the United States. If we want to talk correctly about Puerto Rico, we must begin by calling it a colony.

We must also note, however, that this long history of colonization has not eradicated the people's will to fight back. The sign of the times today is the fact that more and more Puerto Ricans are awakening from their colonial stupor and realizing the need to fight for self-determination, so that the people may be able to control the decision-making process which affects their existence and their collective destiny.

Military Colonialism

Under Spanish rule Puerto Rico was a military bastion designed to protect her commerce with the new world. Her strategic position is what led the United States to take her over. Puerto Rico was soon converted into the Gibraltar of the Caribbean. Thirteen percent of her land was set aside as United States military bases, some of these bases later being converted into arsenals of nuclear armaments. The future of Puerto Rico's youth was put up for barter through the law of compulsory military service. United States Army training centers were established on the campuses of Puerto Rico's universities.

This military colonialism has been the chief target of Puerto Rican resistance in recent years. University students have waged a long and consistent battle against the ROTC. They oppose the idea that their universities should be turned into training centers for the officers of an invader army. Five people have died in this opposition struggle—a laborer, a student, two policemen, and one cadet. Hundreds of students have been injured or have suffered from police repression.

This struggle goes on. The growing intensification of the Vietnam war during the past decade had two results for Puerto Rico: 1) a larger quota of young Puerto Rican men were sent as cannon fodder to southeast Asia; 2) the tiny island of Culebra was increasingly used as a naval training center. Both of these actions boomeranged on the imperialist nation. Young Puerto Ricans waged a real battle against compulsory military service. Hundreds of them flatly refused to serve with the invader army, thereby expressing their solidarity with the people of Vietnam. This struggle against compulsory military service opened the eyes of young Puerto Ricans to the colonial status of their island. The island of Culebra itself became both a symbol and a crisis-point of the military colonialism dominating Puerto Rico. For two years this small island of about only 800 inhabitants fought against its use as an American war base. More recently, substantial segments of our population have protested against the nuclearization of Puerto Rico. The struggle goes on, and in fact it is intensifying.

Economic Colonialism

The key to understanding the colonial status of Puerto Rico lies in the economic exploitation which it suffers. Puerto Rico is a clear example of capitalist colonialism. The island is used in several exploitative ways:

1. It is used as a center for the investment of the excess capital

of the large United States corporations. The much vaunted industrialization of Puerto Rico was designed to benefit the United States homeland. It is an export-minded industrialization, designed to complement the economy of the United States. It is an appendix to the economy of the United States, responding to that economy rather than to the economy of Puerto Rico. It is grounded on the ideal of Puerto Rico being an "investor's paradise"; there are tax exemptions, and wages are kept artificially low. In this way the huge United States corporations often earn a yearly return of 35% on their original investment.

2. It is a center for the sale of United States manufactured products. Puerto Rico is the fourth largest market of the United States, simply because it is a captive market. It is an island that produces things it does not consume and that consumes things it does not produce. It has no power to protect its home market for its own production; nor does it have any power to diversify its foreign trade since it is situated within the tariff barriers of the United States. It is obliged to buy the surplus manufactures of the United States.

3. It is a center for the creation of an industrial labor pool. Puerto Rico's dependence on the United States economy has meant the ruin of its own agriculture, and this has led to a steep rise in the unemployment index. Around 25% of the labor force is unemployed. This rate is maintained by the empire for several reasons: to keep the demands of Puerto Rican workers at a very low level, and to import into the United States a million Puerto Ricans, who serve as an auxiliary proletariat. One third of our nation is struggling for a subsistent livelihood in the ghettos of the United States homeland. They are new Jews in a new Egypt.

4. It is a center of potential mineral exploitation. United States corporations are particularly interested in the island's rich store of copper and nickel. But in recent years there has been increasing Puerto Rican resistance to economic exploitation of this sort. The most promising signs of this resistance have been these:

    a. The struggle to prevent Puerto Rican mines from being exploited for the benefit of United States mining corporations. Under the slogan "Puerto Rican mines or no mines!" an increasing number of people have joined the

battle against the planned plunder of our mineral resources. An extensive campaign of political education
among the common people has been undertaken to make
them aware of what this mineral exploitation would
mean in terms of environmental pollution, dislocation of
small farmers, and the loss of a natural resource that
might serve as the basis for a reconstructed national life.

b. Land recovery. This is not a new phenomenon on the
island. In sporadic form it has been a real part of our
national life. In the last year or so, however, these recovery activities have changed in character and become acts
of civil and political disobedience that challenge the
overall system and confront the existing order of things.
Those involved have appealed to the advocates of independence for support. The new towns that have arisen in
this way often bear the names of patriots or names that
signalize opposition to the existing system. The new
communities not only seek to provide housing for the
homeless but also seek to reconstruct a communitarian
way of life based on the people's self-determination. In
the long run this thrust would mean the end of the
colonial system.

c. The labor struggle. Throughout the decade of the forties,
the labor movement was divided and made impotent.
This was a necessary prelude to a process of industrialization based on the importation of United States capital.
The General Confederation of Workers was fragmented.
Through the use of the Taft-Hartley Act, significant obstacles were placed in the way of union organizing and
the activities of existing unions. For twenty-five years the
Puerto Rican labor movement was impotent, drugged by
promises of the advantages that foreign-based industrialization would supposedly bring. Meanwhile the
large foreign corporations drew off our wealth from the
labor of our workers. In the last two years, however, the
lineaments of a new situation have taken shape. A United Labor Movement has arisen, with the aim of bring-

ing the working class together. A new generation of labor leaders has come to the fore; they are more combative and more clear-eyed politically and ideologically. In the last six months the island has been hit by a series of strikes that have served as an opportunity for establishing ties between the advocates of independence and the workers. This has disrupted the old imperialist strategy in Puerto Rico: i.e., to keep the struggle for national liberation divided from the struggle for working-class rights. From the meeting of these two forces on the picket line there is developing a working class movement that is consciously aware of the need to go beyond the boundaries of trade unionism, and an independence movement that is consciously aware of the need to establish deeper ties in theory and practice with the labor movement. The working-class struggle and the struggle for national liberation are becoming one single, united struggle.

Here lies the key to the future of Puerto Rico. It lies in the realization by the advocates of independence that the working class is the most logical and promising basis for the struggle against imperialism. And it lies in the workers' realization that there is an antagonism between their own aspirations and the existing system of colonial capitalism.

d. In the meantime a third of the nation, now living in enforced exile in the imperial homeland, is also beginning to enter the fray. Their struggle takes two forms. First of all, it is directed against the terrible living conditions to which Puerto Ricans are subjected in the United States. The most recent studies show that they are on the lowest social scale in the United States. They must face the scorn and ridicule of racism. Like Negroes in the United States, they are exploited economically by their employers. And they are secluded in ghettos, where they are plagued by impotence, frustration, and crime. The dream of a promised land has turned into a nightmare, and now the nightmare is turning into an active will to fight. In various ways the Puerto Rican community is beginning to protest against the oppression to which it is subject.

On the other side of the coin young Puerto Ricans, born or raised in the United States, have embarked on a quest for their cultural and national identity. It is a painful, agonizing quest. Many young Puerto Ricans are obliged to affirm their Puerto Rican identity in English, because they have been deprived of the ability to express themselves in Spanish. But an astonishing capacity to resist cultural assimilation is showing up. They are forging a clear awareness of the fact that their destiny and future is linked to that of the struggle for national liberation in Puerto Rico.

These two elements are important. At a critical point in the future history of Puerto Rico it may well be that the Puerto Rican community in the United States will decide, by its activity or its apathy, whether Puerto Rico is to remain a colony or achieve liberation.

Cultural Colonialism

Our colonial status is not just based on political, military, and socio-economic dependence. It also entails cultural subjugation, an internalization of the ruling imperial structures, a general feeling of impotence, a feeling of scorn for what is our own, and a "fear of liberty." Since the beginning of this centruy, the public school system in Puerto Rico has served as a tool for teaching the English language and for imposing the values and symbols of the United States. It became the chief instrument for Americanizing our people. Americanization was not the only aim. It also helped to create subjects who would bow to the process which was turning them into a proletariat. Through the school process they internalized the ideological justifications of their colonial status and of capitalist exploitation. The aim was to fashion a docile Puerto Rican. This led to the rewriting of Puerto Rico's history, where facts were turned upside down and truth was castrated.

The submissive were turned into heroes, the rebellious were turned into traitors.

On another front, the mass media undertook the task of creating a consumer mentality. This was needed for the expansion of markets and for the sale of manufactured products from the United States. So we get an island of poor people with the tastes and consumption habits of an affluent society. This in turn leads to a spiralling whirl of public and private debt. We are eating our future ahead of time.

In the last few years, however, the more advanced segments of our population have undertaken the task of fashioning a culture that truly befits a people struggling for its liberation. Public education has been unmasked as an instrument of domestication and conformism, and the true history of Puerto Rico is now being rediscovered. Its true history is one of oppression and of struggle for liberation, and we are rediscovering men who can be the provocative symbols in our quest: Betances and Albizu in particular. We have also begun to write the history of those "without a history," that is, of the oppressed classes in Puerto Rico.

A socialized press in favor of independence has also come into being. It has broken the monopoly that the consumerist press used to exercise over the people. This press has begun to perfect ways of carrying out its task, which is to spell out for the people the following: the social reality as one of dependence and subjugation; the Achilles' heels of this dominion; and the forms of struggle that suit this moment in our history.

Along with this there has arisen a whole art of defiance and protest: dramas, poetry recitals, puppet shows, paintings, protest songs, and so forth. Their aim is to describe the nature of the oppression and to arouse protest against it in people's hearts.

The Advocates of Independence

In the last five years, parties and organizations advocating independence have developed their ideas on every level. Ideologically speaking, the principal developments have been these:

1. A growing awareness that the struggle for national liberation in Puerto Rico cannot be isolated from the Latin American struggle against imperialism. The empire has tried to isolate Puerto Rico from Latin America. This attempt has been abetted by the imposition of United States citizenship on the population and by geographical isolation. But more and more the Puerto Rican struggle is being seen as a critical symbol of the Latin American struggle. The attempt has been made to turn Puerto Rico into a "bridge between two cultures," that is, into an instrument for colonizing Latin America. Techniques of assimilation are tried out in Puerto Rico, and they are then exported to our sister countries in Latin America. Thus the Puerto Rican struggle is of utmost importance for all of Latin America. It serves as a barometer of Latin America's struggle against imperialism.

2. A shift from slogans advocating independence to a real struggle for liberation, this struggle being viewed as an indispensable precondition for the construction of socialism. The empire managed to keep the independence movement isolated from the people by locking the latter up in an ideology of national sovereignty and cultural identity. This lockup has been broken by means of socialism. It also means that the anti-colonial struggle has turned into an anti-capitalist struggle as well, and that the struggle for political liberty has turned into a struggle to create a new social order.

3. A realization that the working class is the most logical one to carry on the struggle against imperialism in Puerto Rico. It is the most revolutionary class for several reasons. Firstly, because it is the most exploited. The colony is maintained by the profits won from the hard labor of our workers. Secondly, because in strategic terms it has the greatest potential of effectively transforming the system. The workers keep the system functioning, and they can also paralyze it if they choose. Thirdly, the working class is the most revolutionary class because it is the symbol of the future, not of some past that will inevitably be laid to rest. The working class is inextricably tied up with the development of new production forces. Its aim is to democratize these forces through a socialist revolution.

In the realm of political praxis, this ideological development has brought with it a real solidarity between the movement for independence and the exploited classes. Advocates of independence see the exploited classes as the leaven of revolution. The exploited classes see the struggle for independence as an indispensable element in their revolutionary ideology. Thus, in Puerto Rico, we see the major libertarian movements of this century joining forces: i.e., the struggle for national liberation and the struggle to construct and implement socialism.

Christians

The churches have been instruments of cultural penetration. Along with the Protestant gospel came symbols and attitudes that fitted in with imperialism. Until a decade ago, the hierarchy of the Catholic Church was made up of Americans, although the Catholic Church itself is a "national church" with an impressive network of primary and secondary schools. The teachers in most of them are American religious who teach in English and use U.S. textbooks. The church inherited from Spain has served as a center for transmitting that culture.

A rebel church began to appear about a decade ago. It was composed of priests and ministers who had broken with the castrating a priori schemas established for their ministry and who were beginning to commit themselves, in word and deed, to the struggle for liberation. Today the class struggle has penetrated into the church. More and more, Puerto Rican Christians are refusing to talk about reconciliation and unity in an alienating sense. For them, justice is the prerequisite for peace, and revolution is the prerequisite for reconciliation.

14

Cuba (Excerpt)

The Possibilities for Making a "Christian Contribution"

The Christian making the contribution in question here is not some entity fashioned by abstract speculation. It is not "the Cuban Christian" in general. We are referring to the flesh and blood Christians that we ourselves are, the flesh and blood Christians who have made a life-or-death commitment to our own revolution. And of course we are also referring to the whole group of Christians who, like we ourselves, have opted for socialism as the only possible course.

The contribution is not some idealized thing either. It is a concrete reality designed to further the Cuban revolution. We are "Cuban Christians For Socialism in Cuba." In other words, we are working on behalf of a specific political and socio-economic reality: i.e., the revolutionary process taking place on our island. When we talk about a "contribution," we are talking about an activity that must be fleshed out concretely within a specific context—the context of "the Cuban Christian element." Our contribution is meant to directly enrich the Cuban Christian context in particular. But that context is framed within a broader reality, the reality of the socialist revolution, and it cannot be abstracted from that broader reality. In that sense we can say that indirectly we are making a contribution to the revolution. This specification is important because if it were a matter of discussing our direct contribution to the revolution, then all we would have to do is to talk as revolutionaries.

Recognizing that other situations may have their own exigencies, we feel that it makes no sense to talk about a specifically Christian contribution within the concrete context of the Cuban revolutionary process. We cannot talk about a Christian contribution insofar as that might signify something qualitatively distinct and supplementary within the overall revolutionary project.

In considering the possibilities of making a Christian contribution, the first dimension to come under consideration would be the sphere of the ecclesiastical hierarchy. The fact that this sphere does not have any significant impact on our national reality, that it is spiritually absent from the sphere of our real-life problems and issues, does not nullify its objective reality. The churches of the hierarchy are churches "in exile" within Cuba itself. Our concrete contribution would be to "repatriate" them, to help them return to the motherland which they renounced for reasons that are concretely against the gospel.

First of all, there have been situations in which figures in the hierarchy have made some sort of option. When this option was in favor of the revolutionary process, we have made this fact known. They then made a public commitment to the views they had expressed. This in turn led to harsh criticism of them by the most reactionary elements and thus intensified the opposition. All this has helped to radicalize the more honest elements within the hierarchy and to clearly pinpoint the more reactionary ones.

Secondly, we have advocated a minimum of submission to the institutional complex without withdrawing from the context of ecclesiastical authority. Within the Church we can foster dialogue on the concrete problems of the Church as a structure existing within a revolutionary process, and on the ways in which the revolutionary process has made inroads into ecclesiastical life. This is one way of defusing its defense mechanisms and paving the way for its "repatriation." At the same time one must put stress on the class character of existing ecclesiastical structures and point out how they serve the forces of reaction by serving as last-ditch redoubts of bourgeois morality and an individualistic spirit.

A second dimension where we can make a contribution is the Church as a people, as a band of active, "militant" faithful whom we prefer to call worshippers. We are trying to furnish these Christians with evangelical and theological elements which will help them to realize that Marxism and Christianity are not incompatible. To begin with, we try to help them reach the liberating conclusion that a sincere Christian must be as much of an "atheist"—in the Marxist sense—as any atheist is. Why? Because belief—in the authentically Christian sense—is meaningless in the abstract, metaphysical context of philosophical idealism. It has meaning only in the concrete, ethical context of history-oriented theology. Then we try to make people understand, from within the context of real-life revolutionary experience, that faith turns into dogmatics when it is institutionalized as if it were some order in itself; that in the last analysis Christian faith is not just another dogma or institution or religion but rather a life to be lived and an activity to be carried out in the concrete. Thus we try to prevent faith from turning into an alienating factor—a danger that is always present.

Our contribution is aimed at trying to help the worshipping Christian to realize that his adoration is false if it is not lived out in daily life and concretized in works of love. The Cuban Christian cannot engage in authentic worship if he does not have and demonstrate an uncommon interest in such matters as these: increased national productivity, development of technological capabilities, promotion of the common welfare, acceptance of the sacrifices required to build a new society, and defense of our revolution. In short, he cannot measure up to his task unless he immerses himself in the work of man's total redemption that confronts the Cuban people as a whole.

Speculation about the necessity or non-necessity of religion must not become an obstacle to the work that confronts us at the hour of total liberation. It must not prevent us from confronting the imperialist enemy in the day-to-day struggle for liberation. In that struggle there must be a common effort by Marxist and Christian revolutionaries in particular, and by non-Christian and Christian revolutionaries in general. Quite often the radicalization of these small Christian groups into revolutionaries is impeded by some reaction of the hierarchy or by the increasingly reactionary position of the surrounding milieu.

A third dimension where we can make a contribution is the realm of "the Christian" as a dispersed people. Here we are referring to those Christians who, for all practical purposes, have no contact with institutions but maintain their fideistic Christian spirituality so that it is solidified into a moral "ethos." All we can do for this group is to offer them the example of our own lives, showing them how we incorporate ourselves into the reality of revolution and the specific demands of our socialist reality.

Our interest basically is not that this mass of believers should integrate themselves into the congregation. It is that they should integrate themselves more and more fully into the process of integral liberation that the revolution signifies.

Here our contribution is a more difficult thing because it is more complex, thoroughgoing, and decisive. It must be more radical and it calls for greater responsibility. Here, of course, people can see more clearly our own frailties, deficiencies, and insincerities.

Our aim is concrete activity within the revolutionary process. Our aim is total commitment and involvement within that process, designed to fashion a new society. Obviously enough, we do not always manage to do that. If we had managed to do that, then theological reflection would be superfluous. But our charity leaves much to be desired. It has been turned into something that is often inoperative and that corresponds to class interests. But now it is turning into something that is more humane, legitimate, and effective. It is becoming integrated into the project of human liberation embodied in the fashioning of a socialist society and in the struggle of the oppressed against the common enemy, United States imperialism.

The Christian hope we knew in the past was false hope. It was resignation. Our "Christian" pedagogy was a pedagogy of resignation which sought to form a "domesticated" human being rather than a free human being. Our total involvement in the educational task of creating a New Man demands from us an attitude totally devoid of egotism, a sense of absolute commitment to the welfare of others, and a fully developed social consciousness that will enable us to reject self-satisfied ambitions of a vile sort.

Our faith was made up of a series of idols. We Christians adored these idols in place of the authentic God of revolution. We worshiped "alien gods." We worshiped the idols of "individual liberty," "the supremacy of bourgeois man," and "the intrinsic goodness of religious elements." The last item took forms that were specifically idolatrous. We foolishly indulged in the blind belief that everything Christian was superior to everything non-Christian. We even went so far as to worship a pharisaism that nullified genuine adoration. And we believed in the moral superiority and intrinsic spirituality of the believer vis-à-vis the atheist. And so we must begin with an iconoclastic effort within ourselves.

It is necessary to eradicate the moral and dogmatic setting of norms which deadens political, social, and economic activity of a satisfactory sort. Utilizing the inner springs of our spirituality, which we dried up but have begun to well up in our contact with the revolutionary process,we seek to replace outmoded normative elements of a dogmatic sort with normative elements deriving from the real-life context. The Incarnation points us in that direction, a direction which accords with the historical moment in which we are living. What the Marxist revolutionary sees as a positive factor in the creation, consolidation, and development of a new society is something that the revolutionary Christian sees as identical with evangelical charity. It is the gospel itself, with its demands of a social nature, that provides us with the formal elements to be used in explicitating and assimilating this ethics.

PART V

CONVENTION DOCUMENTS

The First Convention of Christians For Socialism was held in Santiago, Chile, from April 23 to April 30, 1972. Approximately four hundred delegates from various countries attended. The majority were priest-members of well known movements in Latin America, but some Protestant ministers and many lay people from the Christian left were also present.

The convention opened on Sunday with various welcoming addresses, the proceedings taking place in a facility provided by a local labor union. Monday and Tuesday were devoted to the presentation of the various national reports. On Wednesday focus shifted to various subcommittees, which did their work at facilities that had been provided by the University Parish of Santiago. A central committee coordinated the work of the subcommittees. It in turn was assisted by an auxiliary committee composed mainly of theologians such as Giulio Girardi, Gustavo

Gutiérrez, and Hugo Assmann. It was this auxiliary committee of theologians that drew up the Final Document of the convention.

During the week of the convention, the delegates visited President Salvador Allende and Cardinal Raúl Silva of Santiago. At the final session on Sunday, April 30, the delegates sent telegrams of support to Fidel Castro, the Premier of North Vietnam, and Bertrand Russell's tribunal. They also sent a protest to the Brazilian government, a letter of thanks to Cardinal Raúl Silva for his hospitality, and a telegram to Pope Paul VI which affirmed their faith in Jesus Christ and the value of Christian witness in history.

The bishops of Chile did not endorse the convention but neither did they prohibit Catholics from attending it. After the convention they called for dialogue to analyze its results and conclusions.

Here we present the inaugural address of Gonzalo Arroyo (Document 15), a brief address by the Bishop of Cuernavaca, Mexico (Document 16), a message from President Allende (Document 17), and the Final Document of the convention (Document 18).

15

Inaugural Address
of Gonzalo Arroyo

Speaking on behalf of the organizing committee of the Chilean delegation, I have the honor of welcoming you all to the First Latin American Convention of Christians For Socialism. Present here are delegates from twenty-six countries in Latin America, North America, Eastern Europe, and Western Europe. Also present are distinguished figures in the Church world, labor, and politics. And finally a large group of Christians in Santiago have chosen to be present at this labor-union site in order to manifest their solidarity with this event and its proceedings. There is no doubt that this convention will have great importance in the life of our churches and in the commitment of Christians to the task of constructing a new socialist society on our continent.

What is the sense and purpose of this convention, which one rightist newspaper has described as an "odd get-together"? It might be well for us to take a brief look at its past history and see how it originated. In April 1971, there was a meeting of approximately eighty priests who live or work among the common people in Santiago and the provinces, and who saw hopes revive in these people when the Popular Unity coalition won the election. Their public declaration marked a step forward in the ideological struggle. They attacked private property and the capitalist system; and they proclaimed their personal commitment to the laboring class. Their faith in Jesus Christ, their solidarity with the exploited, and their scientific analysis of the dependent capitalism prevailing in Chile led them to demand socialism. This group, known as The 80, has been growing in numbers and forming subgroups in various sections of the the country. Nuns

and Protestant ministers joined. A Secretariat of Christians For
Socialism was set up to issue documents, provide for the interchange of personal experiences, and coordinate the various
groups on the grass-roots level. All this demanded much help
and voluntary sacrifice from the members. The contact of this
Secretariat with groups in other nations led to the idea of a Latin
American Convention, and our meeting here today is the fruit of
that work.

The objective of this convention is to satisfy a need that has
arisen. In many cases there is a danger that the voluntary efforts
of Christians will turn into mere activism. We must stop for a
moment to exchange personal experiences, to engage in theological reflection, to offer each other mutual support, and to coordinate our activities so that our commitment to laborers, peasants,
and students will become even more effective. To judge from
your presence here today at the cost of great sacrifice, it would
seem that this need was felt all over Latin America.

Some people feel that this is just another political meeting; that
we priests and ministers are betraying our apostolic mission.
Needless to say, if this were meant to be a political meeting
designed to propagate a particular ideology, there would have
been move effective ways to accomplish that purpose. For example, instead of inviting priests, ministers, nuns, and bishops, we
could have invited representatives of the various political parties
on this continent. We, the organizers of this convention, deny
that our aim is to hold a political meeting; but we realize full well
that it can have political repercussions. If such a large group of
Christians get together to reflect on the situation of injustice in
Latin America, the liberation of the oppressed, the behavior of
Christians in this political struggle, and the impact of the faith on
all this, their meeting will undoubtedly have an impact on the
consciousness of Christians on this continent. And that impact
will be political, even as the episcopal conference at Medellín had
an even greater impact in this direction. If this convention is
political in that sense, and we hope it is, this does not mean that
we are trying to organize a new political party or that we are
trying to create some kind of Christian political organization on
the continental level.

We, the organizers, are very clear on one thing: namely, that

Christian participation in the struggle of the workers implies acceptance and adoption of the discipline and strategy worked at by the organized political forces of the working class. Leftist Christians join these fronts; they do not form parallel organisms of their own. They fight alongside non-believers in these class parties and movements. We, the organizers, feel that whatever leftist option Christians may make, the cause of unity among the people must be an imperative for them. Their chief contribution at this convention will not be to promote party positions but to exert an impact on Christian consciousness in Latin America and the world, thereby helping to destroy the seeming religious legitimacy of the capitalism to which most countries of Latin America and the Third World are accustomed. That is why the holding of this convention coincides with the third convention of UNCTAD here in Santiago. We wanted to demonstrate the revolutionary outlook of Christians vis-à-vis the injustices of world imperialism, and to bear witness to our solidarity with the countries of Asia, Africa, and the Americas in their struggle to destroy neocolonialism and their economic dependence on capitalist countries and conglomerates which make it impossible for them to develop further.

Here at home, this convention seeks to strengthen our committed involvement with the people of Latin America and their struggle for liberation. It seeks to purify our faith of the bourgeois ideological elements that often pervade it, and of the emotional blocks which prevent it from fully expressing the renovating force of the gospel. We Christians cannot approach revolutionary commitment in a triumphalist spirit. We are aware of the fact that the capitalist regime has demonstrated surprising vitality and adaptive capacity amid the ever new twists and turns of history. The reformist forces in the Church, beginning with Leo XIII and then moving on to social-minded Christians, have almost always been behind the times.

Hence at this convention we shall make an effort to unmask the ideologizing of the Christian way of life. It will not be a forum for verbosity and revolutionary rhetoric. It will be a convention of workers in which we shall examine the ideologizing of faith, hope, and charity; the ideologizing of the sacraments and Christian institutions; the simplistic identification of the class struggle with hatred and disunity; and the religious manipulation of such slogans as "democracy," "liberty" and "order"—which are identified with bourgeois society—as well as other slogans of Christian reformism such as "participation," "communitarianism," "self-management," and "workers' enterprise." This is the difficult task we shall try to accomplish in these eight days. Our aim will be to free ourselves from these entanglements so that we may be able to rediscover our adhesion to Jesus Christ and his liberative action in the people in all its purity.

This is a convention of Christians taking place during hard times for our continent. Profound changes are taking place in various countries, and the backlash often leads to repressive measures on the Church and on dedicated Christians who are openly wondering what the real meaning of their Christianity is. Their questions are different from the questions of other Christians who stand outside the revolutionary process and are disconcerted by the drama taking place before their eyes. The latter see a society whose supposedly Christian values and social traditions are crumbling before their eyes. In some this awakens laments, feelings of inner rebelliousness, and even painful results. These traditional Christians are distressed by the unfolding course of this drama for a small minority whose age-old privileges are disappearing one by one.

Revolutionary Christians are clear about a few things. If they want to be consistent with the gospel, then their primary task is to struggle for the liberation of the oppressed. In the concrete that means struggling for the liberation of workers and those exploited by international capitalism. Here there is no need to spell out the theology of liberation which has welled up from the social situation of our lands and which was officially endorsed by the Latin American bishops at Medellín. This theology is both the reflection and the germ of a profound transformation taking place in significant segments of the Latin American Church, which include both clergy and laity. The starting point of this theology is not philosophical reflection on the essence of man in general—as it is in the case of a vague Christian humanism—or the Church's interpretation of divine revelation. The starting point for the reflection of revolutionary Christians is the situation of oppression and injustice in which the people of Latin America lead their lives. This situation is a catastrophe which must be confronted at once. The response of the Christian should take the form of practical action, but this in turn calls for theory.

Through personal commitment and practical action in conjunction with a people on the march, the revolutionary Christian glimpses the activity of Christ himself, who leads this history of struggle, failure, and success and gives it its ultimate liberative meaning. The faith of the revolutionary Christian, then, does not offer a ready-made response to the questions of the world. It challenges him to work this answer out in his praxis, to slowly unravel the mystery in which we live, and to fashion history. It does not teach him some doctrine or some abstract discourse on man and society. Instead it points to the deeper meaning of history as the incarnation of love and the construction of a more just and humane society.

Faith is a critical court of appeal which causes the revolutionary to relativize every human achievement and which impels him towards a greater plenitude. This does not isolate him from involvement with non-believers. The obligation facing him is to rebuild a devastated society with those who are most capable of doing it. He does not have the luxury of choosing his allies. He can only accept those that real life provides. Thus the deepening of his faith brings him closer to those who are collaborating in the common task of human liberation, and the philosophical differences between Christians and Marxists take a back seat to the urgent need for effective revolutionary action.

At the same time, however, the Christian realizes full well that his political praxis cannot be deduced directly from his faith. To do that would be to manipulate Christianity for contingent ends as the right wing does in fact do, to take personal advantage of Christ's message and dilute it into an ideology, to violate man's reason and liberty in order to construct history. In living his faith as a commitment to the liberation of the oppressed and as a fight for a more just and humane society, the revolutionary Christian uses the intermediary help of scholarly science and revolutionary theory to open up pathways in history for his action on behalf of the laboring class and the Latin American people in their journey towards a socialist society. Faith in itself is not socialist. But it implies a perduring effort to break the chains of oppression and to build a new world. This is why faith motivates many Christians to commit themselves to socialism.

An objective analysis of the political reality of Latin America, where the left has failed repeatedly to attract the masses into a determined struggle against the national and international forces of capitalism, leads to the conviction that Christians must be integrated into the revolutionary process in a massive way. As Che Guevara puts it: "When Christians dare to give full-fledged revolutionary witness, then the Latin American revolution will be invincible."

In order to turn this project into a living reality, the most important task facing leftist Christians is the task of helping directly to mobilize the common people in favor of socialism. It is inconceivable that the common people should be won over by the forces of the right—against their own real interests but by virtue of their Christianity; that they should end up in reformism or unorganized conformism. The conditions of structural exploitation, the "institutionalized violence" of which Medellín speaks, will be overcome only if the people themselves take cognizance of their situation and act in an organized way. Therefore, leftist Christians pledge to help the people move out of their delusory notions, their passivism, and their ideologized brand of religion. They seek to motivate the people to act on behalf of their own liberation.

The work of de-ideologizing, then, is a primary task if we are to incorporate the Christian masses in the struggle on behalf of socialism. But it also presupposes efforts by the Latin American left to create favorable conditions for the incorporation of Christians into the struggle. They cannot be regarded merely as tactical allies, to be used for broadening the base of support for the traditional Marxist parties. The left must open up to Christians as they really are—despite the obvious absence of total philosophical agreement. As we see it, this is a necessary precondition if Christians are to be fully and effectively incorporated into the struggle. As Lenin points out:

> Marxism recognizes the most varied forms of struggle. It does not "invent" them. It simply generalizes, organizes, and injects con-

scious awareness into the forms of revolutionary class struggle that arise spontaneously in the course of the whole movement. Marxism rejects unconditionally anything in the nature of abstract formulas or doctrinaire recipes. It demands that one pay most attention to the struggle of the masses in operation . . . . That is why Marxism does not reject any form of struggle outright. It does not restrict itself completely to the forms of struggle that are present or possible at a given moment. It recognizes the inevitable need for new forms of struggle which may be unknown to people acting at a certain period of time but which may appear when a given social setup changes. In this sense we might say that Marxism *learns* from the concrete practice of the masses. Nothing could be further from its mind than the notion that it is to *teach* the masses certain forms of struggle that have been worked up and criticized by ivory-tower systematizers . . . . If one proposed to give a simple "yes" or "no" to a specific means of struggle without giving detailed consideration to the concrete situation of the movement in question at a given stage, that would be equivalent to withdrawing from the terrain of Marxism altogether.

Pardon me for the long quote, but I think it is important for us to realize that the Christian masses have been determined by a series of ethical and cultural imperatives which condition their forms of struggle. Their effective collaboration in the revolutionary process presupposes respect for their manner of being on the part of non-believers, even though this may entail limitations for the political struggle in the short run. Furthermore, one must also realize that revolutionary Christianity has developed further in Latin America over the past few years. It has given such martyrs as Camilo Torres, Enrique Pereira, and Néstor Paz.

In turn, Christians involving themselves in the struggles of the working class must learn how to respect the Marxist forms of awareness which have been refined by a long process of revolutionary struggle but which may not necessarily dovetail with Christian forms of awareness. Real, effective collaboration between Christians and Marxists can give rise to a fruitful synthesis of theoretical positions which will contribute to the real unity of the working class and of the Latin American left.

While leftist Christians see some things clearly, they also face questions for which they do not have any definitive answers. They are aware of the divisions that exist within the churches. They are not satisfied by the formal changes such as those introduced by Vatican II, the Medellín Conference, and the renewal efforts in the Protestant churches. Nor are they satisfied by the changes in ecclesial praxis: e.g., the use of the vernacular in the liturgy, the abandonment of clerical garb, greater lay participation, and attempts to democratize church structures. Traditional religious practices are rejected, but they have not found new forms of Christian living which could give vigor to the activity required in the task of liberation. Leftist Christians want the most weighty portion of the churches to take the part of the oppressed, and they want to see the disappearance of those institutions of Christian inspiration which have created the ruling class. They see that many reforms (pastoral, catechetical, administrative, and so forth) and the political thrust of grass-roots communities often bolster the established system. They are subject to pressure and to subtle but effective persecution by their hierarchical officials and their communities. Leftist Christian leaders are kept out of official and semi-official organizations of their churches. (Some, for example, were positively excluded from the Medellín Conference.) Obstacles are placed in the way of leftist educators and pastors. Institutions such as Adveniat, Misereor, and the Latin American Division of the NCWC deny economic aid to initiatives undertaken by leftist Christians; and the middle classes do not back them up in seeking such aid. They are not invited to participate in the redaction of official church documents.

When Christians at the grass-roots level see that the organisms of the Church do not pay heed to their positions, many of them lose interest in official Christianity. They want to have serious critical dialogue with their hierarchies. The latter, despite some gestures of good will, tend to show a great distrust towards them. There is no doubt that these leftist Christians do not have any desire whatsoever to form a front in opposition to their communities or their hierarchies. Thanks to the discernment of spirits in the Church, the search is a common task which calls for positive and perduring dialogue with the hierarchy.

The questions raised by the ongoing liberation process in Latin America, and by the move towards socialism, run counter to the habitual ways of thinking evinced by large groups of Christians. We must fight against these inertial mental habits. We must bear witness before these Christians, showing them that participation in this process of liberation contributes to our faith and that we have an obligation to proclaim the gospel to the exploited classes of our continent.

Another point about which leftist Christians are not totally clear is their political action. There is no doubt that faith in Christ the liberator has a political dimension, insofar as it motivates us to commit ourselves to the transformation of society. The way we live that commitment requires the intermediation of a revolutionary theory. This theory is not deduced from our faith; it arises from the practical action of the proletariat in its struggle against the exploitative bourgeoisie, and it is grounded on a scientific generalization of this praxis. Hence there are two poles to political action. At one end we have the overall project of history; in the Christian's case, it is enriched by his faith. At the other end we have the scientific rationality of political activity. Fairly frequently the Christian—and even more so, the priest—tends to value the overall project of history but to spurn concrete, objective analysis of the political situation in all its complexity. This tack can lead to positions that are politically naive. If these positions are not incorporated within a concrete program, they run the risk of degenerating into spontaneous gestures of a purely utopian sort. We do not mean to deny the mobilizing power of Christianity in the realm of motivation. But if this does not take place in a dialectical relationship with political analysis, then it ends up in positions that are incorrect from the viewpoint of advancing socialism. We must remember the gospel's admonition: "Be wary as serpents, innocent as doves" (Mt 10:16). It is not a matter of being one or the other; we must be both. Hence it is not enough for us at this convention to offer each other mutual encouragement in our personal commitment. We must also deepen our scientific knowledge of the reality of Latin America and gain an even more correct analysis of the present political situation.

I will close this rather lengthy speech by thanking all those who have made this convention possible. In particular I want to thank the Minister of Foreign Affairs for his presence here. Despite his important work in presiding over the UNCTAD convention, he has taken time out to address us here. I want to thank the Tourist Board, which has taken great pains to obtain material facilities for us. I want to thank all those who have made personal sacrifices so that we could receive the foreign delegates: the families who have taken them in here; those from other lands who helped to defray the travel expenses; the many comrades who voluntarily spent time at workshops to prepare all this material; the officials of the ex-Hirmas labor union who provided this setting, which symbolizes our solidarity with the workers and their solidarity with Christians For Socialism; and the chaplains of the University Parish for providing us with rooms in which to hold committee meetings.

We would also like to remember the various delegates who could not come to this convention because of obstacles posed by the repressive conditions in their home countries. We would like to remember the Catholics of Vietnam, who are suffering brutal bombardment these days from the imperialist forces of the United States. Finally, we would like to welcome the only delegation at this convention which represents a socialist country in Latin America: the delegation from Cuba.

April 23, 1972

16

Address of
Bishop Méndez Arceo

Comrades, independently of my own wishes, I find myself standing in front of you and talking. It was not my decision, and hence it is not a political act. It merely represents my acceptance of the decision cabled to me by the organizing committee.

But my presence here at this First Convention of Christians For Socialism is my decision—a consciously thought-out decision. It is a political act that seeks the transformation of our world in Latin America.

I am here for the same reason that you "conventioneers" are here from all over Latin America, because I share the conviction that our underdeveloped world has no recourse open to it but socialism: i.e., social appropriation of the means of production and authentic representation of the community in order to prevent these things from being utilized as tools for domination by an oligarchy or a totalitarian government.

I am certain that we have not come, as Christians, to forge a Christian socialism. That would amount to absolutizing socialism and relativizing Christianity, just as we have absolutized other things in the past by labelling them "Christian" and have thereby diminished authentic Christianity, the living presence of God in history. I refer to the absolutizing of such things as "Western civilization," "democracy," "humanism," and "religion" itself.

I believe that there is only one system which, thanks to the grace of God, we have not dared to label "Christian" explicitly and directly—even when Christian ideology had reached its most abject levels. I refer to capitalism. Today it seems that we are all agreed that it must be rejected, even though we try to evade the consequences of that decision and look for ways to keep capitalism on the sly. We pretend it is not there or we simply tolerate it, still trying to fit it out as a possible option to socialism.

In any case we have been its accomplices, by defending it and conforming to it. Now we must investigate the extent to which the abstract notions of Catholic theology have had a preponderant influence in the development of the capitalist ideology and in preventing us from accepting other tools for analyzing reality. We must find out to what extent these notions were inclined to conceal the true reality, to what extent they were not subjected to the critical light of divine revelation.

Now we will try to take a closer look at the praxis in which we are personally involved. We will try to revise the theory and to formulate, or reformulate, the historic project of our liberation.

Convinced that God does speak to us in his written word and in the events of real life, in which he is present in a gratuitous but not superfluous way, we believe that we cannot have theology without the cooperation of sociology. For the fact is that the methods of interpreting written divine revelation have been in the service of man's domination over man. For this reason, the contributions of Catholic social ethics and social doctrine were totally inadequate for realizing and carrying out the implications of the faith as a praxis of liberation. We discussed and debated issues within the framework of a sterile Catholic social reformism, out of contact with the analyses which have led human beings to discover the true reality of this world: i.e., the organized praxis of man, which shuns the light when it is not founded on truth.

Truly postconciliar Catholics in Latin America certainly do look to such documents as those of the Medellín Conference, regarding them as points of reference. The oft repeated language of these documents either stimulates real awareness and is deepened in the reality of praxis, or else it turns into mere declamation that alienates people and frustrates their hopes.

The theory of liberation is the direct result of analyzing the failure of developmentalism and the growing burden of dependence. It reformulates the notion of imperialism and many other current notions. We Christians could and should have been able to find all this in the history of salvation, but we did not. It has been handed to us by the social scientists and by the activity of those involved in the revolutionary struggle. Just as we read liberty, equality, and fraternity differently in divine revelation after the French Revolution, so the Old and New Testament passover events now take on a fuller and deeper sense.

Many others feel that that is as it should be. But insofar as we Christians were alert to the Lord's will, we should have been able to descry it ahead of time in our praxis. We should have been able to proclaim it in the framework of our eschatological utopia and to denounce the intervening obstacles openly and fearlessly.

We realize that it is now time for Christians to stop looking like counter-revolutionaries all the time. It is time for us to stop looking like opportunists who are finally urged on by God's message to climb on board the bandwagon belatedly and to eventually join a process whose dynamism leaves us in its wake. It is time for us to stop posing the issue as a choice between God or man, when such an either/or should not have to exist. The real alternative is between God and sin, a sin that is structured in countless ways in the institutions that oppress people.

Priests, in particular, are wont to experience real confusion these days because they have argued and debated in a framework where they were unable to present a salvific message to human beings. The chasm between the exploiters and the exploited is something that crops up for the non-exploiter in the very celebration of the Eucharist, not just in other aspects of liturgical worship or in his other activities. Many intramural questions of the clergy show up as superfluous and secondary in the face of hunger, sickness, the mortality rate, ignorance, alienation, persecution, and torture. We who have met here want and choose to be men of hope. We are spurred on by those who regard the Church as a real agent for change by virtue of her very nature. We cannot forget the surprise evoked by the unexpected spectacle of Vatican II. Nor can we overlook the acceptance people everywhere give to the gospel when it is proclaimed in all its purity, to the point where they forget the inconsistencies of our way of living and of many of our doctrines.

Finally, I want to assure you that I do not feel that I am out of place in your midst, despite the fact that I am a bishop. Each day I try to be a Christian more and more. Apparently it is my fate to be alone. I can recall two other big events. Although many Latin

American bishops are more illustrious graduates of the Gregorian University in Rome, I was the only one to participate in its fourth centenary celebration in 1953. Totally devoid of musical talent, I was the only bishop in the world to participate in an important international congress of liturgical music in Pamplona, Spain.

Right now I do feel alone, even though I am in communion with you people here, with my fellow bishops of Latin America, and in particular with the bishops of Chile. At Vatican II the latter were a real spearhead for reform, and I got much encouragement and support from them in my small efforts to serve God in human beings. As a group, and often as individuals, the bishops of Chile give splendid and courageous example today. We greet them fraternally and respectfully as pastors of the wayfaring local churches of Chile.

Many of our brother bishops regard us with sympathy, accompany us with their prayers, and anxiously await the outcome of our convention. Why? Because we Christians, particularly the ministers who are personally committed to the task of liberation, are a major factor in the whole complex of the local churches in Latin America.

We are not, and do not want to be organized as some bloc or shock brigade within the Church. We take on the painful task of being a leaven and of engaging in humble service. We are part of the local communities. Together with the bishops in charge of these communities, we seek the continuation of Pentecost. We seek to form one person: i.e., the Spirit in many persons. We seek to form a Church that is committed to the full-fledged salvation of man.

Hence we do not claim to be an organization except insofar as that word refers to a process of mutual communication which prevents us from being scattered far and wide and which enriches us with the fruits of shared reflection, shared action, and planned action if necessary.

Permit me to close with a reference to my own country, Mexico. Someone has remarked that the words of our President Luis Echeverría in Chile signify the reintegration of Mexico into the overall Latin American web of liberation—after a long period in which we Mexicans regarded ourselves as singular. Although I should like to believe it, I cannot claim that our presence here amounts to the real-life integration of Mexico's local churches into the overall complex of churches in Central and South America; that it dispels the old prejudice of seeing ourselves as a singular brand of Christianity—which is not the same as recognizing all our distinctive characteristics.

But one thing is certain. We Christians in Mexico and throughout Latin America who are committed to liberation do feel that we are at one with the rest of our brothers in Latin America. We feel at one with the people of Chile and Cuba, in particular, because there decisive events in the process of change are taking place. Christians must resolve to be involved with them, so that they may be able to judge them in the light of the gospel, sharing these human realities with their compatriots from within.

April 23, 1972

17

Message from
President Salvador Allende

One Christian thinker, who was an exemplary fighter and protagonist in our own day, described the revolutionary in these terms. He said that "the revolutionary is a man who is cognizant of the fact that in our countries we cannot feed or clothe or house the vast majority of the people. Cognizant of this, the revolutionary fights against oppressive structures. He does not settle for what is. He promotes union among all the sectors that are exploited in society. In short, he fights for the full-fledged elevation of man."

Although I start from a different philosophical focus, I fully agree with these thoughts of Camilo Torres. At bottom they also describe the vast majority of our people here. After a long and heroic struggle, our people have taken over the government of Chile. Today, with vigor and decisiveness, they are moving towards full takeover of power so that they can fashion a society that is thoroughly fraternal and that eliminates poverty and exploitation once and for all.

The political force which governs Chile today, and which I am honored to represent, is the end result of a permanent, hardcore, unassailable alliance between Christians and non-Christians; between human beings of a different ideological stamp who have come to see clearly that the real conflict of our time—and hence the real dividing line—is not in the realm of religion or of philosophical ideas but is between imperialism and the dependent countries; and that in these dependent countries it lies between the exploitative bourgeoisie and the masses of exploited people.

Your presence here is the result of the decision of revolutionary Christians from all over Latin America and the Third World, from

Mexico to the Democratic Republic of Vietnam. It confirms once again the democratic and pluralistic character of our revolutionary process, the respect and consideration of this government and its people for all your beliefs, and our affectionate relationship with all the churches—in particular, the Catholic Church and its hierarchy.

Your presence is also proof of the growing support which the Chilean revolutionary process is gaining from all sectors of the people and from all peoples.

In addition to greeting you and your convention, may I also extend the best wishes of this government and its people for the success of your labors here. We are sure that it will enrich the broad and deep revolutionary movement that is transforming today's world.

In brotherhood with all those who struggle for a world where men will be brothers, I greet you cordially.

April 28, 1972

18

Final Document
of the Convention

More than four hundred in number, we are Christians who have come to Santiago from all the countries of Latin America. The delegates include lay people, ministers, priests, and nuns; and there are observers from the United States, Quebec, and Europe. With a clear realization of the injustice pervading the socio-economic structures of our continent, we wanted to ponder, in the light of our common faith, what we can and should do at this point in history from within the concrete set of circumstances we face.

We wish to identify ourselves clearly as Christians. We are pondering our faith and re-examining our love for the oppressed from the basic standpoint of the liberation process now going on among our people and of our own real-life commitment to the task of constructing a socialist society. Most of us work with industrial laborers, peasants, or the unemployed. These people are suffering the pangs of poverty, constant frustration, and neglect on the economic, social, cultural, and political level. There is much we have to do. We must do it together with these people, and we must do it right away.

We have come together in Santiago at the same time that the Third World convention of UNCTAD is taking place here. That group is discussing a problem which is growing more acute every day. A relatively small sector of humanity is making greater progress and growing richer every day; but the price for their progress is the oppression of two-thirds of the human race. What pricks the consciousness of the exploited peoples most is the

realization that their precarious economy results from the growing wealth and well-being of the great powers. Our poverty is the
other side of the coin, the reflection of the growing wealth of the
exploiter classes throughout the world.

How are we to confront this clearcut situation of injustice? One
thing, at least, is clear: The peoples dominated by imperialist
capitalism must unite to break away from the situation of oppression and plunder to which they are subject. But this unity, which
seems so logical, is not easy to attain because their dependence
on foreign elements fosters disunity; and in direct or subtle ways
this disunity is fostered by imperialism. United here from all over
Latin America, and in the presence of the UNCTAD convention,
we Christians wish to send out an appeal to the exploited social
classes and the countries under foreign domination; we urge
them to unite to defend their rights, and not to beg for aid.

The economic and social structures of our Latin American
countries are grounded on oppression and injustice, which in
turn is a result of our capitalist dependence on the great power
centers. In each of our nations small minorities serve the cause of
international capitalism and its accomplices. Using every means
in their power, they seek to maintain a situation that was created
to benefit themselves. This structural injustice is in fact violence,
whether it be open or disguised.

Those who have exploited the weak for centuries, and who
wish to keep doing this, use *de facto* violence against them. This
violence is often veiled under the guise of a fallacious order and a
fallacious legality, but it is violence and injustice nonetheless. It is
not human, and hence it is not Christian.

But diagnosis is not enough. By his example Christ taught us to
live what he preached. Christ preached human brotherhood and
proclaimed that love should configure all our social structures.
Even more importantly, he *lived out* his message of liberation to its
ultimate consequences. He was condemned to death. The power
brokers in his nation saw his message of liberation, and the
real-life love to which he bore witness, as a serious threat to their
economic, social, religious, and political interests. Today, as always, the Spirit of Christ is actively giving impetus to history. It

shows up in solidarity, in the unselfish commitment of those who struggle for liberty and evince authentic love for their oppressed brethren.

The structures of our society must be transformed from the roots up. The task is more necessary today than ever before because those who benefit from the unjust order in which we live are defending their class interests in an aggressive way. They use all the means at their disposal—propaganda, subtle ways of dominating popular consciousness, defense of a discriminatory legal setup, frequent repression, and dictatorship if necessary —to prevent a revolutionary transformation from taking place. Only by gaining economic and political power will the exploited class be able to construct a society that is qualitatively different from the existing one: i.e., a socialist society, without oppressors or oppressed, in which everyone will have the same possibilities for human fulfillment.

The revolutionary process is in full swing in Latin America. Many Christians have made a personal commitment to it. But many more Christians, imprisoned in mental inertia and categories that are suffused with bourgeois ideology, regard this process fearfully and insist on taking the impossible pathway of reformism and modernization. The Latin American process is all-embracing and one in character. We Christians do not have a peculiar political approach of our own to offer, and we do not wish to have such an approach. The realization that the process is all-embracing and one in character makes us comrades, uniting all those who are committed to the revolutionary struggle in a common task.

Our revolutionary commitment has enabled us to rediscover the import of Christ's liberative work. That work gives human history its underlying unity. Framing political liberation in a broader and more radical context, it enables us to grasp its true sense and import. Christ's liberation necessarily shows up in liberating events of history, but it is not limited to such events. It indicates the limitations of these events and, even more impor-tantly, leads them towards their complete fulfillment. The real reductionists, who diminish Christ's work, are those who want to separate it from the pulsing course of history where individuals and social classes struggle to liberate themselves from the oppression to which other individuals and classes subject them. The real reductionists are those who are unwilling to recognize the fact that Christ's liberation is a thoroughgoing liberation from every sort of exploitation, plunder, and alienation.

We commit ourselves to the task of fashioning socialism because it is our objective conclusion, based on the concrete experience of history and on a rigorous, scholarly analysis of the facts, that this is the only effective way to combat imperialism and to break away from our situation of dependence.

The construction of socialism is not accomplished by vague denunciations or by appeals to good will. It presupposes an analysis that will reveal the mechanisms which really move society, that will lay bare the existing oppression, and that will unmask and name all those people and things which oppress the laboring class in open or subtle ways. Above all, it presupposes participation in the struggle that pits the exploited class against its oppressors. Authentic charity cannot gloss over the struggle unleashed by those who exploit the people and who seek to defend or increase their own privileges.

We publicize our reflections because we believe that they can help to inspire other Christians and men of good will to reflect along with us and to set out in quest of some way to radically transform the structures that now prevail on our continent.

PART ONE

1. The Latin American Reality: A Challenge for Christians

1.1. The socio-economic, political, and cultural situation of the peoples of Latin America poses a challenge to our Christian conscience. Unemployment, malnutrition, alcoholism, infant mortality, illiteracy, prostitution, ever growing inequality between rich and poor, racial and educational discrimination, exploitation, and so forth: these are the factors that go to make up a situation of institutionalized violence in Latin America.

1.2. To begin with, it is clear that this reality is not the inevitable product of natural inadequacies, much less of some "inexorable" destiny or some implacable "God" who is a stranger to the human drama. On the contrary, it is a process determined by the will of human beings.

1.3. The human "will" in question is that of a privileged minority. It has made possible the construction and maintenance of an unjust society—the capitalist society—based on exploitation, profit, and competition.

1.4. This unjust society is objectively grounded on the capitalist production-centered relationships, which necessarily give rise to a class-based society.

1.5. Colonialist and neocolonialist capitalism is the economic structure that shapes the reality of Latin American countries. In its higher phase, this capitalist structuring leads to imperialism and its auxiliary factors, which operate through many different mechanisms: military and economic aggression, alliances between repressive governments, multinational organizations, cultural domination, the presence of the CIA and the State Department, and so forth.

1.6. Within each country imperialism operates in complicity with the ruling classes or the national bourgeoisie who are dependent on the capitalist setup. The ruling classes, in turn, are allied with the institutional Church.

1.7. One of the last resorts of imperialism is dictatorships and governments of a fascist cast, which spawn repression, torture, persecution, political crimes, and so forth.

1.8. The desperate struggle of imperialism poses economic obstacles to those countries who have opted for socialism. This is true in the case of Cuba and of Chile.

1.9. Imperialism tries to keep the people disunited. It sets Christians against Marxists with the intention of paralyzing the revolutionary process in Latin America.

1.10. False models of economic growth, implemented at the expense of the laboring class and the peasantry, try to distract the people from the real overall goals of the revolution. This is true, for example, of the developmental models worked up for Brazil and Mexico.

1.11. Using all the communication and education media, the forces of imperalism and the ruling classes in the nation impose a dependent form of culture on the people. This culture disguises and justifies the situation of domination. In addition, it forms a human being who is resigned to his alienation. It also stimulates the oppressed to patronize and exploit others in turn.

1.12. The historical process of a class-based society and imperialist domination inevitably leads to confrontation between the classes. Despite the fact that this confrontation becomes clearer every day, it is denied by the oppressors. Meanwhile the exploited classes are progressively discovering and adopting a new revolutionary consciousness.

1.13. The growing acuteness of the class struggle makes it clear that there are only two possible alternatives in Latin America today: dependent capitalism with its resultant underdevelopment, or socialism. At the same time the happenings within each country reveal the historical failure and the impossibility of any middle-ground position between capitalism and socialism, and of any kind of reformism.

1.14. Some leftist national movements have importance for the revolution. But they prove to be inadequate if they do not lead to socialism within the framework of the liberation process now going on in Latin America.

1.15. Whether we realize it or not, the present position of every human being on this continent—and hence of the Christian—is determined by the historic dynamism of the class struggle within the process of liberation.

1.16. Christians who are personally committed to the revolutionary process recognize the ultimate failure of any Christian "third way" in the social realm. Hence they make every effort to insert themselves into the one and only history of liberation that belongs to our continent.

1.17. The intensification of the class struggle represents a new stage in the politico-ideological struggle, and it rules out any pretension to neutrality or a-politicism. The intensification of the class struggle gives the revolutionary process in Latin America its true dimension of totality.

1.18. Scientific analysis and revolutionary commitment to the struggle of the exploited necessarily bring out the real-life elements at work in the present situation: i.e., production-based relationships, capitalist expropriation of surplus value, class struggle, ideological struggle, and so forth.

1.19. In this context, the Cuban revolution and the Chilean transition towards socialism propose a return to the wellsprings of Marxism and a criticism of traditional Marxist dogmatism.

1.20. With the help of all the analytic devices provided, by Marxism in particular, the common people are realizing the need to set out for a real takeover of power by the working class. Only this will make it possible to fashion an authentic socialism, which so far is the only way to achieve total liberation.

2. Attempts at Liberation in Latin America

2.1. A common process of liberation is under way in Latin America. It is in the tradition provided by Bolívar, San Martín, O'Higgins, Hidalgo, José Martí, Sandino, Camilo Torres, Che Guevara, Néstor Paz, and others. It is a second war for independence, bringing together the revolutionary forces of a continent who share a common past—colonization—and a common present—exploitation and poverty.

2.2. The dependent form of capitalism that reigns in Latin America necessarily spawns the laboring classes: industrial workers, manual workers, and peasants. As such, these classes constitute the social base that is objectively revolutionary. They also pose an urgent task of politicization, so that they may gradually acquire the power to destroy the capitalist system and replace it with a more just and brotherly society.

2.3. Numerous attempts at liberation have cropped up throughout the continent, particularly since the Cuban revolution. They are similar in form insofar as they represent a breakaway from dependence and a fight against imperialism. They take on different forms in accordance with the diversity of the various nations in which they take place.

2.4. Despite their differing tactics, these attempts at liberation tend to unify at a higher level. They bear witness to a desire to develop a new strategy which will combine the revolutionary forces in a common attempt at liberation.

2.5. The revolutionary process demands that we overcome sterile divisions between different leftist groups in Latin America, divisions that are fostered and manipulated by imperialism.

2.6. Urged on by the Spirit of the gospel, Christians are joining proletarian groups and parties and accepting the same rights and duties as the other revolutionaries. Christians committed to socialism see the national and continental proletariat as the vanguard of the liberation process in Latin America.

2.7. The growing mobilization of the people makes new demands upon us: e.g., overcoming such things as sectarianism, bureaucratism, corruption in high places, and the inculcation of bourgeois values.

3. Christians and the Process of Liberation in Latin America

3.1. Some Christians are beginning to realize that the reality of Christianity (its institutional forms, its theologies, its consciousness) is not outside of this confrontation between the exploited and their exploiters. On the contrary, it is marked by colonialism and, in many cases, it is allied with our dependent brand of capitalism.

3.2. Groups of Christians, motivated by their faith, are making a revolutionary commitment to the people in growing numbers. And it is evident that they are having greater and greater impact on this continent.

3.3. At the same time Christian and non-Christian groups are showing greater interest in noting and analyzing the sociological impact that Christianity has had and continues to have on the social configuration of the Latin American continent—in both a positive and a negative sense.

3.4. Increasing numbers of Christians are discovering the historical relevance of their faith through their political activity on behalf of the construction of socialism and the liberation of the oppressed on this continent. The Christian faith shows up with new vitality and relevance as a factor for criticism and liberation.

3.5. Real-life praxis alongside the proletariat is destroying ethical and emotional blocks within Christians that have prevented them from committing themselves to the class struggle. By virtue of their historical weight, these blocks are a particularly important aspect of the cultural and educational revolution.

3.6. Priests and ministers are making a growing commitment to the poor, the oppressed, and the working class. Enlightened by a new type of theological reflection, they are discovering that their specific mission has new dimensions. Their personal commitment induces them to take on a political responsibility, which is required if they are to effectively display the love for the oppressed that is demanded by the gospel. It also immerses them in the prophetic thrust that is part and parcel of the process of divine revelation. Sometimes grouped together in specific organizations of their own, they represent a positive contribution to the Latin American process of liberation.

3.7. There is a growing awareness that revolutionary Christians must form a strategic alliance with Marxists within the liberation process on this continent. Such a strategic alliance goes beyond the tactical alliances of a temporary or short-run nature. It signifies a common journey towards liberation in history through joint political action. This indentification with Marxists in political action within history does not mean that Christians are abandoning their faith. To them it represents revitalized faith in the future of Christ.

PART TWO

1. Some Aspects of Our Revolutionary Commitment

1.1. Revolutionary commitment entails a comprehensive historical project: the transformation of society. Generosity and good will are not enough. Political action calls for a scientific analysis of reality. There is a constant interaction between political activity and critical analysis. This particular brand of analysis has its own peculiar scientific rationale, which is qualitatively different from the rationale of the bourgeois social sciences.

1.2. The social structure of our countries is based on production relationships (predominantly capitalistic and dependent on worldwide capitalism) which are grounded on the exploitation of the workers. Recognition of the class struggle as a fundamental fact enables us to arrive at an overall interpretation of the structures of Latin America. Revolutionary praxis discloses that any objective, scientific interpretation must resort to class analysis as a key.

1.3. Socialism presents itself as the only acceptable option for getting beyond a class-based society. The fact is that social classes are a reflection of the economic base which, in a capitalist society, sets up an antagonistic division between the possessors of capital and those who are paid for their labor. The latter must work for the former, and thus they are an object of exploitaiton. Only by replacing private ownership with social ownership of the means of production do we create objective conditions that will allow for the elimination of class antagonism.

1.4. The takeover of power that will lead to the construction of socialism has need of a theory that will criticize the capitalist society. Laying bare the contradictions of Latin American society, this theory reveals the objective revolutionary potential of the working classes. The latter are exploited by the system; at the same time, however, they have the capacity to transform it.

1.5. To attain socialism we need not only a critical theory but also the revolutionary praxis of the proletariat. This entails a change of consciousness. That is to say, the present gap between the societal reality and the consciousness of the workers must be overcome. To effect this change in consciousness, we must unmask and denounce the ideological mystifications of the bourgeoisie. In this way the people will identify the structural causes of their wretchedness and conceive the possibility of eliminating them. At the same time, however, this change of consciousness requires popular parties and organisms, and a strategy that will lead to a takeover of power.

1.6. The construction of socialism is a creative process that has nothing to do with dogmatic schemas or an uncritical stance. Socialism is not a complex of historical dogmas but a constantly developing critical theory of the conditions of exploitation and a revolutionary praxis. Operating through the takeover of power by the exploited masses, this praxis leads to social appropriation of the means of production and financing and to comprehensive, rational economic planning.

1.7. Inadequate comprehension of the rationale proper to the class struggle has led many Christians to a defective kind of political involvement. Failing to appreciate the structural mechanisms of society and the necessary contributions of a scientific theory, they try to deduce their political approach from a certain kind of humanistic conception: e.g., the "dignity of the human person," "liberty," and so forth; this is accompanied by political naiveté, activism, and voluntarism.

2. Christianity and the Ideological Struggle

2.1. The class struggle is not restricted to the socio-economic level. It extends to the ideological realm as well. The ruling class fabricates a set of ideological justifications which impede recognition of this struggle. The ideology of the ruling classes, spread among the people by the communication and education media, produces a false consciousness in the dominated class. This false consciousness acts as a restraint on revolutionary action.

2.2. For this reason, revolutionary action places great value on the ideological struggle and regards it as an essential component. Its aim is to liberate the consciousness of the oppressed.

2.3. The dominant ideology takes in certain Christian elements which bolster it and diffuse it through vast segments of the Latin American population. At the same time, the dominant ideology to some extent finds its way into the expression of Christian faith—in particular, into Christian social doctrine, theology, and Church organizations. One of the central tasks of the ideological struggle is to identify and unmask these ideological justifications that are supposedly Christian.

2.4. The deeper core of the faith which we profess, and which is Christ's gratuitous gift, requires us to be critical of the ideological use to which it is put—often in subtle and unnoticed ways. The task of unmasking this sort of use, in which the Christian faith is impoverished and made to serve certain interests, is an exigency of the gospel itself. But it also requires a satisfactory scientific methodology and a real-life commitment to the poor, the oppressed, and the working class. The aim is not to use the faith as a tool for other political ends; rather, it is to restore its pristine evangelical dimension to it. On our continent that task is an urgent one, because the ideological use which people make of the faith paralyzes its liberative, evangelical force that is so important right now.

2.5. The dominant culture imposes an image of man as a being who is summoned to accept an already established order. The latter is presented as the objective order which is founded on human nature itself and which finds expression in natural laws and natural rights. Existing inequalities, dependence, the division of labor, and the chasm between the people and political power are presented as natural necessities of society. This hides the fact that these relationships are rooted in the capitalist system itself, and it undermines the tendency to look for radical, all-pervasive change.

2.6. The dominant culture imposes an individualistic conception of man, picturing him with capabilities, tasks, and goals that are purely individual. In its various forms—liberalism, humanism, and personalism, for example—this culture presents itself as the defender of personal liberty, private property, free trade, open competition, and love reduced to the interpersonal plane entirely. In this way it conceals the structural features of social relationships and the contradictions engendered by the system.

2.7. The culture of the prevailing system imposes a "spiritualistic" idea of man. It explains his behavior and history as if they were grounded mainly on moral ideas and attitudes, as if the ills of the world were based solely on ideological or moral deviations of a purely individual cast. Without at all denying the creativity and the moral worth of the individual person, we feel that the prevailing culture diverts attention away from scientific study of the economic and social mechanisms which fundamentally govern the movement of history. It conceals the fundamental role of structures in the oppression of individuals and nations. It hides the basic impact of the economic factor, of class relationships in particular, on man's political, cultural, and religious life. Hence it sloughs off the idea of seeking change through a transformation of the economic system.

2.8. Using the gospel in a partial and distorted way, the dominant culture imposes a pacifist notion of society. It describes the contrasts, the forms of dependence, the division of labor, and the privileges of some as so many forms of pluralism and complementarity that are required for order and the common good. Hence it promotes "collaboration" and "dialogue" among the classes and the nations. In this way it conceals the conflict-ridden nature of the relationships between classes and peoples and of any authentic process of liberation. It disguises the institutionalized violence of the prevailing system, reserving the label "violence" for the struggle against the dominant class and in favor of revolution. In this way it ultimately retards any authentic communion between human beings.

2.9. The underlying basis for most people's block vis-à-vis the class struggle is the class struggle itself. It works all the more effectively when it works without the oppressed taking note of its influence and its mechanisms.

2.10. To a large extent, the alliance between Christianity and the ruling classes explains the historical forms that Christian awareness has taken. Hence Christians must take a definite stand on the side of the exploited in order to break this alliance. Such a stand, verified in concrete praxis, will enable us to discover a revitalized Christianity. In a sincere effort to be faithful to the gospel, we can recover the revolutionary, conflictive character of its pristine inspiration.

3. Faith and Revolutionary Commitment

3.1. One of the most important discoveries being made by many Christians today is the convergence between the radicality of their faith and the radicality of their political commitment. The radicality of Christian love and its required note of efficaciousness impels them to recognize the specific rationale of the political realm, and to accept the full and logical implications of the tie-up between revolutionary action and scientific analysis of historical reality.

3.2. The real-life presence of the faith in the very heart of revolutionary praxis provides for a fruitful interaction. The Christian faith becomes a critical and dynamic leaven for revolution.

Faith intensifies the demand that the class struggle move decisively towards the liberation of all men—in particular, of those who suffer the most acute forms of oppression. It also stresses our orientation towards a total transformation of society rather than merely a transformation of economic structures. Thus, in and through committed Christians, faith makes its own contribution to the construction of a society that is qualitatively distinct from the present one, and to the appearance of the New Man. The specific nature of the Christian contribution should not be viewed as something prior to revolutionary praxis, as something readymade that the Christian brings with him to the revolutionary struggle. Rather, in the course of his real-life experience in that struggle, faith reveals its capacity to provide creative contributions which neither the Christian nor anyone else could have foreseen outside the revolutionary process.

3.3. But revolutionary commitment also has a critical and motivating function vis-à-vis the Christian faith. It criticizes the open and the more subtle forms of complicity between the faith and the dominant culture during the course of history. It gives new impetus to the faith insofar as it compels the Christian faith to set out on new and unforeseen pathways in order to maintain its vitality. Christians involved in the process of liberation vividly come to realize that the demands of revolutionary praxis and the changes in outlook and discipline entailed in this praxis force them to rediscover the central themes of the gospel message —only now they are freed from their ideological dress.

3.4. The real context for a living faith today is the history of oppression and of the struggle for liberation from this oppression. To situate oneself within this context, however, one must truly participate in the process of liberation by joining parties and organizations that are authentic instruments of the struggle of the working class.

3.5. The Christian involved in revolutionary praxis discovers the liberative power of God's love, of Christ's death and resurrection. He discovers that his faith is not the acceptance of a world already made and a history already determined; that it is an existence which creates a new world of fellowship and a historical effort seeded by Christian hope.

3.6. In real-life commitment to the revolution, the Christian learns to think and to live in terms of history and conflict. He discovers that a love which brings about transformation is lived out in antagonism and confrontation, and that the definitive goal is approached and constructed in history. He begins to realize that no neutrality is possible in the struggle to create a different society, that the humanity of tomorrow is fashioned in the struggles of today. Finally, he discovers that the unity of the Church comes about through the unity of humanity. Hence the revolutionary struggle, which reveals the superficial unity of the Church today, is fashioning the authentic unity of the Church of tomorrow.

3.7. Reflection on the faith ceases to be abstract speculation outside of commitment in history. Revolutionary praxis comes to be recognized as the matrix that will generate a new theological creativity. Thus theological thinking is transformed into critical reflection in and on liberation praxis—in a context of permanent confrontation with the exigencies of the gospel.

Theological reflection assumes that an indispensable prerequisite for carrying out its task is a socio-analytical methodology that is capable of critically grasping the conflictive nature of historical reality.

3.8. This leads the Christian, in a spirit of authentic faith, to a new reading of the Bible and Christian tradition. It poses the basic concepts and symbols of Christianity anew, in such a way that they do not hamper Christians in their commitment to the revolutionary process but rather help them to shoulder these commitments in a creative way.

CONCLUSION

We leave this convention and return to our tasks with a revitalized spirit of personal commitment. We take as our own the words of Che Guevara, which we have put into practice to some extent during these past few days: "Christians should opt definitively for the revolution—particularly on this continent where the Christian faith is so important among the masses of the people. But in the revolutionary struggle Christians cannot presume to impose their own dogmas or to proselytize for their churches. They come without any intention of evangelizing Marxists and without cowardly concealing their faith to assimilate themselves to the latter.

"When Christians dare to give full-fledged revolutionary witness, then the Latin American revolution will be invincible; because up to now Christians have allowed their doctrine to be used as a tool by the reactionaries."

April 30, 1972

PART VI

POST-CONVENTION DOCUMENTS

On September 11, 1973, a military coup toppled the coalition government of Marxist President Salvador Allende. The Christians For Socialism movement was outlawed and many of its members forced into hiding or exile.

The impact of the movement continues to be felt, nevertheless, throughout Latin America and beyond. In this final section we include a lengthy document published by the Chilean bishops analyzing the relationship of Christians to the political process and prohibiting the participation of priests or religious in the Christians For Socialism movement. This significant hierarchical statement has been widely circulated and has already been influential among hierarchies outside Chile.

We conclude with an article by Gonzalo Arroyo, S.J., the chief organizer of the First Latin American Convention of the Christians For Socialism. These reflections on the impact of the hierarchy's reaction to the coup were written prior to the publication of the bishops' statement; they appeared in the Paris periodical Politique Aujourd'hui *(January-February 1974).*

19

Christian Faith
and Political Activity:
Declaration of the
Chilean Bishops

In the regular plenary session of the Chilean episcopate, which was held in Punta de Tralca from April 6-11, the participants explored in detail and at length the whole theological and pastoral question of the doctrinal and disciplinary orientation of priests and religious. The bishops arrived at this conclusion: "No priest or religious can belong to the movement known as 'Christians For Socialism' " (Session XVI, April 11, 1973, n.139).

It was agreed, however, to postpone the publication of this pastoral norm until we had put together a doctrinal statement which would explain the outlook that served as the foundation for this norm.

The basic content of this doctrinal statement—that is, its fundamental perspectives, its main lines, and its resultant norms—was worked out in the course of the sessions held in Punta de Tralca in April. The broad outlines of the document were formulated then under the provisional title: "Concern for the confusion surrounding the mission of the Church in the world."

The plenary session of the episcopate delegated to its standing committee the task of drawing up the final, definitive text of the aforementioned doctrinal statement. It also allowed time for the bishops to offer their own suggestions and comments regarding the original draft. Various observa-

tions of merit were incorporated into the text, and in the following months the standing committee devoted its time and effort to the elaboration of a final version. It approached the task by studying all the literature available that came from the Secretariat of Christians For Socialism, the groups in Santiago and Concepción, and the informational bulletins that were published periodically in connection with workshops, meetings, and so forth. There is no plethora of citations and footnotes in the final text, but the content of these various publications has been kept in mind at all times during the preparation of our final document.

It took much time to work up the final text because much thought went into its preparation. We were well aware of the fact that even though the document originated within the episcopal conference of Chile, it would undoubtedly have large repercussions in Latin America. So we felt a sense of responsibility and involvement vis-à-vis the other episcopal conferences of the continent.

In the meantime it became known that the Chilean episcopate was preparing this document. A report was circulated that the then President of the republic had taken steps to make sure that our document would not see the light of day. This rumor was passed along by certain news agencies in Latin America. The truth is that no such steps were ever taken. Indeed when some Catholic politicians active in leftist parties became acquainted with the content of this document in a more thorough way, they fully realized that it was a doctrinal statement on the Church and that it was not a political document. And the fact is that the aim of this document is to clear up and bring an end to the ambiguities surrounding the matter of the Church's mission.

The definitive text of this document was ready around the middle of August. Even though the president and the secretary of the episcopal conference has been authorized by the standing committee to proceed with its publication, it was decided to wait for a final reading of it at the next session of the committee. That session was to have taken place on September 12. Final approval of the text came in a session held on September 13, 1973, after certain observations had been made.

Events which took place in the public domain on September 11 greatly altered the historical situation in Chile. Certain sections of this docu-

*ment were rendered irrelevant because they referred specifically to the
general Chilean context during the first half of 1973, the period during
which they had been drawn up. But it was decided to publish the
document as it stood, without reworking it, because events had not
affected its doctrinal or disciplinary sections.*

*Finally, we should like to point out that this present document is
wholly consistent with previous collective statements of the Chilean
episcopate that deal with similar topics—ranging from the one issued
September 24, 1970, right up to the present day. In particular, it
dovetails with the resolutions formulated by the regular plenary session
held in Temuco (April 1971), and with its draft document entitled*
Evangelio, política y socialismos *["The Gospel, Politics, and Brands
of Socialism"]. The most novel feature of this present document is the fact
that its main concern is not the area of discipline. Its deeper purpose is to
clarify the mission of the Church in the context of Chile and its history.*

Santiago   *Carlos Oviedo Cavada*
October 16, 1973   *Auxiliary Bishop of Concepción*
                                    Secretary General of the
                                    Episcopal Conference of Chile

INTRODUCTION

Political Pressures on the Church

1. Today the nation is undergoing social transformations.
Naturally enough, Christians cannot remain indifferent to this
process. It has profound moral and spiritual consequences for the
lives of believers and for the life of the Church herself. By the
same token, as faith grows more mature and embraces existence
in its totality, it becomes the underlying principle that serves as
the inspiration for the various socio-political options and commitments of Catholics. But it is a source of growing concern for
us, the bishops of Chile, to see what certain sectors try to do in the

heat of national political debate. They try to assign tasks to the Church, or to seek signs of involvement and support from her which are not in accord with her proper mission and which may even distort that mission on substantive matters of faith or evangelical morality.

2. Faced with this sort of pressure and its disorienting impact on believers, we feel it is our duty to speak the truth clearly and to adopt disciplinary measures that will safeguard the authentic mission of the Church and her hierarchy. Hence we direct our words to those who are sons of the Church, or who wish to be so; to those who share our solicitude for all human beings; and to our brothers and collaborators, the priests. We want to direct our attention, in particular, to the movement known as "Christians For Socialism," and to other Christians who wittingly or unwittingly use the Church and the gospel to defend their own opinions and their own political interests. We do this in response to numerous inquiries from the faithful. And in so doing, we have taken into consideration the various documents that have been published in the territory of the nation.

3. The group mentioned above uses the name "Christian" and is under the direction of priests. But it takes positions so clearly and decidedly political that it is indistinguishable from political parties or similar currents of opinion and activity. This would be legitimate in itself, at least for lay people and within the framework of liberty and pluralism that is properly theirs, if it were not for the fact that the content of this option leaves much to be desired from the standpoint of doctrine and praxis. Furthermore, this group sets up its program of action as a Christian norm, as the program which the Church herself should adopt if she wants to remain faithful to her mission. The result is to disqualify other Christians who do not think the same way or who hold contrary opinions.

4. Other Christians regard certain institutions and traditional patterns of society as things that should not be touched. When they see these things being called into question or jeopardized, they urge the Church to organize for the defense of these institutions in the name of democracy, liberty, the family, religion, and so forth. But they do not distinguish adequately between the

essential Christian values of the social order and those more contingent institutional forms which the Church does not have a mission to guard or defend—however much Catholics, freely exercising their personal liberty, may feel that these latter forms are better or even necessary within the boundary lines of faith.

5. To avoid misunderstandings, we feel it is well to repeat the sentiments we expressed in our draft document entitled *Evangelio, política y socialismos* ["The Gospel, Politics, and Brands of Socialism"]. We do not deny the possibility or the legitimacy of Catholics adopting leftist positions and working in leftist parties so long as they do this in line with the preconditions governing the political involvement of any and every Catholic, whatever his or her position may be (see EPS 67; see note 1 below for all abbreviations). If we devote particular attention to the movement mentioned above rather than to deviations at the other end of the spectrum, we do so because the latter deviations are political in character and do not claim to formulate a new idea of the Church and its relationship with the world. The movement known as "Christians For Socialism" does make such a claim as part of its program, and its doctrinal error calls for equally explicit clarification from pastors.

6. There is nothing new in this attempt to use the Church as support for a temporal order deemed better or more legitimate. Nor is there anything new in the urge to commit its hierarchy and its organic structure to the support of one's own political stance. But today this whole phenomenon bursts upon us in clearcut forms, and it is highly disorienting and combative in character. Because of its doctrinal consequences, we want to examine and analyze it in detail. In line with this analysis, and with the whole affair and its attendant circumstances, we also want to formulate certain general principles for the temporal activity of Christians.

7. Our aim is to get away from any and all improper utilization of the Church in the civic domain. We assert that the above mentioned modes of thinking and acting disfigure the Church and the gospel, obscure its universality (its "catholicity"), diminish its credibility, distort its truth, and impede its authentic activity. Behind these tendencies we can glimpse the witting or unwitting desire to manipulate the Church and the gospel to the

benefit of specific political interests, and to make propaganda for specific temporal options by using the name of Christianity on their behalf.

The Mission of Lay People and the Mission of the Church

8. The outcrop of such polarizations does not surprise us. At bottom we find authentic aspects of the whole matter of the Church's relationship to the world. We are now far removed from the prejudice which circumscribed faith within the private domain of the individual conscience and left history—the profane history of institutions, laws, and regimes—to its own course in time without any possible connection with personal salvation. Such a thing is impossible; we do not live in limbo. The destiny of mankind—its eternal destiny—is played out within the societal and political life of peoples and nations; and that life always entails serious moral problems. The Church carries on Christ's mission on this earth: "to liberate all men from the slavery to which sin has subjected them—hunger, misery, oppression, and ignorance, in a word, that injustice and hatred which have their origin in human selfishness"(MED II, *Justice*, n.3). And this holds true even though the end result will always be less than complete and perfect on this earth. Today more than ever before the Church must pass judgment on social doctrines and situations and motivate its faithful to take action within every human institution.

9. Hence we can readily understand what happens to people who make Christ's salvific will their own and then flesh it out in a specific ideology or political position. They end up concluding that their option is a perfect expression of the gospel message and consubstantial with Christ's manifestation in the world—so much so that other options, different from theirs or opposed to theirs, seem to be downright opposed to the gospel itself. And the universality of the Church, which tolerates and even fosters political pluralism within its precincts, seems to them to represent a lack of definiteness or outright evasion vis-à-vis the grave problems of the day. Or, still worse, it may seem to be complicity with specific temporal interests.

10. But there is an improper inference in this view of the matter, and we cannot pass over the error in silence. These Catholics, feeling that a specific course of social or political action is an imperative, invest it with a character that is proper to the Church as a corporate body. They feel that this course of action cannot simply be their own personal course as lay people and Christian citizens; that it should also be the joint undertaking of the whole people of God—lay people, priests, and hierarchy. Perhaps quite unprepared as lay people to conjugate the "I," they look to the "we" for support. And instead of applying this "we" to the components of a particular group—which would be legitimate—they apply it to the whole ecclesial community. Thus they confuse and indentify the temporal mission of the laity with the universal and supernatural mission of the Church itself and its hierarchy. The mission of the laity is in fact the task of ordering temporal affairs in accordance with the spirit of the gospel. The mission of the Church and the hierarchy, on the other hand, is not that of resolving temporal questions: economic, social, juridical, and so forth. The mission of the Church and the hierarchy is to sanctify, teach, and rule—supplying the faithful with the re-vivifying energy of grace which they in turn will project in their work as citizens. In so doing, lay people will act on their own initiative and at their own risk, exercising the liberty and personal responsibility that is properly theirs as lay people.

11. In temporal matters, then, we insist that this fundamental distinction be made between the civil, secular task of the laity and the activity of the Church itself and its hierarchy. Vatican II, in fact, urges Christians "to make a clear distinction between what a Christian conscience leads them to do in their own name as citizens, whether as individuals or in association, and what they do in the name of the Church and in union with her shepherds" (*Guadium et spes,* 76). Both bishops and priests as well as all the faithful form a vital, operative part of the people of God. The Holy Spirit has been poured out into the hearts of all of them; and today, more than ever before, we appreciate the sanctifying value of the lay person's life in the world. But the rights and duties of the two groups vis-à-vis temporal activities are very different. Lay citizens act in their own name. They represent only them-

selves. They have undergone a human preparation and they possess certain political, professional, and occupational talents which do not come from the Church but from their own human effort. They have certain claims and rights which they must win from society for themselves as every other citizen must. At the same time they act in accordance with their Christian conscience, which has been enlightened by the gospel and the social teaching of the Church. This commitment is one that they made their own in a form that is equally laical. That is to say, it does not implicate in it the hierarchical Church or the rest of the faithful.

12. We bishops and our co-workers, the priests, act "in the name of Christ, the head of his Mystical Body" in the Church. Our pastoral duty vis-à-vis the laity is to lead them to a meeting with the Lord, "who is the source of all holiness"; and to form them in the faith and its social ramifications. This supernatural task requires that we respect their liberty in their own temporal commitments insofar as the latter contain contingent and debatable elements. We are pastors of a Church which does not identify itself with any particular civilization, culture, regime, ideology, or party in this world (see *Gaudium et spes,* 76). Hence we take a standpoint that is distinct from the particular options of the laity. We simply judge these options in the light of gospel values, making sure that they stay in line with the exigencies of Christian faith and morality.

13. To proceed otherwise would be to risk converting the Church into just another element of the world, which is not what Jesus wanted: "I am to stay no longer in the world, but they are still in the world, and I am on my way to thee. Holy Father, protect by the power of thy name those whom thou hast given me, that they may be one, as we are one . . . . I pray thee, not to take them out of the world, but to keep them from the evil one" (Jn 17:11-15). The Church lives to unite human beings with the living God, the Father of Jesus Christ; to incorporate them in a vital and conscious way with the person of Jesus; to transform them into temples of the Holy Spirit and instruments of his activity in the world.

14. Hence Vatican II has this to say: "Christ, to be sure, gave His Church no proper mission on the political, economic, or social order. The purpose which He set before her is a religious

one. But out of this religious mission itself come a function, a light, and an energy which can serve to structure and consolidate the human community according to the divine law. As a matter of fact, when circumstances of time and place create the need, she can and indeed should initiate activities on behalf of all men. This is particularly true of activities designed for the needy, such as the works of mercy and similar undertakings. The Church further recognizes that worthy elements are found in today's social movements, especially an evolution toward unity, a process of wholesome socialization and of association in civic and economic realms. For the promotion of unity belongs to the innermost nature of the Church, since she is, 'by her relationship with Christ, both a sacramental sign and an instrument of intimate union with God, and of the unity of all mankind.' Thus she shows the world that an authentic union, social and external, results from a union of minds and hearts, namely, from that faith and charity by which her own unity is unbreakably rooted in the Holy Spirit. For the force which the Church can inject into the modern society of man consists in that faith and charity put into vital practice . . . " (*Gaudium et spes,* 42).

15. But here again the Church must not arrogate to herself a responsibility or management that is not properly hers. To do that would be to infringe upon the autonomy of the temporal order. By the same token, however, it is not human science or human desires that determine the proper mission of the Church; that mission is determined by the mandate of Christ, her founder. We cannot ask non-believers to look at the Church with other than worldly eyes, but we can ask them to take note of, and show appreciation for, the way in which she sees herself. And we can go so far as to insist that believing members of the Church look at her with the eyes of faith, view her in the spirit of faith rather than in the spirit of the world (see 2 Cor 5:16; 1 Cor 2:13-3:1) and with the wisdom of God rather than worldly wisdom.

THE GROUP KNOWN AS "CHRISTIANS FOR SOCIALISM"

16. We have read most of the documents published by this group.[1] Their representation of the Church and their doctrinal formulations are varied and unequal. In them the group does not

claim to present an exposition of the faith or a systematic presentation of theological doctrine. Many important aspects of Christian faith are omitted by them. The thinking evident in them is not worked out fully. Their positions, concepts, and language are diffuse and indefinite. Particularized statements are intermingled with universal pronouncements; no further attempt at precision is made. Emotional feelings and reactions are intertwined with ideas that claim to be scientific and scholarly. Formulations associated with scholarly disciplines and sciences—e.g., economics, sociology, and history—are combined with principles related to the faith. There is a real vagueness between what they say and what is left in the readers mind; between what they believe in general and what they think in particular cases; between what they practice and what they write or preach. Many articles limit their attention to some specific event; they are based on situations of the moment. In general, they deal with calls to concrete action that are directed at Christians as such. Despite this lack of precision, however, certain underlying attitudes reveal the persistent lines of their approach and their outlook.

Anxious Concerns and Positive Contributions

17. In the aforementioned documents we do find positive elements. We also find intuitions and anxious concerns that should be given their due, even though we can only mention them briefly. They represent seeds sprouting from the Spirit which Jesus gave his Church and are ever present in her. We would like to make sure that they develop further. They are:

a. The summons to review the task of the Church so that she does not become enslaved within specific social or institutional forms; so that she may divest herself of special interests and of any concern for human prestige, thereby remaining free to be herself and to help those who need her most.

b. The impulsion of Christians towards the problems of the world, particularly towards the problems of social justice, the transformation of society, and the struggle against poverty and oppression.

c. Sensitivity to structures and a keen sense of the socio-economic factors that condition the moral and spiritual life; the obligation to get beyond structures that condition customs and people's outlook in a negative way, and the need to give structural expression to their personal desires for justice and charity.

d. The vitalization of theology by bringing it into open contact with the historic problems of the present day; the impulse to form new theological categories that will foster real encounter with the contemporary sciences.

e. The yearning to get the Church truly involved in the world of the manual laborer and the peasant; the need to proclaim the good news to the poor, this being a sign of the kingdom's arrival (see Lk 7:22); and, by the same token, the need for the Church to take in the outlook and values of the world in its own expression of the faith, morality, and liturgy.

f. In general, critical re-examination of all ecclesiastical institutions so that they may truly mirror the poor in spirit who are to have the kingdom of heaven.

Unjust Accusations against the Church

18. In these documents, however, a defective notion of the Church becomes more and more apparent. It leads to ecclesial activities that are equally defective. This notion must be pinpointed and corrected so that these priests do not end up by falsifying the most basic truths of the faith and thereby harming or scandalizing the faithful who have been entrusted to their care. For as priests, they enjoy a high degree of credibility among their faithful.

19. In the view of the Church held by this group we see an obsessive and exaggerated emphasis on the socio-political realm, and a strong tendency to reduce the whole dynamism of the Church to this one dimension. It leads these people to distort even the temporal role that has been played by the Church in history. In the most recent documents of the Secretariat of their organization, the socio-economic and political point of view

overwhelmingly affects their conception of the Church and the way people should belong to her and act within her precincts—so much so that we find it difficult to see her authentic supernatural and spiritual nature in their distorted image of her.[2] The hierarchy has stressed the non-political character of the Church's mission, the primacy of the spiritual, and the universality of Christian values: e.g., charity, overcoming class confrontation through justice, reconciliation, and peace. In so doing, this group maintains, the hierarchy is putting itself in the service of bourgeois ideology and its class interests, and is therefore an ally and defender of the oppressive structures of capitalism. This has been said repeatedly by spokesmen for Christians For Socialism.[3]

20. Many who speak thus may not really know our characteristic outlook and approach, or the concerned work of the Church on behalf of those who are poorest. Perhaps that is why they are uninformed or unduly forgetful of the role of the Church and Christians in the social history of the country. We must mention just a few facts here. The peasant and labor-union movements, as well as the work of educating and training these groups, has in large measure been the fruit of actions undertaken by people and institutions of Catholic inspiration; and they have had the full backing and support of the Church. The peasant effort to gain possession of land also got a concrete and timely response from the hierarchy; it initiated agrarian reform on Church lands as best it could. Moreover, scores of Catholics in our nation, motivated by the Church's social teaching, have dedicated their time and effort to all sorts of efforts in the realm of social justice; and they continue to do so today. They have in no way felt that they were allied to oppressive systems or structures. Most important and essential of all, above and beyond the complex and pluralistic political stamp of the faith's expression in the temporal sphere, is the undeniable fact that the Church has carried out an extensive pastoral effort in the realm of the laborer and the peasant. She still continues to do this in her own proper way, without partisan interest; her only commitment is to achieve and embody union with Christ, the eternal high priest.

21. Ignorance or forgetfulness of these facts, and ill-considered judgments, lead the members of Christians For Socialism to make

unacceptable and injurious statements. What is more regrettable, they cause priests to do this in the exercise of their ministry, thus exploiting the office and the trust which their superiors have conferred on them for very different ends. We note with surprise that they make these accusations on the one hand, yet verbally profess a desire to stay in communion with the hierarchy on the other hand. And we are saddened to see that these accusations are echoed by "Christians," who claim to derive them from a "scientific analysis of reality . . . which reveals the objective conditioning factors behind the various forms of religious ideologization."

22. It is not difficult to surmise the underlying inspiration for these judgments: It is the Marxist-Leninist method of interpreting history in economic terms. This method reduces the religious life of humanity to an ideology reflecting the economic infrastructure and the class struggle. In every instance where religion claims to be a-political, to be above and beyond conflicting dialectics in the social struggle (e.g., that of the bourgeoisie and that of the proletariat), this method sees alienation on the one hand and complicity with the dominant social groups on the other hand. It is not for us here to spell out to what extent this method can contribute valid elements to the social and historical sciences, and hence to people's social and political action. But we certainly can state that many of its elements and its essential postulates—e.g., materialism, dialectics, atheism—are not scientific at all; nor can they claim the label of science in order to disqualify the spiritual and supernatural import of the Church's life. We can also say that these presuppositions and conclusions, which are formally philosophical and ideological in character but not scientific, are contrary to and incompatible with the most elemental fundaments of the Catholic faith. As the magisterium of the Church has repeatedly pointed out, they do not dovetail with the existence of God, human liberty, the autonomy of moral and spiritual values, and so forth.

23. It is regrettable that a priest of Christ would take this method to be scientific and enlightening and—with certain vague limitations or mental reservations—regard it as the key to unlocking the secret of history, while at the same time giving up the

fundamental ethico-religious sense of salvation history. There may well be an acceptable sense in which one can adopt certain elements of this methodology within a Christian vision of history, but it is not evident in the tack taken by these priests. In general, they do not give any indication that they possess the required theological, philosophical, and scientific training for such a task. They have simply taken over the main features of the Marxist methodology wholesale, adding to it the remnants of Christian truth that remain after they have applied this same methodology to the Catholic faith in their own way.

24. This means that adherence to Christ becomes relative. That is to say, it is allowed on condition that a certain methodology intervenes in the picture. These people refuse to interpret history, the class struggle, and Marxism itself in the light of the gospel and an unconditional faith. Instead they interpret—or rather, re-interpret—Christ on the basis of a human, cultural instance which starts out from atheistic premises and ends up by distorting him at the very least. Starting from the premise that they will follow the "scientific"thread of this methodology, they do not see why this analysis should stay within certain limits and view only certain affirmations of faith as "bourgeois ideologizations." The underlying presupposition of this methodology is the reduction of every religious reality to the conditioning influence of the infrastructure, and its whole drift is dominated by atheism. This drift can easily be glimpsed in the analyses alluded to earlier, even though it is disguised under other categories. They would like to reduce Catholic faith and the Church's dogma and morality to "post-religious Christianity" and "Christian commitment to liberation," and both of these terms are understood in an increasingly temporal and materialistic sense.

25. We feel that in this case it is not right or honest to evade the dramatic but indispensable conflict that conscience faces when it is confronted with the alternatives posed by Christ: "He who is not with me is against me, and he who does not gather with me scatters" (Mt 12:30). It is our wholehearted wish that this crisis of conscience would be resolved in favor of full and total adherence to Christ and the Church. We would hope to see a repeat of

Peter's ardent act of faith, voiced at a time when other followers were leaving Jesus: "Lord, to whom shall we go? Your words are words of eternal life. We have faith, and we know that you are the Holy One of God" (Jn 6:68-69). In this hope we urge the priests involved in this movement to come to a clearcut decision. But our pastoral confidence and trust cannot be with them in the ambiguous, undefined, and indeed contradictory situation where this crisis of conscience is evaded in a welter of doctrinal and moral confusion that falsifies the two terms of the alternative.

26. The Church did not wait for the rise of a revolutionary ideology in the nineteenth century to fight for human and evangelical values; to denounce all sorts of idolatry and oppression; to show her concern for the poor; and to make every possible effort to bring education, assistance, and the light of faith to the neediest peoples and nations. She has done this in every age. When people who call themselves "Christians" take up the "scientific analysis of reality" and the "rational praxis of the class struggle"—to the extent that such a tack is possible at all, they should not deform their loyalty to the Church in the process. They should not judge her role over the past twenty centuries in what is clearly an anachronistic and unjust way. This applies to her educational and civilizing role—not to mention her history of holiness and heroism. That history still is her most precious treasure today, yet these people would gainsay it by accusing her of "objectively" having served the dominant class and its economic interests.

27. No Christian could possibly recognize his mother, the Church, in that analysis. We are very saddened that these sons of hers, brought up in the faith of the Church, would thus distort the image of their mother by an ill-considered application of fallacious ideological reasoning (see Col 2:8); that they would end up by repudiating her under the pretext of loving her better, accusing her of prostituting herself to the idols of the day. They do not advert to the fact that they themselves are puffed up with false science, that they have prostrated themselves before new gods that cannot save them. No one has the right to keep calling himself a Christian if he has vitiated his faith to that extent.

The Church and the Political Realm

28. There is one aspect of the question which we feel must be clarified in the minds of the faithful. The group insistently maintains that the Church cannot help but be political; that she is favoring one of the parties in the class struggle whether she wants to or not; that any claim to be a-political would be naive —or worse still, a covert way of supporting the established order.

Starting from this point, one can easily go on to reduce the substantive reality of the Church to her political import or influence. In practice that would lead her to condition all her activities by the interpretation that the political organs of society might put on them. The result would be to shackle her freedom and her own style vis-à-vis the temporal realm.

29. It is easy enough to detect the hidden presupposition underlying this view: namely, that the substantive and ultimate conflict in human history is the economic conflict, the class struggle, and the resultant political battle. In this view the struggle between sin and grace, between good and evil, is an accidental and non-substantive one. This notion is rather difficult to imagine if there is a heaven and a hell. Or else, in their view, the struggle between good and evil is simply the moral expression of the class struggle and political confrontation. That, at least, seems to be what the group known as Christians For Socialism would reduce it to in the last analysis. In either case the Church would not possibly be a-political. She would have to avow militancy in the class struggle and in the battle of political parties who seek to embody this struggle in their quest for power.

30. Quite logically we confront the problem from the basic standpoint of salvation history: i.e., that in the lives of individuals and nations, in the hearts of all human beings, there is a struggle going on between grace and sin, good and evil. These forces may have many varied relationships with the various elements involved in social and political conflict—i.e., with classes, structures, and parties—but they can never be totally identified with them or reduced to them. The reason is that no group or structure in this world is the clear and simple embodiment of

good or evil—neither socialism nor capitalism, proletariat or bourgeoisie. There is no clearcut territorial or social frontier which divides the invisible forces that wage war in each and every human heart. And this is the substantive, definitive struggle of human existence, on which we will be judged by God in the final accounting.

31. Hence the socio-political realm is not an absolute. Political life is lived in varying degrees and forms. Politics can be a profession—the discharge of public functions on behalf of the common good. There are political parties and analogous groupings which are united by a common philosophical ideology and by a concrete program for social liberation. We uphold the nobility and dignity of this task, to which many lay Christians and other men of good will dedicate themselves in a disinterested and constructive way. But whether they operate within or outside such channels, all citizens are called upon to carry out certain duties and to exercise certain essential political and civil rights. Many of these rights are prior to any concrete political regime: e.g., the right to life, work, education, and freedom of conscience—with their attendant obligations.

32. Hence there are a host of activities and institutions which have some relation to politics but which are "social," properly speaking. Their main stress is on education, work, culture, science, sports, welfare, juridical matters, and so forth. They are embodied in such entities as schools, labor unions, small business associations, universities, military corps, and other groups. Even though they are dedicated to various aspects of the common good, they are not political in a partisan sense; nor should they be. And the fact is that people do not want to see them politicized or put in the service of a partisan cause, for that would lead to discrimination against certain people and a loss of the proper autonomy and purpose of these groups. Today in Chile there is an evident temptation to subordinate this whole realm, which is political in the broad sense of the term, to partisan activity. Instead, politicians should put themselves in the service of these other related activities which promote the common good, and should foster their development in a disinterested way.

33. We look with growing concern on the excessive politicization of the nation, not only because it menances the Church but
also because it threatens the whole life of the nation. When
everything in the country becomes political, then politics itself
becomes insane because it takes over areas of life that are not
proper to it. Other autonomous roots and other human resources
are destroyed. If they were allowed to exist, they would
humanize life and would make political activity in the strict sense
more sane and creative. Partisan tensions cannot be allowed to
destroy these other life-giving roots whose sap will fertilize the
life of the community. It cannot be allowed to destroy spirituality,
science, scholarship, work, art, technology, and culture. When
all the life-giving juices of the nation go to nourish one
branch—i.e., political partisanship—then the result will be a
monstrously deformed flower. Politics is ennobling and wholesome when it permits the existence and further growth of all the
other domains of life above and below it: the family and home
life, work and study, science and art, culture and leisure, thought
and religion.

34. Let no one think that it is the professional politican or the
party activist as such who bears the major share of the country's
burden and holds the complex threads of its institutions together
from day to day. This task if far more tied up with the daily effort
of human beings, from the lowliest worker to the most brilliant
professional; and it is bound up with all the interwoven strands of
the common good—home life, economic life, cultural life, union
life, and so forth. So we are increasingly disturbed by the deteriorating condition of political relationships in the national
sphere, and also of work relationships. The loss of discipline and
of work habits causes deep moral damage in people's consciences
and visibly affects the prosperity of the country in an adverse
way.

35. Insofar as the Church is in the world (see Jn 17:11) and in
history, insofar as it is the work of man and for man, it is a part of
the social realm. From this standpoint no one would deny that
the activity of the Church is in some way political. It is political
even as man himself is a "political animal," even as all human
relationships are political: e.g., family life, science, art, and so

forth. But one must understand and appreciate the difference between politics insofar as it underlies every social reality, and politics insofar as it is a partisan activity. The latter is the concrete, tactical, strategic, and combined effort undertaken by a group of people with a specific ideology to win positions of power and carry out their political philosophy. In the latter area the activity of the Church is very different. There the Church exerts an influence insofar as she educates her lay sons in a faith that does not lack a social dimension and social implications. They in turn flesh out these implications on their own initiative and at their own risk, acting as citizens of the world. The Church also exerts influence insofar as her social teachings can and hopefully will be heeded by society as bearing upon the great moral principles underlying the social order. But it is captious to interpret this influence in terms of power, no matter what "science" one may claim to base this interpretation on.

36. There is no denying that throughout the course of church history some people have tried to make use of this influence and to convert it into temporal power. But it would be naive to judge those situations in past ages without trying to understand the contemporary historical circumstances which made them possible and which are very different from our circumstances today. Our feeling is that all "clericalism" is to be repudiated; and by "clericalism" we mean clerical domination of the world and ecclesiastical supervision of temporal institutions. For this very reason we are distressed by the rise of new forms of this evil today. They reappear when people try to dissolve the Church in the current of civil causes and parties, turning her into nothing more than an energizing force for temporal progress, or a liberating ferment in the class struggle and the buildup of a better world. Both the old and the new forms of clericalism end up as the same thing. In both cases it is ecclesiastics who seek to direct politics. Only the thrust and sense of the politics has changed.

37. The members of Christians For Socialism profess to be a-political to a certain extent because they do not seek to be a political party or to serve any particular party. But this supposedly non-partisan character soon reveals itself to be nothing more than a political tactic or strategy. It is designed (1) to unify

the political parties and groups of the left and (2) to win support for this cause from Christian individuals and groups who might not see this as a partisan commitment right away. The tactic or strategy is abetted by the supposedly non-partisan character of the movement and the fact that its leaders are priests. But this does not alter the fact that its militancy and activity are clearly political. Its supposedly non-partisan character is simply a means for operating more effectively within its own specific situation. Its aim is to foster what is intrinsically political activity of a Marxist-Leninist stamp. Anyone can readily see that this sort of "a-politicism" is totally out of line with the a-political character of the Church and her priests.

The Church is Not Neutral in the Struggle for Justice

38. The authentic influence of the Church in society is quite different. When the Church intervenes officially in the problems of the world, she seeks to enlighten men's minds, motivate their wills, and set their hearts ablaze. And she does so in terms of the great moral values and goals of man's life in society. These values and goals fall within the perspective of the gospel message, even when they relate to specific problems and transient events. If the pope and we bishops were to speak out on these matters in terms of special interest or temporal power, or even in disinterested but contingent and debatable terms, if we sought to sway the opinion of the faithful solely in terms of what seemed right to us without it having any essential relationship to the gospel message, then we would be betraying our charism and our function.

39. The Church is not neutral insofar as justice is concerned. She can and ought to pass judgment on social and political matters. But she does not judge such matters on the basis of political criteria. Instead she judges them on the basis of the gospel and its exigencies, that is, in terms of the moral kernel which many social and political problems contain. She cannot choose between various economic, social, and political solutions, just as she cannot choose between various juridical, scientific, and artistic options. She must pass judgment on moral and

religious terms. Starting from a social and political ethic grounded on the rights of all men and on God's vision of man, she goes on to judge the truth or falsity of political doctrines and the justice or injustice of *de facto* situations. And she has the loftier liberty of voicing her judgments precisely because she does not allow herself to be taken over by any party or social group. Lay Christians certainly can and should assume commitments of that nature, but they will do it freely and responsibly as individual persons, exempt from any trace of clerical paternalism.

40. Thus the Church can truly say that she is a-political—in two basic senses. Firstly, because she does not offer any political model as such that is properly her own; that is not her job. Hence she never identifies herself with any such model (see *Gaudium et spes*, 76; Synod of Bishops, *Justice in the World*, II). Secondly, because her mode of action is not that peculiar to political activity. She does not try to be effective by exercising power: "The Church seeks no power on earth except that which will enable her to serve and to love" (Paul VI, Address at closing of the third session of Vatican II, 16). As he says elsewhere: "Founded to build the kingdom of heaven on earth rather than to acquire temporal power, the Church openly avows that the two powers—Church and State—are distinct from one another; that each is supreme in its own sphere of competence" (*Populorum progressio*, 13, TPS 12:148).

41. Through her social teaching, the Church continually motivates her faithful to take decisive action in favor of justice. In Latin America she has done this with great insistence, and we in Chile have done the same. In so doing, we have set great value on the efficacy of political activity as such. We have tried to move the laity away from harmful abstentionism, to get them to shoulder their task in this area in a free and responsible way. But it has become clearer and clearer to us that the more insistent our appeal becomes in that respect, the more necessary it becomes to make sure that the Church, as an official community, does not undertake any political activity or flesh out this appeal in any concrete way that would fail to show respect for the free option of the individual citizen who is also a believer. Hence we ourselves and those who share our pastoral responsibility try to spell out

our real motives time and again. We want them to be the motives of Christ himself. He asked the shepherds of his flock not to act like those in authority among the Gentiles. Instead of lording it over their charges, his apostles were to serve those entrusted to their care (see Mk 10:42-43).

42. No doubt there will be times when, in the flurry of partisan emotions, the activity of the Church will seem to be welcome interference to one political group and unwelcome interference to another group. Jesus himself, who came to convert all human beings to the kingdom of God and who acted as the servant of all, was brought before a political tribunal. So we would ask Christians to abandon all interpretations of that sort; to set aside passion and appreciate the loftier truth of the Church; never to reduce the Church to just another political factor; and in this way to help us lead the people of God in line with its authentic mission.

Defective View of the Gospel and the Church

43. In their documents, the members of Christians For Socialism describe the constitutive elements of the Church, her mission of liberation, the activity of her members, and the spirit of charity that is peculiarly hers. We find their description inadequate. Indeed their views seem to be equivocal on all these matters, when not actually erroneous.

44. As we see it, they lay such stress on socio-political liberation that in practice they pay mere lip service to essential aspects of Christian liberation and to the proper way in which the Church is to promote justice in the world.[4] In reality they lose sight of these points. The activity of the Church becomes indistinguishable from any other political current.[5] One indication of this is their tendency to limit man's encounter with God and Christ to participation in a very specific revolutionary process.[6] The primary and essential mission of the Church, it would seem, is to mobilize the masses in favor of one specific type of revolution.[7] Or, at best, the suggestion is that if the Church wants to carry out her authentic task some day, then she should first do all she can to foster the establishment of a particular kind of social order: socialism.[8] The

work of evangelization is either subordinated to revolution or made indentical with it.

45. This tack inevitably leads to confusing the Church with the world, and salvation with human progress (or a rather dubious version of progress, even in the temporal sphere); to reducing the person of Christ to a mere human leader, the prophet of a new earthly order and the director of the proletariat. Thus stripped of its supernatural dimension, the gospel is turned into nothing more than another human factor fostering civilization, socialization, and worker solidarity. Is this not the vision that drives these people to associate themselves with what they regard as the liberation movements of the age? They seem to think that certain social processes, by virtue of the mere fact that they occur in history, are "signs of the times" willed by God; that they are new incarnations of Christ in history. For once salvation history is made identical with profane history, then the mere occurrence of some process in history will erroneously be viewed as a "sign from God" summoning us to collaboration.

46. The Church holds many things which are opposed to this way of thinking and acting. History is not infallible; sin exists. Sin is not restricted to economic alienation nor to social injustice. There are true and false kinds of liberation. Christian liberation stems from Christ's resurrection, and not from social processes or struggle and not from human decisions. It calls for the construction of a better world within history, but it also projects its gaze towards the kindgom; the latter is the soul of history on the one hand, but it also transcends history on the other hand. The kingdom, including its historical dimension, is not identical with any process or economic structure or political regime in this world. The person who accepts this kingdom into his heart, the new man vested with Christ, is not merely a good citizen or a staunch promoter of development. He is also a human being reborn of water and the Holy Spirit, a son of God, a new creature. Christ himself is not just a temporal leader; he is God made man, the Lord of the universe, the judge of the future world. While his kingdom is already in our midst, it will only reach its perfect fulfillment in a real order that is far beyond man's manner of thinking.

47. Pardon us for feeling that we must reiterate these basic notions of the catechism. Social liberation, as the bishops affirmed at Medellín, is a consequence of Christ's redemptive work and our liberation from sin. For this reason, the proper task of the Church is to work directly for the transformation of human beings, so that they in turn may transform structures (MED II, *Justice*, 3). We have often affirmed the present-day need for structural change, precisely because structures condition the hearts of human beings. It is more difficult to train and form the new man within unjust and oppressive structures. But we must recall the fact that the ministry of the Church is a ministry of the Spirit (see 2 Cor 3:4-8). Its aim is to renew human beings interiorly so that they may dedicate themselves to the struggle for social justice.

48. Christ knew full well that the people in whom the good news of the kingdom was planted would live their lives within those institutions; and also that they would find specific ways to embody the gospel in them, thus vivifying them with the life-giving juice of the kingdom. He also realized that this effort to order the temporal realm in accordance with the faith would be an essential dimension of salvation history, since man's life formed a unity. But this projection of the gospel was to be effectively carried out to the extent that the hearts of his disciples were converted to it out of faith and love.

49. Hence we are surprised by the odd interpretation of the gospel which is proposed by the members of Christians For Socialism. As they see it, the gospel message is not primarily an ethico-religious one which then becomes social. The contrary is true. They see the supernatural realities of the gospel message —charity, the kingdom, the sacraments—as signs and images of temporal realities (regimes, classes, structures) in which the words and intentions of Jesus are to be fleshed out and fulfilled. This fulfillment has had to wait nineteen centuries for the appearance of an intermediary "science"—the Marxist methodology—which teaches us that structures transform the human heart—not vice versa. Now this view in turn leads to a total re-interpretation of the gospels in which their deeper and original sense is brought out: i.e., liberation as revolution. We affirm that this supposed exegesis is nothing but a complete

inversion of Jesus' work and word, of his parables and miracles, of his life and death and resurrection. All these mysteries have always been understood by the Church in their basic and original sense, the sense in which they were understood by the apostles. We received that sense through apostolic tradition, without the mediation of any "science" which, under the pretext of throwing more light on the gospel, ends up by distorting or even reversing its real sense.

50. In the context of this upside-down symbolism, peoples signify classes, virtues signify systems or regimes, beatitudes signify structures, conversions signify revolutions, and sacraments signify social parties or groups. If Christ had intended that, he would have let us know. He would not have left us wandering in error until the arrival of nineteenth-century sociology and political economy. That upside-down interpretation is not right. As the successors of the apostles, we affirm that Christ was pointing beyond the historical vagaries of institutions to the very depths of the human heart. It is there that the transformation of the human person takes place in contact with the person of the Lord. It is there that the invisible activity of the Holy Spirit and man's free decision give shape to our eternal destiny. It is there that man is freed from inner bondage to sin and its trappings: injustice, exploitation, hatred, egotism, haughtiness, lust, sloth, greed, and so forth. Only then does man become capable of expressing himself in free, liberative institutions. But then he has not only the capacity but also the duty to do so: "Love must not be a matter of words or talk; it must be genuine, and show itself in action" (1 Jn 3:18).

51. To say this is to say something that is both obvious and profound. It is to say that the gospel operates through man and his personal liberty; that we cannot liberate institutions from injustice unless we liberate people's consciences from individual and social sin. As is true of every living thing, redemption grows from the inside out. It does not come from external violence directed against the forms of societal life. The gospel strikes roots first in the inner personality of individuals; then it manages to impress its mark on the spirit of a community, but always in an imperfect form. From these personal and social depths it generates the creative strength to fashion social and institutional

changes, as well as new forms of culture, societal life, and political organization.

52. Today man is discovering the many and varied factors that condition his moral conduct. These factors are chemical, biological, psychic, social, economic, and so forth. With its realism, Christian morality has always recognized conditioning factors of this sort. Hence it has always been prudent enough to descry the limits and limitations on human liberty. (You will never hear the Church talking about absolute liberty, which is an absurd illusion, because it is the very limitations of liberty that give liberty real meaning.) Understandably enough, it is not faith but science and scholarship that is called upon to spell out the mechanism of such conditionings. Today, however, a sense of euphoria surrounds transformations that seek to modify human behavior by working from the outside in, by merely manipulating these mechanisms in a skillful way. We must underline the dangerous and inhuman element in this effort, however much people may label it "liberation." The fact is that, except in extreme or pathological cases, the conditionings surrounding human conduct are not causal determinations. The truest and loftiest fruits of human action—justice, love, beauty, truth, holiness—will never be achieved by external or perhaps even violent manipulation of a scientific or technological nature. Such manipulation of the human conscience will never produce those fruits. They can only be achieved by moral self-determination; that is true liberty. They can only be achieved by real love and conversion, by opening up to others, by unleashing the creative power and generosity of the human heart.

53. For some materialistic ideologies and materialistic lines of praxis concerned with social liberation, which claim to be a "science" or a "technique" of human redemption, the project of the Church in history naturally has an air of poetic revery and magic about it. For this project is based on the coming together of two imponderable factors: the activity of the Holy Spirit and the free decision of human beings. As we see it, it is a sad and tragic fact that Christian people, including priests, would want to stay on the surface level of social mechanisms and to achieve liberation in that way—using violence if they deemed it necessary. For,

as Paul VI points out, this liberation can only be achieved through individual conscience and personal conversion: "Today human beings yearn to free themselves from need and from control by outsiders. But this sort of liberation starts with interior liberty, which must be regained with regard to one's own possessions and actions. Interior liberation cannot be won, however, except through a transcendent love for man and a genuine readiness to serve. Otherwise, as one can plainly see, the most innovative and revolutionary doctrines lead to nothing but a change of masters. These new masters, once in control, surround themselves with privileges, restrict liberties, and permit new forms of injustice to become established" (*Octogesima adveniens,* 45; TPS, 16:159).

Evangelical Love and Class Struggle

54. As the members of Christians For Socialism see it, membership in the Church is conditional upon a political option.[9] Adherence to Christ is equated with commitment to the poor. Christ is in them. From there one moves on to a revolutionary commitment to the working class.[10] Thus conversion to the living God and love of neighbor is necessarily equated with the adoption of a revolutionary stance in favor of one social class against the other.[11] If conversion to Christ is not to be abstract and illusory, then it must pass through this intermediary step.[12] And this whole outlook is dictated by the Marxist analysis of social classes and their struggle with each other.[13]

55. In this same outlook, one comes to identify the people of God with the proletarian class that is conscious of its situation. It is this class which shows up as the locus of the Spirit's manifestation, and indeed as the new incarnation of Christ.[14] Through the mediation of social and structural factors, Christian charity is turned into "revolutionary charity." Not surprisingly, therefore, these people end up by viewing the activity of the Church as framed within the rigid boundaries of class struggle, and indeed as identical with it. The impression is that class struggle is the only mode of salvific activity.[15] That is what is said about evangelization, about the internal buildup of the Church, and about her involvement in the problems of society. As one can

readily see, this comes down to re-interpreting the whole content of Christian faith and morality in terms of the Marxist schema of class struggle. This schema is viewed as "scientific"; and it is accorded a credibility and an imperative nature that is equal if not superior to that of divine revelation itself.

56. Confronted with these assumptions and assertions, we must underline the ideological, artificial, and prefabricated character of what Marxism, and Christians For Socialism in turn, call the "class struggle." It is not a reality or an evident thing deriving automatically from the social conflict we certainly do witness in everyday life. Instead it is a complex, artificial mock-up that is superimposed on the latter fact in the light of certain ideological and philosophical categories. The so-called "class struggle" is posited as an irreconcilable dialectical antithesis that divides humanity into two self-enclosed worlds, one world being the total negation of the other—as the dialectical method demands. This conflict between contraries—between exploiters and exploited—is regarded as the motive force and guiding thread of history. Only the further exacerbation of this antithesis and the eventual outbreak of revolution will produce the desired synthesis: i.e., the classless society, the "reign of liberty," which is the final result of the destruction of the bourgeoisie and the dictatorship of the proletariat.

57. Between these two classes there can be no bridge of communication or understanding grounded on a higher justice or a justice common to both. Such a bridge would merely be a way for the bourgeoisie to solidify its domination more effectively. The same alienating character would ultimately show up in any kind of tie or court of appeal above the struggle itself: e.g., in the notion of a universal morality or some morality not grounded on class, in common law, or in some universal culture or religion. The fact that these Marxist postulates are not always explicit or fully adopted by Christians For Socialism does not alter the basic situation. This in fact is the perspective from which they analyze events and ask us to reinterpret the Catholic faith and the mission of the Church.

58. We fully realize the extent to which Chileans are divided by the class struggle, and we also realize that it affects other national

communities in varying forms and degrees. Far be it from us to claim that Marxism fabricated this struggle, which is due to a multitide of very real causes. Among these causes are the demand for justice on the part of the poor, who seek a more dignified human life, and the insensitivity of those who have more when they are confronted with such demands. But we cannot accept this interpretation of social conflict. We cannot accept this dialectical vision as "science," since it is riddled with ideological and mythical elements of a Manichean cast. Nor can we, as Christians, hope that the social struggle will take this virulent and irreconcilable form. We do not believe that man can arrive at the "reign of liberty" by exacerbating the conflict to the utmost. Behind the dictatorship of the proletariat we cannot help but see the same things we see in every other dictatorship: oppression and political tyranny. We cannot accept at all the proposition that "bourgeoisie" and "proletariat" signify absolute, irremediable opposites; or that any mediating point between these conflicting parties would come down to bourgeois cunning or complicity with capitalism.

59. Still less can we accept the notion that the universal aspiration of Christ's Church—which is situated above classes and nations and in which there is neither Jew nor Greek, slave nor freedman (see Gal 3:28)—is a "bourgeois" pretention or an objective support for the capitalist structure. Like Christ himself, we pastors find ourselves faced with a human being, not a class. Behind every mask and trace of class we detect a human being, a person, a child of God whose ultimate and decisive conflict is one between grace and sin. For this reason we refuse to talk about good or evil collectivities, or about the redeeming clash of social forces. As we see it, the faith we have received is a higher gift from God. We feel it is a crass doctrinal and moral error to re-interpret it from such weak and negative principles.

Loving the Poor Is Loving Christ

60. To be sure, loving the poor is loving Christ himself. He indentified himself in singular fashion with those who had nothing (see Mt 25:40). Living for Christ rather than for our-

selves (2 Cor 5:15) means loving with the same sentiments that Christ had (2 Cor 1:8) hence it means showing the same predilection for the weak and the oppressed. Jesus makes it clear that our love for him and his Father is off-base if it does not find direct expression in our attitude towards our neighbor (Mt 5:23). We do not seek to water down this deeply evangelical mandate; indeed we want to solidify its roots more surely. That is why we feel obliged to state that our encounter with Christ has a solidity of its own. It transcends and goes beyond all other intermediary encounters precisely because it serves as their foundation. Loving God in Christ unconditionally is the radical and ultimate act of the Christian life. Christ manifests himself to us in the poor especially, but he himself is more than the poor. The latter we will have with us always (see Jn 12:8). It is he who deserves the unreserved homage of our love first and foremost.

61. It is our love for the person of Jesus, true God and true man, that puts an evangelical stamp on our brotherly love—not vice versa. It is that which prevents Christian brotherhood from degenerating into mere philanthropy and humanitarianism, into an impersonal passion for some collectivity or some particular way of life. Hence we are greatly distrubed by the fact that in the documents studied by us this personal attachment to Christ, above and beyond any intermediary attachments, is so diluted that it is scarcely perceptible at all.[16]

62. The fact is that certain basic Christian values do not get the attention they would merit in the overall Christian conception of society. We refer to such values as the transcendence of the human person above and beyond classes and structures, and of the person of Christ himself first of all. In the impersonal schema proposed by this group, what room is left for prayer, contemplation, the priestly ministry, humble pastoral service devoid of direct temporal implications, love exercised beyond the boundaries of structures, and the folly of the cross? If a priest finds himself wholly caught up in the class struggle and the quest for social justice, will he be properly disposed to nourish his interior life with prayer, adoration of the Eucharist, and devotion to Mary? And will he then be able to nurture similar dispositions in

the souls of the faithful entrusted to his care? Will he not end up by deprecating all those personal practices and those ministerial concerns that do not have a direct and visible impact on the social struggle? Yet these practices are an indispensable part of the priestly apostolate and, within the context of the communion of saints, they are also indispensable for the cause of social justice.

63. In the documents of this group, love is not well defined. What is really an end result of love is presented as an absolute first principle. Love for the poor, made identical with one class (the proletariat) and with one system (socialism), is turned into the heart of charity and its criterion of validity and effectiveness.[17] We have already indicated that love for the poor is a deeply evangelical notion. But the root of this love, as presented by Christ, is not to be found in the justice or injustice prevailing among human beings. It is to be found in the mandate to imitate the love of our heavenly Father "who makes his sun rise on good and bad alike" (Mt 5:43-48). The difference in motivation here causes us to have serious doubts about the evangelical cast of this "revolutionary charity."

64. Love for the poor is the most luminous indication that we are not loving for external or selfish reasons; that we are loving someone because he is a human being and a child of our one and only heavenly Father. It is then that we love to some extent as God himself loves us. He freely chose to love us first (see 1 Jn 4:10), "not for any good deeds of our own but because he was merciful" (Ti 3:5). Christian love for the poor, which calls for active and effective concern for justice (see Jas 2:14-17), is a consequence of God's gratuitous love for all human beings. No earthly mediation of a "scientific" or political sort can condition this love to the point where it alters its motivation or restricts its scope (e.g.: to one class alone). The thrust of this love is so universal that its other distinctive feature, which is just as necessary as love for the poor, is love for our enemies. Reading the documents of this group, one cannot help but notice that they foster animosity towards those who do not adopt their position.[18] Thus the radical supernatural demand to love one's enemies and to pardon offenses is transformed into open and systematic hos-

tility towards large groups of human beings. Yet this tack does not hesitate to go under the name of charity, although it is an abuse of the term.[19]

65. We are not unaware of the difficulty that is sometimes to be found in reconciling the struggle against injustice with love for those whom we deem unjust. But the obligation remains, especially for those who guide other Christians, to seek this reconciliation with priestly dedication. One cannot deliberately set off on the wrong track, seeking to promote hatred and violence. We cannot minimize the Lord's command. We cannot adapt it to our own viewpoints and emotions, and then dub the resultant sentiment as "evangelical." We, too, believe that among the poor of our nation one can find lively sentiments of generosity and solidarity. It is a fact attested to over the centuries. But we also know that it has an unconditional and universal character. Precisely because they are poor in spirit, they do not set limits on their love. It would be very sad if we let some social theory, some "science," or some intervening structural factor snuff out this spirit in them. That spirit could make a major contribution to the renovation of society. We cannot allow it to be replaced by exacerbated class hatred, for underlying the seeming "necessity" of this hatred is a new kind of exploitation in disguise.

The Christian View of the Poor Differs from the Marxist View

66. Moreover, we cannot accept the complete restriction of the "poor" in the gospel to one social class, the proletariat, which is viewed in the light of a specific socio-political ideology. None of the ethico-religious categories of the gospel—e.g., poverty, wealth, justice—can be made wholly identicial with socio-economic categories bearing the same names, even though there may be a close relationship between the two groups. The poor and lowly in the Bible cannot be indentified with one social class. Nor can the social class embracing the most deprived people be identified with the "proletariat" in the Marxist analysis, for the latter category is laden with *a priori* ideological elements. On the basis of a social and economic analysis, a person may decide that a particular class has an irreplaceable task in history and

that this task represents a thing of moment in the earthly career of salvation history. But he cannot appeal to the authority of Christ and Scripture if he wishes to make this class the sacrament instituted by God in Christ as the efficacious sign of universal reconciliation.[20] Socio-economic analyses by a group of priests do not share in the infallibility of the Church. Even if they were completely precise and accurate as scientific analyses, they could not claim the character of revelation or of proceedings that found a new covenant between God and human beings. In the authentic new covenant, the messianic people has been convoked and brought together "not from a perishable but from an imperishable seed through the Word of the living God, not from the flesh but from water and the Holy Spirit" *(Lumen gentium, 9).*

67. The Christian understanding of the poor is different from the Marxist notion and evaluation of the proletariat. In the Marxist view the proletariat is the industrial worker—in the first stage at least. Then it comes to include other sectors who are conscious of their unjust situation. They organize and, under the lead of the one and only party of revolution, they fight for their rights. The Church cannot identify herself solely with the proletariat, for that is only one segment of the world of the poor. To do that would be to commit herself to one specific political party, a party which defines itself as the vanguard of the social revolution. The Church cannot abandon the immense multitude of the poor and suffering who are not identified with that social class. They represent the suffering Christ also, and hence they deserve her understanding and help.

68. If the class struggle were the proper modality of the Church's salvific activity, then the Church would find herself diminished and set within narrower limits. She would also find herself locked in a framework where she could not exercise the critical function which recent theology has discussed so much. We, for our part, state categorically that the class struggle is not the specific means which Christ gave his Church to contribute to the ultimate triumph of justice in the world. It is quite incredible, and contrary to Scripture and the magisterium, that the true sense of the gospel message would have been kept hidden for almost twenty centuries, hidden from Peter, the other apostles,

their successors, and the Fathers and Doctors of the Church; that only now its true substance should be handed to us through the intermediary of a socio-economic "science" inspired by atheistic premises; that the content of revelation would have remained hidden until the advent of a methodology deriving from Marxism, a methodology that has enabled us to discover a revelation within divine revelation as it were; that the mystery hidden from all ages would be the class struggle as the focus and thread of salvation history.

69. Inspired by Christ's word and activity, the Church believes that it is not the class struggle which overcomes evil; that there is a more excellent (see 1 Cor 12:31) and effective way. We must overcome evil with good. We must suffocate evil in a superabundant measure of good. We must live by love in order to disarm and convert those who had been our enemies (see Rom 5:5-11; 12:14-21). No doubt this seems to be silliness and outright folly to human wisdom and the spirit of aggression. It may even seem to be scandalous, enabling our enemy to win more power over us. But that is how the spirit of Christianity overcame slavery in the ancient world, and that is the law of the gospel. If someone opts for the wisdom of this world instead of the wisdom of God and the folly of the cross (1 Cor 1:20-25), why should they want to retain the epithet "Christian" for a "science" of liberation that appears to be self-sufficient as an instrument of salvation?

70. In saying these things, we certainly are not asking people to set aside their legitimate quest for justice for the working class and the poor in our nation. This is a fundamental moral duty, which religious faith only makes more intense and passionate. We are trying to make it clear to the children of the Church that when they look to the gospel message for the inspiration of their temporal activity, they cannot forget the most essential aspects of the Lord's activity. They cannot overlook those very aspects through which he "conquered" the world, according to Scripture (Jn 16:33). On occasion it may seem that these latter means put them at a clear disadvantage vis-à-vis those who entertain no such scruples. But they must realize that moral rectitude and God's grace engender forces of a deeper, more subtle, and enduring sort, even in the temporal domain. The experience of history over the centuries, as witnessed by the Church, bears elo-

quent testimony to this fact. It is less ostentatious but no less real and sagacious.

71. Most of all, we are asking that they do not demand something from the Church which is not her mission. We are asking that they do not reduce the evangelizing activity of the Church and her presence in the world to a convenient way of recruiting people for their revolution. It may seem to them to be the present trustee of justice and social liberation,but that is on the basis of a human and perfectly fallible analysis. The Church really would not be necessary to achieve that liberation; at most she could be useful. But Christ did not establish the Church to be anyone's lackey. As we pointed out earlier, various churchmen in other ages succumbed to the tempation of linking the ferment of Christianity to the cause that seemed to embody the true sense and trust of history at the time. With the passage of time, the temptation proved to be misleading and it brought sorrow rather than effectiveness to the Church. We do not want to see those past mistakes repeated in our country today.

Division in the Church and its Pastoral Consequences

72. For the members of Christians For Socialism, Scripture as interpreted by the Church's magisterium ceases to be the ultimate criterion of Christian truth. They give the clear impression that they would locate this criterion in their personal faith, which is bolstered and supported by a biased selection and interpretation of scriptural texts.[21] Instead of allowing those texts to open up their minds and issue a summons to them, they take hold of the texts and use them for their own ends.[22] The texts are made subject to external exegetical norms that are alien to the Church. They are taken out of context and inserted into a new framework that is ideological in character and alien to the Church's magisterium. Any believer informed in the faith can readily see how much manipulation is necessary to get Scripture to say what those priests claim it says. Needless to say, we cannot accept their methods of biblical interpretation or their arbitrary norms of Christian truth.

73. Throughout their analysis they start from the unfounded

assumption that Marxism and Christianity are compatible, even convergent. [23] In affirming the incompatibility of these two doctrines, we are not engaging in politics or ideology. We are simply making a basic moral and religious judgment which has been firmly established by the magisterium many times. It grieves us that these people do not heed the warnings of the magisterium. Jeopardizing their souls and confusing the faithful, they devote themselves to the impossible task of reconciling the supernatural and divine meaning of existence with dialectical and historical materialism. They readily accept Marxism's criticisms of religion—not just those that might apply to a distorted practice of the Christian faith but also those which attack the very foundations of the faith. On the other hand they do not undertake any in-depth criticism of the postulates of Marxism. They promptly accord the label of indisputable science to Marxism. [24] They have denigrated and rejected our observations on this whole subject (see EPS 31ff.). And this is aggravated by the fact that they allow the postulates of Marxism to substantively affect the way in which they interpret the doctrine and activity of the Church.

74. Hence it is not surprising that they detract from the nature of the Church and her essential institutionality. This leads to a "new Church," without a supernatural dimension, a hierarchical ministry, or sacraments. We cannot see this image as a simple "renovation" of the perennial Church. It is simply a different institution with different roots, means, and aims. It is, in short, a new sect. The fact is that the practical actions of this group come dangerously close to being just that, more markedly as time goes on.

75. Today there is much talk of "desacralizing" things. "Demythologization" is applied to sacred areas where in fact it makes no sense. The priests in Christians For Socialism are not beyond this tendency. Yet at the same time they end up by sacralizing certain historical realities that are profane in themselves: e.g., social processes and political causes. The social revolution is made identical with a manifestation of God's kingdom and the industrial proletariat is given the character of a messianic people, thus duplicating the temporal messianism that is latent in the Marxist vision of the proletariat. Through the use of the term

"liberation," the salvation of Calvary is watered down to the eventual arrival of socialism. Thus this group inevitably ends up by somehow "sacralizing" its own cause and making it a Church within the Church—or rather the "true Church," a new sect, only marginally associated with the hierarchical ties of the ecclesial community.

76. One might say that the Secretariat of Christians For Socialism exercises a kind of teaching function parallel to that of the bishops. It feels obliged to dictate what the stance of Christians should be vis-à-vis this or that given situation or problem.[25] Its pronouncements lament the lack of unity and coordination with the hierarchy. One gets the impression that they are meant to correct or complete what its official documents have to say about the same matters. This parallel magisterium is manifested in many different ways. One manifestation is the widespread diffusion of what might be called a popular catechism. In fact it contains nothing but ideological and political indoctrination, which any group of a similar cast might formulate.

77. On repeated occasions we have made appeals to those people who, by virtue of their office and ministry, show up as official representatives of the Church. We have asked them not to organize publicly in favor of one specific group or party. We have directed these appeals to priests, deacons, religious, and lay people who hold managerial positions in pastoral endeavors of the Church. By banding together they are abusing the trust and confidence which the Church has placed in them; they are casting doubt on the credibility of ecclesiastical ministers in general; and they are driving away from their ministerial service those faithful who do not think as they do. They have no right to abuse the moral authority which their office gives them by promoting or attacking partisan positions. This line of conduct cannot help but twist and deform the deepest sense of their ministry (see EPS 69-71).

78. The group of people who direct Christians For Socialism contradict our disciplinary directives in full view of the faithful.[26] Giving direction and Christian support to lay people who have taken a particular political option is one thing; involving the ministry itself in the framework of a specific political program is

something else again.[27] In the latter case, the function of active propagandizing ends up destroying the function of the ministry itself,which is to fashion and build up the Christian community through the ministry of God's word and the sacraments. Equipped by the Holy Spirit to act "in Christ's name and person," they end up by regarding their essential task as a secondary one—if not downright useless.

79. Their reinterpretation of the Church within the dialectical framework leads them to foster political controversy and ideological debate among the faithful. This, they say, should come before the fashioning of the ecclesial community itself.[28] Thus they vitiate the whole trust of pastoral activity as a service to the cause of ecclesial unity, designed to make Christians one in Jesus Christ (see Gal 3:27). We fully realize that class differences, political divisions, and other tensions of that sort make it very difficult for people today to discover the higher unity of the faithful in Christ in the concrete context of their daily lives. This very fact imposes on us, Christ's ministers, a more urgent responsibility to help Christians get beyond their legitimate differences—not by some naive or intolerant reduction of some differences to others, but rather by a deeper harmonizing of their lives with the person of Jesus Christ. We are convinced that this fundamental unity of the faithful, and its varied expression in brotherly love, understanding, dialogue, and living together, can help to soften sore points and to make the moral climate of the country more humane and serene. It will have a positive effect on social and political aggregations themselves. The formulated positions of Christians For Socialism with regard to the work of the Church are directly opposed to the pastoral bearings we propose.

Membership in Christians For Socialism Prohibited

80. To sum up: The activity of the group known as Christians For Socialism is riddled with ambiguity and calls for clear definition on its part. If this group seeks to form a front for penetrating into the Church and converting her into a political force from within, with the aim of tying her to a specific program of social revolution, then it should state this honestly and openly and stop

regarding itself as an ecclesial group. In that case it would be more proper for it to take the name of a political group, join the party or current it deems most suitable, and give up the practical and propagandist advantages it enjoys insofar as its members are Catholic priests. The ambiguity cannot continue because it is prejudicial to the Church and causes disorientation in many of the faithful—besides being an abuse of the faith and the priesthood in itself. The Church of Christ will not tolerate this sort of damaging harm. *For this reason, and in the light of what we have said above, we prohibit priests and religious from belonging to that organization; and also from carrying out the kinds of activity we have denounced in this document in any form whatsoever—institutional or individual, organized or unorganized.*

OTHER GROUPS OF CHRISTIANS

81. It would be unfair of us not to allude to other positions, as if the group known as Christians For Socialism were the only one to exhibit distortions of the Church's temporal role. We have dealt with that group in greater detail because it is an organized group whose positions have been published in written form during the past three years and spread throughout the country. This fact enables us to systematically analyze what is acceptable and unacceptable in its stance. The utilization of the faith in the opposite direction is just as regrettable. But it does not call for such extensive examination for obvious reasons. It is not crystallized in organized groups, it does not have the same impact on public opinion, it does not invoke the label "Christian" so explicitly, it does not entail militancy on the part of priests and religious, it is not formulated in written documents, it does not propound a distinct doctrine or vision of the Church, it does not call the fundaments of the faith into question in the same way, and it does not oppose the ecclesiastical hierarchy in the same measure.

Political Utilization of the Church

82. Even though it does not take systematic and programmatic form, however, the practical utilization of the Church by these

sectors and the confusion created in many faithful grieves us deeply. It takes the form of presenting the Church as a force in opposition and conflict with the present-day government and the political currents that support it. It is a more diffuse and subtle outlook, but it also goes against the authentic mission of the Church. In practice it, too, foments divisions within the Christian community and discomforts those who are damaged by it.

83. It grieves us to see what this utilization of the faith, more veiled and at times even unconscious, produces. Because of it, Christians belonging to leftist parties are more and more emphatic in insisting that their own position is demanded by the gospel message; that it is the only position in line with the mission of the Christian as opposed to the type of religiosity that is tied up with the feudal trappings of bourgeois ideologies. They feel that up to now their position has been viewed as being incompatible with the Church, and that they must still confront the inertia which finds support in the very principles of the faith. To break up this prejudice and to counteract the anti-leftist propaganda which other political groups formulate by expropriating Christianity, they feel they must adopt an attitude of intransigence and aggressiveness, not only in the political arena but also within the Church itself.

Diverse Applications of the Church's Social Doctrine

84. We do not share this judgment, but we do recognize the reality of certain facts which lend support to it. We have often heard the gospel presented in such a close tieup with a particular political credo, a particular social reform, or simply the maintenance of the established order, that the unwary Christian has felt obliged by his Christian faith to commit his support, his vote, or his efforts to that particular position. Various political tendencies have sometimes given in to the temptation to present their ideology, not as one among several possible embodiments of the Church's social doctrine vis-à-vis a given situation, but rather as *the* embodiment of that doctrine. Thus they have invested the Christian faith with an ideological character which in fact it does not have. Even when such positions are compatible with Chris-

tian social doctrine, or even inspired by it, people err when they try to turn these positions into *the* concrete expression of the Church herself. Conversely, people err when, in calling these positions into question, they feel they must also attack the Church by that very fact.

85. We must be clear on this point. When Christians constitute the active majority in some political party or current, they must make doubly sure that it is clear to people that their activism as citizens and their membership in the Church are two very different things in themselves. This is true even though the two things are very much tied together within their own consciences, as is the case with every commitment that is at the same time temporal and Christian.

86. Furthermore, one must not confuse the ideological or programmatic formulations of political groups with the actual activities of the groups and their members. As the old proverb tells us, it is a long way from word to deed. The point here is that even though a political doctrine or program may take its inspiration from a Christian view of the social order, that alone does not mean that the *de facto* activities of its spokesmen and followers are Christian. Nor does it insure that they will display moral uprightness or political astuteness. Their activities may be very much open to question. On the other hand, many Catholics may be doing splendid things for the common good in their daily work without espousing any explicit ideology or program or seeking any partisan endorsement. Thus, in his recent letter commemorating the eightieth anniversary of the encyclical *Rerum novarum*, Pope Paul VI stressed the importance of such temporal activity by many Christians. He alluded to those Christians who find their inspiration in the principles of Christian social doctrine rather than in some explicit ideology, and who try to put these principles into practice outside of a narrow partisan framework by freely using the forms and modalities they deem suitable.

87. For these reasons we would ask all Catholics to exercise great discretion as believers in their public activity. We would ask them not to use their status as Christians to push their positions or programs of a temporal sort. Such programs should recommend themselves on their own merits as human proposals.

88. Here the only thing we can add is a statement by Vatican II: "Often enough the Christian view of things will itself suggest some specific solution in certain circumstances. Yet it happens rather frequently, and legitimately so, that with equal sincerity some of the faithful will disagree with others on a given matter. Even against the intentions of their proponents, however, solutions proposed on one side or another may be easily confused by many people with the gospel message. Hence it is necessary for people to remember that no one is allowed in the aforementioned situations to appropriate the Church's authority for his opinion. They should always try to enlighten one another through honest discussion, preserving mutual charity and caring above all for the common good" (*Gaudium et spes,* 43).

89. The approach of some Catholics, stemming from mental laziness or selfish interests, causes us far greater apprehension and disgust. They try to link the doctrine or activity of the Church with the property system of liberalist capitalism, its political schemas, and its social immobility. We do not think these things are in line with the gospel message at all, but they are all too ready to label them as "sacrosanct," "inviolable" elements of "Christian civilization." As far back as 1962, we had this to say in our pastoral letter: "The Church has condemned the abuses of liberalist capitalism . . . . What is more, it is unacceptable that we should continue to maintain in Chile . . . a situation which violates the rights of the human person, and consequently Christian morality. Catholics have an urgent and serious duty to work for a quick and thoroughgoing reform of this unchristian state of affairs." And we went on to say: "We urge everybody to open their eyes and see. To see the suffering of others even though it is an accusation against ourselves. Perhaps then we will recognize Christ's call in the poverty that surrounds us . . . . We have contracted an obligation with Christ to change the real situation of the country as quickly as possible, so that Chile may be the homeland of all Chileans equally. We do not want superficial and violent approaches which leave the situation of misery intact. Neither do we want to rest content with leaving things as they are, offering vague promises for a change that never comes . . . . We will be recognized as disciples of Christ by the

depth and effectiveness of our approach to this brotherly task"
(*El deber social y político en la hora presente*, n. 25 and 39; "The Social
and Political Duty of the Present Moment").

Respect for the Diversity of Political Options

90. Among believers it happens at times that a legitimate difference in political opinions leads to violent mutual hostility
which is not at all legitimate. As a result, each side claims exclusive right to the label "Christian," but their common faith is not
equally effective in fostering fraternal charity between them and
promoting their higher union in Christ. In such cases, it seems to
us, personal opinion dons the absolute character which really
belongs to the dogmas of faith while the latter take on the relative
character that is really proper to any and every human opinion.
Thus their roles are reversed, so that faith is used as the tool of
opinion. People feel more united with those who share their
opinion, even though they do not possess the faith, than with
those who share the same faith even though they hold a different
opinion. People are intransigent where they should be tolerant:
i.e., in matters of opinion. And it sometimes happens that such
people are quite willing to yield on matters in which they should
stand firm: i.e., in the essential content of their faith.

91. We ask Christians never to succumb to this reversal of
principles. When faith and love and the desire for social justice
are in their proper place, one is much more readily inclined to
meet and understand those Christians who do not share one's
own political opinions. In their relationships with each other, the
faithful must preserve the proper hierarchy as expressed in the
classic phrase: in necessary things, unity; in debatable things,
freedom; in all things, charity. Instead of trying to reduce one
attitude or approach to another, we must grant our brother the
possibility of thinking differently from ourselves. In this way we
will foster the loftier unity of all believers in Christ, and this
harmony will have a beneficial impact on the plane of political
relationships.

92. So we reiterate that the Church has no political expression
of her own. Many different political expressions are entertained

by Catholic citizens. None of them compromises or commits the hierarchy, precisely because they are all lay options. None of them has such an intrinsic or necessary relationship with the gospel message that it can represent the Church in the civil realm or turn its proponents into the intermediaries between the Church and the public domain. Any intimation of this sort would threaten to deprive the hierarchy of its moral authority and its autonomy in its own proper sphere. The hierarchical Church would not be able to freely offer any pronouncements, since its official acts and its magisterium would be distorted by political factors and their repercussion in that sphere. We do not wish to see our voice dimmed or silenced by such factors.

93. It is our feeling that many of our statements have in fact been received in this manner. And here we are not referring so much to non-Catholics. All we can ask them to do is to show us the respect that citizens should show to a-political institutions. Here we are referring to some of our own faithful. Instead of adapting their own attitude to the directives of their bishops, in the spirit that these directives are presented, they look for their political implications in order to see which side they favor. As a result, we witness a kind of paper guerilla warfare. Passages are taken out of context and interpreted as one sees fit. And those passages which seem unacceptable are attributed to partisan political motives.

The Desire of the Hierarchy

94. So we appeal to Christians in general, and in particular to priests who share our pastoral responsibility. We ask them to work with us to heal these situations. We ask them to help people understand and appreciate the true mission of the Church and her hierarchy, which represents her as a total community.

95. In particular we ask all priests to refrain from taking part in partisan politics, whatever the group in question may be. Such participation can only help to increase the existing confusion about the role of the Church vis-à-vis temporal problems. In a particular situation that is exceptional in nature, we may judge it necessary to set limits on the legitimate political pluralism of the

faithful because that course is clearly in the best interest of the common good of the Church and society. When we judge that we must direct them towards one specific course in a situation of that sort, we ourselves will announce our decision as members of the hierarchy.

FINAL REFLECTIONS

96. In this document we have said certain things to specific individuals or groups. We do not want our remarks to be taken as a denial of the right of Christians to interpret their political options in the light of their faith and to shoulder their social responsibilities as a real Christian commitment. The Church has consistently stimulated lay people to act in that manner. We, in union with the bishops of Latin America, have done the same with regard to our faithful; for we have fully realized that the existing situation of poverty and social inequality calls for urgent and necessary changes. But in shouldering their responsibilities connected with this task, Christians must not distort the true face of the Church in the process.

97. Our sole aim is to build the true Church. Love for God, fraternal charity, the sacraments, and Christian understanding are a source of inspiration and spiritual strength which Christians need to give life and vigor to new cultural forms or new sociopolitical structures. One will look in vain to Christians for action if the religious wellsprings of their creativity are dormant or stopped up.

98. For this reason, we also want to accept what is positive in the formulations and inquiries of the groups and individuals to which we have alluded above. Our concern over certain dangers does not diminish our desire to hear what they have to say, or to hear the voice of God speak through their anxious concerns. We know that many of them possess a solid spirit of faith and charity. We believe that all those who truly love the Church will be wise enough to cultivate these positive elements without deforming their involvement in the body of Christ. Indeed we are sure they will be able to find their inspiration more truly in the gospel, in the spirit of prayer, and in living and life-giving contact with the

fonts of grace. The social, cultural, and political creativity of Christians can only hope to increase insofar as it is matched by corresponding growth in their docility to the creative, manifold Spirit who was given to us at Pentecost. It is He who stimulates our searching and who enriches the discoveries of God's people in the course of history.

99. Brothers in the Lord, we are aware of the great problems that afflict our society and our nation. We are aware of the enormous tasks that confront Christians in their effort to solve these problems. We are convinced that our best way of collaborating in these tasks is to make sure that the Church is truly the Church: one, supernatural, living, faithful to Christ and in service to the poor. The Church is meant to be the salt of the earth: "And if salt becomes tasteless, how is its saltiness to be restored?" (Mt 5:15) If the Church is turned into a political or temporal faction, who will save us? Nothing makes a more effective contribution to the problems of the world than the spiritual dynamism of the Christian life. There are always ethical and religious roots underlying social and political conflicts. The deteriorating institutional setup of a community conceals underlying factors: weariness of spirit, moral infirmity, degradation of mind and heart, failure in communication, and the absence of God. Economic and political diagnoses are always necessary, but they are not enough because they do not go to the roots of the human mind and conscience. It is in those depths that the grace of God goes to work, unleashing new energies that will create a new social order founded on justice, liberty, and love.

100. We do not want to end our message without making an appeal to our sons in the Lord. We realize that today we are speaking very different languages. But we sincerely believe that our priests, and all those who want the Church to be Christ's leaven for the world, can and should understand the language we have addressed to them if they ponder it in the presence of God. With the Lord, who has made us pastors of his Church, we appeal to them: "He who has ears to hear, let him hear."

NOTES

1. From the extensive literature consulted by us, we would specify the following items as being most indicative. The opening label for each is for shorthand reference.

a. Participación."The participation of Christians in the construction of Socialism in Chile," Press communiqué by a group of 80 priests, Santiago, April 16, 1971. Text in *Los cristianos y la revolución: Un debate abierto en América Latina,* Santiago de Chile, 1972, pp. 175-176.

b. Reflexiones. "'Reflexiones sobre el Documento de Trabajo 'Evangelio, política y socialismos'," Coordinating Committee of the workshop cited in note 1a. They deal with the political commitment of Christians. Mimeographed text. Also reprinted in *Cristianos latinoamericanos y socialismo,* Bogotá, 1972, pp. 117-136.

c. Marxistas y cristianos. "Marxistas y cristianos en edificación del socialismo." Press conference at end of workshop cited in 1a. *El Mercurio,* Santiago de Chile, April 17, 1971.

d. Jornada Escuela Católica. Workshop on the "Escuela Católica en la construcción del socialismo," October 30 to November 1. Mimeographed.

e. Primer Encuentro. First Latin American Convention of Christians For Socialism. Preparatory documents, addresses, national reports, commission reports, final document (see some of this material in this volume). Texts in *Cristianos por el Socialismo,* Santiago, 1972.
Fede come prassi di liberazione: Incontri a Santiago del Cile, Milan, Feltrinelli, 1972.

f. Mensaje a los cristianos. Message to the Christians of Latin America by a group of twelve Chilean priests, members of the Secretariat of Christians For Socialism. Mimeographed. Also in *Punto Final,* Santiago, n. 154, March 28, 1972.

g. Racionalidad socialista. J. P. Richard Guzmán, "Racionalidad socialista y verificación histórica del cristianismo," in *Cuadernos de la Realidad Nacional,* n. 12, April 1972, pp. 144-153.

h. El cristianismo. H. Assmann, "El cristianismo: su plusvalía ideológica y el costo social de la revolución socialista," in *Cuadernos de la Realidad Nacional,* n. 12, April 1972, pp. 154-179.

i. Edición Popular. Popular edition of the conclusions of the First Convention of Christians For Socialism. Mimeographed (April 1972). *El pueblo camina . . . ¿y los cristianos?,* published by Christians For Socialism, Santiago, Prensa Latinoamericana (1972).

j. Lucha de clases y Evangelio. R. Muñoz, "Lucha de clases y Evangelio." Additional reflections by P. Richard; further discussion of the theme by P. Richard, D. Irarrázabal and C. Johanson. Talca, Chile, Cuadernos de la Fundación Obispo Manuel Larraín, July 1972.

k. Communicado I. Communiqué from the National Secretariat of Christians For Socialism, August 10, 1972, mimeographed.

l. Comunicado II. Communiqué from the National Secretariat of Christians For Socialism, October 20, 1972, printed.

m. JN 1972-Documents. Four documents and additional material (report for the National Workshop (Jornada Nacional).

n. JN 1972-Summary. Summary of the work of the commissions and of the main lines of thought, mimeographed.

o. Student Division of Christians For Socialism, Declaration of October 27, 1972.

p. ¿Qué hacer? National Workshop 1972. Diego Irarrázabal C., "¿Qué hacer? cristianos en el proceso socialista," published in 1973, mimeographed.

q. Declaración. Declaration of Christians For Socialism, March 16, 1973, mimeographed.

r. Comunicaciones. Communiqués of the Secretariat of Christians For Socialism, March 1973, mimeographed.

s. Los cristianos. *Los cristianos y la revolución: Un debate abierto en América Latina*, Santiago, E. Quimantú, 1972.

t. Ateismo. J. Pablo Richard, "Ateismo antimperialista camino para cristianos," in *Punto Final*, n. 185, June 5, 1973, pp. 24 f.

u. *Comunidad cristiana y nueva sociedad*, C. J. monthly bulletin, Concepción Local, n. 2, Christians For Socialism.

v. P. Richard, "La burguesía se refugia en la Iglesia," national bulletin Concepión Local, n. 3, Christians For Socialism.

w. P. Richard, "Los Obispos y la prédica de la pequeña burguesía, *Punto Final*, n. 188, pp. 26-27.

x. P. Richard, "El Cristianismo de la pequeña burguesía," *Punto Final*, n. 189, p. 19.

We have also taken into account several documents relating to the movement known as Christians For Socialism:

y. Commentary on document 1b above. Letter of Cardinal Raúl Silva Henríquez to the directors of Christians For Socialism, Santiago, September 4, 1971.

z. Letter of Cardinal Silva to Father Gonzalo Arroyo, S. J., regarding the Convention of Christians For Socialism, Santiago, March 3, 1972. See this volume, Document 7.

aa. Letter of José Manuel Santos, Bishop of Valdivia and President of the Chilean episcopal conference, to Gonzalo Arroyo, S. J. , on the Latin American Convention of Christians For Socialism, Santiago, March 9, 1972.

bb. Letter of the Bishops of Chile to the priests who endorsed the message cited as 1f above, Punta de Tralca, April 11, 1972.

cc. Christians For Socialism Commentary, "Pensamiento y Acción," July 1972, pp. 29-35.

dd. "Primer encuentro latinoamericano de Cristianos por el Socialismo," Internal draft document prepared by the Jesuit Secretariat for activities relating to social and economic development, Rome, October 27, 1972.

The following abbreviations are used in this translation, in the main body of the text:

EPS *Evangelio, política y socialismos* ("The Gospel, Politics, and Brands of Socialism"), draft document, plenary session of the Chilean episcopal conference, Temuco, April 1971.

MED Documents of the Medellín episcopal conference, 1968, in English translation. *The Church in the Present-Day Transformation of Latin America in the Light of the Council.* 2 volumes. United States Catholic Conference, Latin American Bureau of the Department of International Affairs, Washington, D. C., 1970.

TPS *The Pope Speaks Magazine,* Washington, D.C.

Biblical citations are taken from *The New English Bible,* with the Apocrypha (New York and London: Oxford University Press and Cambridge University Press, 1970).

Citations of conciliar documents are taken from Walter M. Abbot, S.J. (ed.). *The Documents of Vatican II* (New York: Guild-America-Association, 1966).

2. See note 1e, Draft Document and Final Document, *passim;* also note 1, documents l,m,n,g,h,o, and p.

3. See J.L. Segundo, "La Iglesia chilena ante el socialismo: una opinión desde Uruguay," in *Cuadernos fundación Obispo Manuel Larraín J.,* Talca, April 1971; also note 1, documents g and p.

4. See note 1 e, Draft Document (p. 210) and Final Document (p. 286); also note 1, documents i,m, and n.

5. See note 1, documents a, e (Draft Document),i,n,p,r.

6. *Ibid.,* documents b,i,p.

7. *Ibid.,* documents e,h,i,n,p,r.

8. *Ibid.,* documents e (Draft Agenda) pp. 19-27; also documents i, m, n, o, p, t.

9. *Ibid.,* document e (Final Document, *passim);* also documents n and p.

10. *Ibid.,* document e (Final Document); also documents i, j, n, and p.

11. *Ibid.,* documents m, n, p.

12. *Ibid.,* documents g, m, p, t.

13. *Ibid.,* document e (Final Document); also documents g, n, p.

14. *Ibid.,* documents p and q.

15. *Ibid.,* documents d, h, m, n, p, t.

16. *Ibid.,* documents b, m, p.

17. *Ibid.,* documents a, b, e, g, j, p.

18. *Ibid.,* documents f, e, k, l, p.

19. *Ibid.,* document p.

20. *Ibid.*, documents b, p, and *passim.*

21. *Ibid.*, documents a, n, p.

22. *Ibid.*, document e (Final Document); also documents v, w, j.

23. *Ibid.*, documents c, e, j, s.

24. *Ibid.*, document e (Draft Agenda and Final Document, *passim);* also document g.

25. *Ibid.*, documents a, e, l. Also see Fernando Vives, SS.CC.,"Nueva educación al servicio del proceso histórico de transición al socialismo," Concepión Local, n. 2: "ENU," Press announcement, March 29, 1972, Secretariat of Christians For Socialism, Santiago.

26. See note 1, documents e and n. Also see "Open Letter to a group of priests and seminarians concerning the priesthood and political commitment," in *Iglesia de Santiago,* May-June 1972, 66:6.

27. See note 1, documents n and p.

28. *Ibid.*, document n.

20

"Christians, the Church, and Revolution"

By Gonzalo Arroyo

In my opinion, the military coup of September 11, 1973, enables us to decide how truly open the institutional Church is to the forces for revolution in Latin America. It also enables us to decide how valid has been the practice of the Chilean left vis-à-vis Christians.

The behavior of the Chilean hierarchy as a whole—and specifically that of the Cardinal of Santiago, which has drawn much attention—does in fact legitimate the military junta even though its aims are humanitarian. Though it seeks to obtain certain guarantees on behalf of the persecuted and to protect Christian institutions, it has led some people to say that in Chile the bourgeoisie has "recovered" the Church.[1]

Does that mean that the socialist Christians of Chile, who had been committed to the struggles of the people, were fleeting birds of summer who could not survive the sudden winter of repression? Christians and Marxists had tasted the effects of joint collaboration in the struggle, and there was reason to hope for benefits to both sides: i.e., new forms of Christian living on the one hand and new forms of socialist organization and culture on the other. Was that a vain hope, shattered in the light of day? Must we now wake to a capitalism that is adopting repressive measures while the Church tolerates them and accommodates herself to them?

In other words, has the coup in Chile proved that the expectations placed in Latin American Christianity were an exception which proves the leftist rule in the past? Impressed by the revolutionary behavior of Chilean Christians and by the loyal collaboration of the bishops with the Allende government, the left had begun to abandon its traditional stance towards Christianity.[2] Must we now say that the traditional image of the Church as a conservative force, as a barrier to social change and a guarantee against the expansion of communism, has won out over the newer and more novel image? Has the latter image failed to hold up, despite the impressive and active presence of avowed Christian Marxists within the revolutionary process?[3]

Proof for Marx's Position?

If the answer to the above questions is "yes," then it is clear that Marx's position has won out over that of Engels. Marx espoused absolute atheism and viewed Christianity as an embodiment of capital and a higher form of alienation. Engels had done a more serious and meticulous analysis of the history of religions, of Christianity in particular, and he saw in it positive aspects from the political viewpoint.

If the answer to the above questions is "yes," then Marx's position has also won out over the view of other Marxists who feel that Christianity contains certain values that can be assimilated by Marxist humanism.[4] Although this topic is not our main concern here, it is worth pointing out that a "yes" answer would also reinforce the dominant if not official position of communist parties and most Marxists: i.e., that the active, militant communist cannot be religious as an individual in his private life. To act thus, in the eyes of Marx, would be to succumb to an intolerable dualism. One would be privately adhering to a practice that directly contradicted his public behavior.

To put it another way, I would say that a "yes" answer to the above questions would perpetuate in Latin America the basic schema that is predominant in the socialist world. One tolerates

Christians, but that does not rule out combatting a religion that is to disappear with the advent of communism. One can "dialogue" and collaborate with Christians, but they are not to be brought into the political project and invested with equal rights and duties. If the progressivist phase of the Church and the involvement of socialist Christians has come to an end with the military coup in Chile—because henceforth the Church is inextricably bound to an economic system that now has assumed fascist and repressive forms in the political arena—then the traditional socialist schema would seem to be forced on the Latin American left once and for all.

Here I feel it is worthwhile to advance several hypotheses of a sociological nature regarding the behavior of Christians after the military coup in Chile. First of all, it seems to me that events in Chile lend support to the following proposition: *Institutionalized churches and religions are integral parts of the overall socio-economic system; insofar as the latter system alters its political structures, the former tend to adapt themselves to the new circumstances.* In the particular case in question, the economic system has moved from a liberal, democratic political structure to a fascist, totalitarian one; and the institutional churches have given up their reformist and progressivist modes of conduct, reverting to doctrinal positions that are more traditionally conservative and to regressive patterns of conduct within their own communities.

However, I think that I should put forward two subsidiary hypotheses at the same time. This accomodation to the new political situation is all the more difficult for the churches insofar as they have been clearly and deeply committed to progressive views prior to this accommodation—through the views of their official representatives and through the appearance of active revolutionary positions and commitments within their confines. After such a new and unexpected experience, a sudden turnabout becomes very difficult. If it takes place quickly and obviously, then it will cost them. They will lose their credibility in the eyes of the popular masses, particularly in the eyes of those who were most actively involved in politics.

The second subsidiary hypothesis is this: Events in Chile will not automatically lead to the disappearance of revolutionary Christianity as a current of social thought and a form of political involvement. In the short run, revolutionary Christianity may have been harmed by repression both inside and outside the religious institution. But it can also penetrate even more deeply into the masses of Christian people. Its authenticity can be verified by its continuing commitment to liberation in accordance with its interpretation of the gospel, and also by the repression it suffers along with the popular masses.

What I propose to do now is to explore these hypotheses in a little greater detail.

Three Currents of Social Christianity

On the Latin American continent we can discern three major currents of social Christianity that are to be associated with political happenings here,[5] and with changes in the Catholic Church and Protestantism due to political developments in Western Europe and elsewhere. This is not the place for a general historical study of the topic, which is a very difficult and ticklish one.[6] Here I shall merely present a few elements that lend support to the hypotheses presented above.

The first current prevailed in Latin America, almost without countervailing forces, until the publication of the papal encyclical *Quadragesimo anno* in 1931. It was the social viewpoint of *traditional Christians* who were politically conservative and religiously faithful to the practice of the sacraments. They carried on the age-old collusion between the colonial government and local hierarchies. From the institutional point of view, one must say that it would have been hard for them to escape this sort of collusion. Later on, it became collusion between confessional parties and the Church.[7]

This current has been steadily losing strength in recent decades. This has been particularly true in Chile, where the Christian Democratic Party made its appearance towards the end of the thirties. Sprung from the papal encyclicals and from the social Catholicism of Europe, it reached its acme right after World War II ended.[8] As the revolution advances, traditional Christians grow more radical by adopting ideological positions of an integralist cast.

The second Christian current is *reformist* in nature. It is closely bound up with the strong growth of the Christian Democratic Party in certain countries (Chile, Venezuela, some countries of Central America, and so forth), and with its impact on the rest of the continent. It also is in line with the reformism that exists in the Catholic Church as a whole, which found its chief expression in the pastoral constitution *Gaudium et spes* that was promulgated by Vatican II. In the Latin American Church that reformism is mirrored in the Medellín Conference,[9] which did present certain original elements of its own, however, by comparison with European praxis at the time.

This particular current of thought was the dominant one among Christians in Chile at the time of the recent military coup. One may group most members of the episcopate here. These Christians talk about social reforms and about "revolution in liberty," to use a slogan from the days of Frei. Subsequently some of them have grown more radical, proposing a "communitarian and democratic socialism" as did Tomic, a candidate who was defeated by Allende in 1970. Basically this kind of prógram claims to be looking for some middle road between capitalism and Marxist socialism. As the revolutionary experiment in Chile proceeded, this current provided the ideological foundation for growing opposition to the Popular Unity coalition from within the ranks of the Christian Democrats. It ended up in an amalgam with the rightist forces that staged the coup.

Christians in this group are particularly susceptible to bourgeois ideology of a reformist cast. They have internalized a whole set of abstract, a-historical ethical values: e.g., democracy, participation, liberty, non-violence, and so forth. These values structure their thinking in such a way that they are incapable of participating in an historical process which, for all its ambiguities and contradictions, is trying to establish in Chile the socialism they claim to profess.[10]

The third current is embodied in *revolutionary Christians*. It appeared on the Latin American continent in the early sixties, and its appearance is probably related to the success of the Cuban revolution. To cite some examples of this current, I would mention the Popular Action movement in Brazil. It was a political movement that arose around 1960 among Catholic university students who did not accept the political directives of the hierarchy. Then there was the United Front movement which arose somewhat later, and which Camilo Torres tried to get going in Colombia. It sought to unite Catholics, Marxists, and all those who wanted to fight on behalf of the exploited class and against the reigning oligarchies and imperialism.

The Medellín Conference

The revolutionary current picked up impetus in the wake of the episcopal conference in Medellín, but not as much impetus as the reformist current did. At the Medellín Conference, Latin American bishops openly declared the commitment of the Church to the task of liberating the peoples of Latin America from neo-colonialism and "institutionalized violence." The latter was evident, they said, in the economic, social, and political structures of our continent which are, in the words of Paul VI, in bondage to the "international imperialism of money."[11]

Even before the Medellín Conference, at the time of Vatican II, a group of bishops from the Third World had taken a stance in favor of socialism. They had been led by Helder Camara, the Archbishop of Recife (Brazil). Before Medellín there had also appeared the "Third World" movement in Argentina and the ONIS movement in Peru. These were groups of priests who had also opted for socialism. But it is correct to say that this third current has taken on greater force because of the political situation, particularly in Chile, and because of the growth of the "theology of liberation." The latter is the first theology to give expression to a distinctively Latin American line of thought rather than merely mirroring European theology.[12]

In Chile the "Young Church" movement began in 1968, and "The 80" priests stepped into the picture in 1971. They publicly espoused socialism, and this led to the creation of "Christians For Socialism" in 1972. Initially the latter organization was composed of priests and ministers who lived and worked among the common people. Gradually it took in the more aware sectors of the Christian working classes, radicalized sectors of students, and the petty bourgeoisie. Disappointed by the failure of Frei's experiments at revolution and in concrete contact with the struggles and sufferings of the exploited, these Christians had come to realize the necessity of rejecting "third alternative" solutions based on the social doctrine of the Church. [13] These solutions were seen to be deceptive and disappointing, designed not to liberate the masses but to put through improvements which would ensure the continuance of centuries-old exploitation of the many by the few. Socialist Christians judged that the real choice was between capitalism and socialism, that there was no third alternative, and that Christians and Marxists should unite around the project to implement socialism. [14]

It is important to point out that these socialist Christians did not try to derive their political stance from their faith, even though they felt that it dovetailed with the gospel message and with Jesus' predilection for the poor and their liberation. They derived their political stance from an analysis which they wanted to be as objective and scientific as possible, and which they saw authenticated by the political praxis of the workers and their avant-garde. But they asserted that their Christian faith was enlivened and vivified by their political activity—that is, by their active involvement in history with the working class and its liberation.

Christians For Socialism

The First Latin American Convention of Christians For Socialism took place in Santiago, Chile (April 1972). The hierarchy had reservations about it and did not participate in it, but more than four hundred delegates did attend (one bishop, some two hundred priests and Protestant ministers, theologians, and lay people). It had considerable impact throughout the Americas and also in Europe. [15] Leftist Christians in Chile were wholly involved in the revolutionary process that had been initiated by the election victory of Allende. For them socialism was no longer a mere word.

This Christian current was a force within the Popular Unity coalition, and within the left as a whole, due to such parties as MAPU and the Christian Left. [16] This gave a singularly pluralistic character to the Chilean way towards socialism, and it allowed us to hope for significant results from the revolutionary collaboration of Christians and Marxists. But the importance of this Christian current was not limited to that fact. By rejecting the reformist position of the Christian Democratic Party, which claimed to flow *de jure* or *de facto* from the gospel message itself, the current of revolutionary Christianity deprived this "third alternative" of its ideological legitimation and its camouflaging of class oppositions. By the simple fact of their existence, socialist Christians helped to strip capitalism, in its outmoded reformist dress, of its ideological justification. It helped to mobilize the working class and the members of the lower middle class. It undermined the prevailing notion that the class struggle was incompatible with the gospel message because it was fed by hatred and led to violence (though admittedly the violence came from people who were oppressed!).

Though this current of revolutionary thought among Christians was a minority one, it had great weight because it was espoused by priests and religious working among the poor and also by eminent theologians and intellectuals. This fact had some bearing on the attitude of neutrality which the hierarchy adopted towards the 1970 elections in Chile, and then on its attitude of collaboration and good relations with the predominantly Marxist government of the Popular Unity coalition. Nevertheless the fact is that the relationship between revolutionary Christians and the bishops never came easy. But no complete rupture took place. The bishops accepted, at least to some extent, the legitimacy of opting for socialism and even Marxism. Revolutionary Christians did not want to break with the hierarchy, both for theological and political reasons.[17]

Christian Reactions to the Military Coup

I would be the first to admit that this typology of Latin American Christianity, particularly in Chile at the time of the coup, is probably too sketchy in nature. It does not take account of other features of Latin American Christianity. For example, it does not consider popular religiosity, a religious phenomenon that existed with some impetus of its own and with some autonomy vis-à-vis the hierarchy. Nor does it consider various forms of the charismatic movement which existed in the country due to the strong impact of the pentecostal movement. My three categories refer primarily to the social and political dimensions of the faith. In my opinion they enable one to better understand the reaction of Christians to the military coup of September 11, 1973, and the subsequent fascist repression.

In line with my first hypothesis above, the Chilean Church would presumably react to the coup in a way that would justify the general norm espoused by the Latin American left. In short, it would bolster the leftist view of Christianity which it had been undermining by its conduct during the Allende regime. Institutional religion in Chile would not prove to be an exception to the rule after all. Its collaboration with a socialist regime during the three years of rule by the Popular Unity coalition would prove to be basically a tactical maneuver. Once the overall system in which it was integrated no longer allowed for legally effected structural changes in the economic and political realm, it would cease to manifest support for the socialist program. Once capitalism shed its reformist mask, it no longer tolerated the overall transformation of society by legal, democratic means. At that point institutional religion, being a support for the system, would tend to regress to conservative positions in ideology and doctrine, thus clearly espousing anti-communist positions.

Events in Chile seem to give clear support to the view that the Chilean Church reached its moment of truth at the time of the coup. Here there is no need to repeat what has been said in many other places about the actions of Cardinal Silva Henríquez and other Chilean bishops.[18] The position of the Cardinal could be identified with that of the "third alternative" espoused by the reformist wing, and he loyally maintained this position during the three years of government by the Popular Unity coalition. One cannot say as much for the majority of Christian Democrats. Immediately before the coup he even tried to find a solution to the political impasse by seeking to restore dialogue between the left and the opposition forces. But such dialogue proved to be quite impossible.

Because of its professed a-politicism, the Church abstained

from politics to a certain extent—particularly after the decline of Frei's administration, the appearance of splits in the Christian Democratic Party, and the formation of MAPU. This won for it the enduring hatred of the right, which still prevails, and came down to indirect support for the ruling government. When workers saw the Cardinal taking part in various demonstrations sponsored by the Workers' Central, which was dominated by Marxist parties, they began to believe that the hierarchy was with the poor. But after the coup, the Cardinal's declarations and actions no longer were consistent with his previous ones. Increasingly they tended to move in an unfortunate direction and to provide justification for the junta.

I do not want to go into great detail here, but it would be well to recall his statements on November 5, 1973, to *L'Osservatore Romano*. In the name of the Church he offers the new government "the same collaboration it had offered to all those works on behalf of the common good that had been sponsored by the Marxist government of President Allende." In other words, the two governments are equally legitimate! There is no word of condemnation for the thousands killed, for the 20,000 political prisoners, for the 15,000 refugees, for the flagrant violation of the most basic human rights—all of these actions performed by a junta whose members profess themselves to be Christians![19]

The silence of the Cardinal, and of most of the churches in general, seems quite unjustifiable in the light of the facts. The events in Chile have been labelled as closely akin to "genocide" by some people. How, then, do we explain the silence?

Three explanations might be offered. The first is that such silence was necessary to help those who were being pursued and arrested by the junta. In order to be of real help to the prisoners and to win better treatment for them, it was necessary to negotiate with the junta. If that be the case, the practical results of this tack are far from evident.[20] There is no question of denigrating the rescue work which many priests and Christians undertook at great personal risk. But the fact is that in the name of individual charity, or in the name of "social" charity if you prefer, people allowed far more serious things to go on unquestioned; and the latter things affected society as a whole. No one expressed opposition to the fascist behavior of a junta whose members professed to be Christians. Indeed, in no time Christians were collaborating with the junta and thus giving it legitimacy.

The second explanation has to do with the underlying ideology of "a-politicism" proclaimed by the Church. The Cardinal and the bishops have repeatedly told priests who were actively involved in politics that they should abstain from such activities. Unlike the laity, they were not to get involved in partisan politics since the mission of the Church is a religious one. Leftist priests replied that even though all were not called to active militancy, abstention was as impossible for them as it was for lay people and bishops. Indeed, they said, the abstention of the bishops was a particularly serious matter. Their a-politicism left the field open to regimes which did not allow the popular masses to participate effectively in government power. It left the field open to regimes in which the people surrendered their destiny to others: e.g., the ruling classes, the armed forces, state organisms.[21]

The third explanation goes right to the heart of the problem. Accepting and recognizing the junta enabled Church authorities to save the institutional Church and its works. When the junta intervened in the affairs of the Catholic universities, the ecclesiastical authorities kept silent. After the coup they juridically ratified the appointment of the Admiral who had been forced upon the Catholic University of Santiago as its Rector. Yet that is a pontifical university, of which the Cardinal is the chief Chancellor. In other words, the religious institution lives by the sociological norm that ensures its own survival; and it does this even when it must openly contradict the principles which brought it into being and which represent its true goal and purpose. Insofar as they are institutions, the churches —represented by their hierarchies —cannot escape the conditions imposed by the ruling class in Chilean society. These conditions become stricter when one enters a political phase marked by fascist militarism, and they can only be broken by charismatic figures such as Helder Camara.

The behavior of other reformist Christian groups also tends to confirm our first hypothesis. The majority of Christian Democrats have welcomed the coup with unfeigned joy. Their betrayal of the democratic principles which they professed to believe, and their complicity with fascism, will cause them to pass into the pages of history as branded hypocrites. Although there are exceptions, some of their top leaders make no sense at all when they talk about a "parallel army of 30,000 men" (Frei in the Madrid journal *ABC*), or when they say that the Allende regime was a totalitarian system "comparable to that headed by Hitler or Ulbricht" (Aylwin addressing the CDU in Hamburg).

These absurd statements are the product of a bad conscience which leads those people to self-justifying rationalizations. They grab on to straws in the wind, alluding to a supposed coup planned by the Allende government itself ("Plan Z"). The junta propagated this story to justify the brutality of its own coup.[22]

Here one must underline the responsibility of the Church for this behavior. The "social doctrine" of the Church implanted in the Christian conscience a variety of abstract, a-historical values which I touched upon earlier and which are fertile soil for bourgeois ideology. Thus the Church's social doctrine allowed the Christian Democratic Party to camouflage its true class nature. President Allende was betrayed by his trust in democracy. His trust enabled the opposition to mobilize against him under the pretext that his government could represent a threat to liberty. In the name of democratic values, people gave the green light to the military coup. And these people included judges and lawyers, defenders of a lawful government such as the Christian Democratic Party, and "democrats" such as Mr. Frei.

Liberal democracy is a fiction, an ideological ruse which safeguards the interests of the ruling classes and functions exclusively within the confines of the capitalist system. If the reproductive capabilities of the latter are threatened, then liberal democracy is choked off at its roots by the bourgeoisie— shamelessly and, in the case of Chile, without any pretense. By preaching a set of a-historical values, the social doctrine of the Church certainly bears a large share of responsibility for the establishment of fascism in Chile.

Socialist Christians and the Future

The military coup also presents socialist Christians with their moment of truth. There is no doubt that in Chile, and to some extent throughout the continent of Latin America, they are suffering direct repression. We know that the ecclesiastical authorities in Chile were contemplating a declaration that would have forbade priests and religious to participate actively in the Secretariat of Christians For Socialism. The declaration was widely known in ecclesiastical circles even before the coup.

Other steps have been taken against the "theology of liberation." It is not simply a matter of holding critical attitudes towards this theology. These steps represent nothing less than an organized campaign against this theology.[23] Does all this portend the imminent death of the revolutionary current of thought among Christians? Are we to conclude that henceforth revolutionary opposition will be ruled out among Christians who remain associated with the religious institution?

In my opinion, such a view is not justified. The subsidiary hypotheses presented above suggest that the socialist current of thought can increase its influence among the Christian masses, at least over the long haul, despite its present persecution. To some extent, this will depend on the attitude adopted by the hierarchical authorities towards the fascist repression that is growing throughout Latin America.

It seems likely that persecution will support the authenticity of socialist Chrsitians in the eyes of the people, that the coherence between their practice and the principles of the gospel message will identify them even more closely with the liberation of the poor and the oppressed. The feelings of solidarity towards them and the concerned interest they have aroused in the countries of Europe and North America suggest that they will be looked on favorably by increasingly large circles of Christians in Latin America itself. This may be particularly true among the masses in less secularized countries, where the Church has been identified with the hierarchy up to now.

The attitude of the various hierarchies will be important. In Chile, for example, there seems to be only two feasible alternatives: Either one is for or one is against the coup. Excessive accommodation to shifting circumstances will cause a loss of adhesion and obedience to the hierarchy among large segments of the Christian population. This will be particularly true among the working class, among other segments that are greatly persecuted by the junta, and in general among the more politicized Christians.

This is all the more true because there has been no other instance in history when the Catholic Church, through some of its bishops (e.g., the Cardinal of Santiago), has gone so far in giving support and displaying political collaboration, of an indirect sort at least, with a government that was predominantly Marxist and that sought to establish socialism. To put it another way: The opportunistic behavior of one church sector (i.e., the hierarchy and Christian institutions) contrasts sharply with the behavior of revolutionary priests and Christians. The latter made no accommodations and suffered persecution alongside the working class. This contrast will undermine the social and political credibility of the Church, which is represented by its episcopal authorities in the eyes of the people.

Their prior support for Allende may have been a tactical maneuver. But they cannot make an abrupt about-face and adopt a completely contrary position without losing credibility. Institutional religion cannot help but appear to be inconsistent. The policies of the new authorities are violent and repressive. Offering support for these policies can only diminish the influence of the hierarchy on the Christian masses, and hence denigrate the reformist socialist positions it espoused before the coup.

The institutional Church certainly did try to save political leftists and others who were being persecuted by the military junta. This work was carried on more effectively in Santiago than in the outlying provinces. There is no doubt that this rescue work may distract people's attention from something that is even more important: the way the churches have accomodated themselves to the new government.

This rescue work was carried on by certain bishops, priests, and Protestant ministers. It was grounded on the institutional power of the churches and on the mediating role accorded to them by the junta—all of that worked out in negotiations with the junta that were public knowledge. Initially people's advertence to this humanitarian and charitable action may obscure the accommodation of the ecclesial institution to the junta and the opportunism of the various hierarchies. This is all the more possible since the gospel message does stress helping the perse-cuted, visiting prisoners, and so forth.

Over the long run, however, matters should take a different turn, particularly when the repressive crimes of the junta become known to the people and when an attempt is made to mete out punishment to the guilty. Ruling out any immediate possibility of the junta being overthrown, one cannot exclude the possibility that the Armed Forces themselves will go through some sort of internal shakeup in order to evade political responsibility for these crimes. In any case, the complicity of the institutional churches in the initial legitimation and subsequent political con-solidation of the junta will become clear to vast segments of the population. Even if it were merely the fact of their complicity by silence, they will be judged by the people at large, not just by the left. Their complicity will seem to stand in direct contradiction to the preaching of Christ, who spoke not only of helping the persecuted but also of liberating the oppressed. The latter action necessarily has implications in the area of political structures. Hence the Church institution will lose some of its capability to impose its hierarchical norms on the social domain and to claim that it is a universal representation of Christianity.

Whatever may happen from here on in, the more or less favor-able reaction of bishops to the junta and the corresponding re-pression of leftist Christians should make new segments of Chris-tians more independent of the normative influence of the reli-gious institution on them in the realm of politics. Up to now this influence has been exerted on them principally through the "so-cial doctrine" of the Church and through parties inspired by Christian social principles in one way or another. More and more, ecclesiastical authorities will find themselves forced to grant freedom of action in this domain to Christians. Under the dynamic impulse of their faith in the gospel of liberation, in which they will certainly detect revolutionary strains, Christians will manage to abandon the abstract ideology of reformism. In the political arena they will decide to start with far more objective analyses of social reality, and this decision will be particularly rich in consequences when these Christians come from the proletariat or the common people.

In conclusion, I would say that the coup has not been without consequences for Christians and the churches. It has brought them into a crisis, forcing them to take a stand and to make political choices that are irrevocable in the accelerated flow of current history. Over and above their personal involvement in the revolutionary struggle, the political task of socialist Christians is to be found primarily in the domain of ideology. This task will be made easier for them, since a "third alternative" between fascism and revolution becomes more and more impossible every day for the popular masses and politicized Christians. The reformism of Christian social doctrine, of men like Frei and Tomic, has been laid to rest by the machine guns and bayonets of the military junta. That much is clear at least. Socialist Christians in Latin America now have that much to their advantage in the struggle that lies ahead. The question now is whether they can carry on this struggle within the institutional Church or whether they will be forced to carry it on outside the Church.

NOTES

1. See Jean-Noël Darde and Isabel Santi, "La junte n'est au bout de ses peines," in *Le monde diplomatique* (December 1973).

2. See G. Arroyo, "Le coup d'etat au Chili, interrogations et réflexions," *Etudes* (December 1973-January 1974).

3. The unusual element here, of course, it not the existence of socialist Christians; similar cases can be found in Europe. For example, there was the worker-priest movement in France after World War II. The novel element in this case is the fact that these Christians carry on their political activity within the revolutionary process itself. They do not give mere intellectual assent to a methodology they deem to be the most adequate.

4. See the study of Georges Morel, "El ateismo del marxismo," *Mensaje* (Santiago), May 1971, pp. 130-140.

5. The Latin American continent possesses vast natural resources, but it is plagued by weak economies, underdevelopment, and dependency on international capitalism. After the success of the Cuban revolution in 1960, it began to go through a period of social and political ferment.

6. See G. Arroyo, "La Iglesia en la década de los 70," in *América 70*, Santiago: Ed. Universidad Cátolica, 1971.

7. In the nineteenth century two kinds of parties predominated. The

confessional party was conservative; the anti-clerical party was liberal. Both had ties with the oligarchies embodied in the large land owners and the business world, and both excluded from their ranks the great mass of peasants, craftsmen, and native Indians.

8. The Christian Democratic Party arose from the younger members of the Conservative Party. In 1938 it would have been condemned by the bishops of Chile if Bishop Manuel Larraín had not stepped in at the decisive moment. He would later found the Conference of Latin American Bishops (CELAM).

9. The episcopal conference in Medellín (Colombia) in 1968 went further than Vatican II. There the bishops committed themselves, in the name of the Church, to the task of liberating the peoples of Latin America. This commitment had political implications. See their "Message to the people of Latin America" at that time.

10. Given such names as "self-managing" or "communitarian" socialism.

11. The fact is that Medellín gave support to the "theology of liberation," even though the bishops may not have wanted to do this intentionally. This is particularly evident in its documents on peace, which helped to radicalize the Christian movement.

12. The main theologians in this area are the Peruvian Gustavo Gutiérrez and the Brazilian Hugo Assmann. The major book by Gutiérrez has been translated into several languages by now, including English: *A Theology of Liberation,* Eng. trans. Caridad Inda and John Eagleson, Maryknoll, New York: Orbis Books, 1973. See also Hugo Assmann, *Teología desde la praxis de la liberación,* Salamanca: Ed. Sígueme, 1973.

13. In other words, derived principally from the social encyclicals of recent popes, starting with Leo XIII. See Pierre Bigo, *La doctrine sociale de l'Eglise,* Paris: PUF, 1965.

14. This position is based on the tenet that the chief contradiction is not between Christians and Marxists but between exploiters and exploited.

15. The Final Document of that Convention (see above Document 18) was distributed throughout Latin America, and subsidiary groups of Christians For Socialism grew up in various countries. It was also utilized by already existing groups such as ONIS in Peru.

16. These resulted from divisions within the Christian Democratic Party. MAPU arose in 1968; the Christian Left arose in 1971. The former claimed to be grounded on Marxist-Leninism, but effective cooperation has become a reality between militant Christians and militant Marxists. There are also Christians in MIR, in the Socialist Party, and even in the Communist Party.

17. Much discussion surrounded the 1971 pastoral document issued by the bishops: "The Church, Politics, and Various Brands of Socialism." This document was criticized by "The 80" priests. See in this volume the national report on Chile, Document 11.

18. See *Politique-hebdo,* n. 103, November 15, 1973, pp. 22-24; also the article in *Etudes* cited in note 2.

19. However, friction between the Cardinal and the junta has not ended. The political right has not forgiven the Cardinal's cooperation with the Allende government. His statements in *L'Osservatore Romano* drew down the wrath of the military government because he had publicly placed the two governments (Allende's and theirs) on the same level. The right-wing press later attacked the Cardinal directly. Since censorship is strict in Chile right now, their attack must have been approved by the junta.

20. Might not a clear stand against the excesses of the junta by the Cardinal have been more effective than aid to the persecuted on an individual basis? Aid measures, such as refugee camps, were given institutional form after a few weeks. In turn, however, the Cardinal had to concede to the junta the mission of "telling the truth about Chile" to the outside world.

21. In fact, however, some priests were active in grass-roots organizations of various sorts: labor unions, political parties, and so forth.

22. The "white paper" of the junta has no internal coherence and it is not based on objective facts at all. Yet it has found even more credibility in Chile than in the outside world.

23. We might mention several things here: the 1972 statement by the social commission of CELAM on the subject of socialism; the steps taken by Father Arrupe against the Mexican Jesuits who have been collaborating with the Secretariat of Christians For Socialism; the decision of several bishops not to renew the contracts of leftist Spanish priests in Chile. In addition, a variety of steps have been taken in reaction to the theology of liberation. New officials have been appointed to CELAM, theological study centers have been set up (particularly in Bogotá) to dispute its scholarly underpinnings, and credit has been granted in Europe to encourage opposition research.